THE
SIX-SPOKE APPROACH **TO GOLF**

THE
SIX-SPOKE APPROACH **TO GOLF**

TOM PATRI AND JULIE L. MORAN

FOREWORD BY
Fred Couples

INTRODUCTION BY
Jimmy Roberts

Photographs by Evan Schiller
Illustrations by Charles McGill

THE LYONS PRESS
Guilford, Connecticut

An imprint of The Globe Pequot Press

To buy books in quantity for corporate use
or incentives, call **(800) 962–0973, ext. 4551,**
or e-mail **premiums@GlobePequot.com.**

The Lyons Press is an imprint of
The Globe Pequot Press.

10 9 8 7 6 5 4 3 2 1

Printed in the United States of America
Produced by Print Matters, Inc.
Designed by Compset, Inc.
Photographs © 2005 by Evan Schiller
Illustrations © 2005 by Charles McGill

1-59228-541-4

Library of Congress Cataloging-in-
Publication Data is available on file.

*To my son P.J., my reason for living,
I love you more than life. You are
my light!*

—DAD

*For Seanie, Katie, and Sean, with love,
and in memory of Mom & Dad.*

—JULIE

CONTENTS

ACKNOWLEDGMENTS

I grew up on a busy 27-hole public golf course on Long Island where my father ran the food concession. I got my first club at age 11: a Sam Snead Blue Ridge Wilson 5-iron I found in the parking lot, broken in half. It had probably been snapped over someone's knee in anger and left for dead. I took it into the pro shop, where a friend of my dad's sliced the jagged edge off the end of the shaft and replaced the grip. I went off and began whacking balls with reckless abandon, and as I recall I was instantly hooked on the legal drug we call golf. Little did I know that this day would have a profound impact on the course and purpose of my life. (P.S. I constantly hope that I'm having a positive effect on each and every life I touch in golf.)

Although I spent part of my life as a competitor, on both the collegiate and professional levels, now, some 35 years later, I have been coaching golf for more than 20 years. During this time I have developed my own philosophy as to learning the great game of golf. However, there are people who have deeply influenced me and my career along the way, and to whom I would like now to offer my most profound thanks.

An enormous amount of credit for helping me goes to the late Bill Strausbaugh, 1992 National PGA Teacher of the Year and former golf professional at the Columbia Country Club in Chevy Chase, Maryland. I met Bill by chance back in 1988 at the PGA Merchandise Show. That coincidental meeting led to a deep friendship, which I was truly blessed to have had, cut short only by Bill's untimely death in 1998. Bill touched my life on a daily basis through phone conversations, letters, and time spent coaching alongside one another in the early days of TP Golf Schools. We conducted clinics, seminars, and speaking engagements together. Every time I was with Bill, I realized he had amassed an incredible amount of knowledge: Over a lifetime he had probably forgotten more than I will ever know. He was a wonderfully talented, patient man, a friend, mentor, father figure, and someone I miss every single day. With the exception of my own parents and my own son, I've never missed anyone more in my life. A part of him is always with me, and as such he is a large part of this book and its teachings.

There are so many teachers out there I'd like to acknowledge. While it's impossible to try to name them all, certainly one of the people who unknowingly influenced me a great deal is Jim Flick, one of Bill's longtime friends. I understand there are a lot of competent people in the teaching world, but I think Jim Flick—well known as he is—continues to be underrated for his ability to communicate the golf swing in a clear and precise manner.

I'd like to thank Mike Wands, formerly of Middle Island Country Club, and Loring Hawkins, a retired professional from Spring Lake Golf Club (the two clubs where I grew up around in

Middle Island, New York)—each man, in his own way, helped shape and influenced me; and Charlie Robson, the executive director of the Metropolitan PGA, and Jeannie Schneider, the first organizer of the Met PGA Junior Golf Tour, for their wonderful mentoring and continued friendship. I am also grateful to John Kennedy, a longtime friend and director of golf at Westchester Country Club, for giving me countless chances and unlimited freedom to expand my knowledge and chase information. They are all true friends.

There are so many people out there who have touched me in my career, but I would be remiss in not mentioning all of my students who, over the years, have made me think and rethink the golf swing, ball flight, and how best to get the job done. Every student I've ever had a lesson with has, in some way, contributed to this book.

Most recently my little boy, P.J., now four years old, has motivated me to a rebirth in my career because of my need to take care of him, nurture him, and watch him grow. He certainly doesn't realize the influence he's had on me in getting this book done. Someday I hope he does. P.J. is my life. God gave me the greatest gift possible in P.J.

In addition to those who have influenced my life and career, I'd like to thank those people who have contributed to this book—some knowingly, others unknowingly.

First, I want to thank Julie Moran, who wrote this book for me, for her patience and understanding, for her support and push in putting my thoughts on paper. I also want to thank her husband, Sean, for his legal expertise, and for being the one who pushed me to strive to make this book a reality for Julie and me. Sean is a student, but first and foremost a dear friend.

Finally, Julie and I would like to extend our grateful acknowledgment to the following individuals for their generous assistance with this book: Tom McCarthy and Holly Rubino, our editors; Michael Snell, our agent; Evan Schiller, our photographer; Charles McGill, our illustrator; Fred Couples and Jimmy Roberts, for taking the time to write the foreword and the introduction; Kathy Hanna, my former director of operations; Kathleen Dwyer and Kevin Lumpkin, our research assistants; and Eanna Rushe, Dr. Rick Jensen, Peter Sanders, Dane Wiren, Peter Harris of Titleist Custom Club Fitting, Bobby Jones Clothing, Patricia Upham, Lisa Lumpkin, Sue Larson Pascoe, Madelyn Cain, Miriam Kadar, Stephen Lupcho, Lynn Burlin, and Rose Zuniga.

This book has been a wonderful journey through my golf life. To all those mentioned above, thank you.

FOREWORD

When Tom and I met, I wasn't Fred Couples the Tour Player and he wasn't Tom Patri, One of the Top 100 Golf Teachers in America; we were just two kids in college chasing a dream. I was at the University of Houston and Tom was at Florida Southern College. During the spring of my sophomore year and his junior year, we met while playing in the 1980 NCAA Championships at Ohio State on their fabulous Scarlet Course.

The University of Houston was a perennial favorite, and Tom had qualified as an individual by finishing second in the NCAA Division II Championships. Though we'd met briefly the fall before, we ran into each other again at Scarlet during the practice rounds and on the range. We talked at length and just seemed to hit it off. (I'm pretty quiet by nature, and if you haven't met Tom in person, let's just say he isn't.)

The NCAA had a 54-hole cut for both teams and individuals and, although I'd made the cut as an individual, both the University of Houston and Tom found themselves just outside the cut line. Later on, I found Tom trying to make a plane reservation home. Since my team and I were trying to escape the wrath of our coach, Dave Williams, for missing the cut, we were on our way to play at nearby Muirfield Village and asked Tom if he would like to join us. He quickly dropped the phone, and we were on our way. That afternoon, we had a blast. We've been good friends ever since.

Since then, I have watched Tom's career grow, and have witnessed the development of his sound teaching philosophy, the Six-Spoke Approach, which I support wholeheartedly. Tom's Six-Spoke Approach to Better Golf—or, as he also calls it, a "blueprint for learning"— is an outstanding method for improving your play. When Tom first discussed it with me, I knew that he was on to something that would help players of all levels reach their potential. I saw, too, that his approach mirrored the approach that a lot of us on the PGA Tour utilize on a day-to-day basis.

Many of my peers work with a sport psychologist—not merely to survive, but to find the edge that will take them to the next level. A very high percentage of us work on our physical well-being, especially through the use of exercise programs specifically aimed at improving the physical skills needed to play golf as well as prevent injury. I personally have had to work very hard on my fitness to ensure that I can play the events that are important to me and my career.

In addition, most of us chart our progress statistically, many with computer-assisted analysis. This is the only truly objective method of uncovering where valuable shots are lost. Time

management is certainly one of our biggest challenges, and one that all Tour players face. We are all interested in tweaking our equipment and finding that edge through the latest technology. And hardly any of us do not work with a coach to refine our technique on a regular basis.

Please allow my pal Tom to help you design your blueprint for success using the Six-Spoke Approach. We both wish you great success on your journey.

Sincerely,
Fred Couples

INTRODUCTION

I can still remember the first time I met Tom Patri as if it was yesterday. It was March of 1989. I was working for ESPN and preparing a feature story on Nick Faldo for our *Sports Center* coverage of the Masters. I had called Westchester Country Club to ask if I might use the course as a backdrop for the feature's "standup"—the part of the piece where the reporter appears on camera. It's a frequent practice in the industry . . . shooting the standup at a location that is related in theme to the subject of the feature, but vague enough in identity to suggest the reporter is actually at the specific site. (There, now you know one of TV's dirty little secrets.)

The people at the club didn't know me, and while they couldn't have been more cordial, they insisted on assigning me a "chaperone" while on the grounds—I assume to make sure I wasn't secretly doing some type of exposé on the club itself. (A decade later, the Westchester Country Club either came to trust me or had a total lapse of judgment, as I was admitted as a member.) The person they assigned to watch over me that blustery March day was Tom. He fixed me with an expression that, I have since come to understand, is not *really* a maniacal grin, extended his hand, and said, "Hi, Jim, how are you? Tom Patri, Golf Professional."

My instant impression was that this was a pretty intense character. He then grabbed my hand to shake it, and my instincts were confirmed. He readjusted my grip to a more "golf proper" position.

I had known Tom Patri all of 15 seconds, and I'd already had my first lesson.

It was far from my last, and not because I had become disgusted with the state of my game (although I had). It was because he was relentless. He shamed me into practicing. Insisted I take lessons. Mocked my complaints when he noticed how few rounds I had taken the time to play. In short, he was one of the most dedicated professionals I had ever met. I guess I shouldn't have been surprised when I found out his dad had been a marine drill sergeant at Paris Island.

And it wasn't just dedication that made Tom stand out. I remember covering an event on the PGA Tour's Southern Swing not long ago, the same week Tom had been tabbed to do an instructional bit in *Sports Illustrated*. I was chatting with Fred Couples after his round and asked him if he had seen the piece. "No," said Freddy, "but I'll tell you what. Tom really knows the golf swing."

And that's hardly by accident. He's been a student of great teachers such as Bill Strausbaugh and Jim Flick. For the handful of years the great Harry "Lighthorse" Cooper taught

at Westchester, Tom was like a wide-eyed assistant following a Nobel laureate around campus.

So let's see. Tom knows the swing. He's dedicated. (Make that *consumed.*) He's not just talking off the top of his head: He won the NCAA Division II Championship (I think it was about the time electricity was invented). But most important of all . . . he's got a system. And what a system it is.

The Six-Spoke Approach to golf is a complete reflection of Tom's personality: It is logical and disciplined. It is also the product of 23 years of thought—not only about the golf swing, but the player who makes the swing. Tom's theory holds that there are six major components involved in a player's improvement: Body, Mind, Analysis, Time Management, Equipment, and Technique. Each of these Spokes supports the process, which you might think of as a wheel. Where they converge in the middle is the ideal point where they all function in harmony.

Since that blustery March day when I first met Tom 15 years ago, I've learned a lot about him. I'm guessing he wrote this book because he couldn't help himself. He just can't stand to think that anybody out there *isn't* playing their best golf. And if you are playing a substandard game, don't get in his way . . . unless you want to get better.

Jimmy Roberts
Commentator for NBC Sports

HOW TO GET THE MOST OUT OF THIS BOOK

You're a far better golfer than you realize. My teaching philosophy, known as the Six-Spoke Approach, will allow you to tap this vast potential in all areas of your game: the full swing and short game, mental and physical preparation, and course and time management skills, all of which work together to enable you to reach your personal best.

I sincerely believe, after having observed hundreds of my students literally transform their games, that every man, woman, and child can play golf at a much higher level than they've ever imagined. I developed the Six-Spoke Approach to learning golf through trial and error over the course of more than 20 years of teaching. In that time I've seen hundreds of individuals of varying physical, mental, and innate athletic abilities achieve remarkable results using this approach.

Within these pages I will speak to you the way I would speak as a coach to any of my students. What I ask of you is that you be willing to put in the necessary time to thoroughly understand the concepts presented, as well as the many hours of practice needed to incorporate these concepts into your game. I promise that, if you do this, it will revolutionize and elevate your game to a level you probably never thought possible.

This approach is geared not to any particular handicap but to those who are serious about improvement, from beginner to advanced player. To succeed with the Six Spoke Approach, all it takes is a solid work ethic and a passion for the game. That passion, that enjoyment, is far more important than your handicap or score, since it gives you the sense of purpose needed to carry out the Six-Spoke Approach. Bring with that passion the simpler determination often found in children—the lack of fear, the willingness to try, and the ability to fail and get up again.

Learning golf is not a fixed or static event, but a lifelong process. In golf you never "arrive." *It's a journey, not a destination*—a journey of constant learning and improvement. Without passion and joy, this process becomes a chore.

As my dear friend and mentor, the late Bill Strausbaugh, taught me years ago, proper golf instruction is based on a *few key* principles that are "learned, earned, and then worked on *forever*." This is the true essence of proper learning, as opposed to jumping from one thing to the next, seeking that one single trick that will finally allow you, with little effort, to "get it" and never have to work on technique again. Unfortunately, many students of golf seem to believe this is possible. They are only kidding themselves. There are no shortcuts or false promises here. I will not lie to you: Golf is a complex motor skill that takes time and effort to learn.

TECHNIQUE MADE SIMPLE

This does not mean golf is or should be overly complicated. It is my belief that golf instruction has become too complex; it is severely *overtaught* and *undercoached*. As the late great sports columnist Jim Murray said, "If they taught sex the way they teach golf, the [human] race would have died out years ago."

One of the things that has struck me the most as a golf teacher is that the overwhelming focus in golf instruction is on technique. Of course, without technique there is no swing, and thus no game. Yet merely learning technique is not a complete approach to learning golf. It is only one of the six essential Spokes, or elements, of golf. The Six-Spoke Approach combines all six of these elements—Body, Mind, Analysis, Time Management, Equipment, and Technique—to give you a complete, integrated approach to learning golf.

You will notice that Technique is the sixth and last Spoke. Without the other five Spokes in place, there is no reason to proceed to Technique. That is where traditional approaches to learning have been unsuccessful, because they cause people to work simultaneously *with* and *against* themselves. For example, if your body does not have the requisite strength or flexibility to make a proper golf swing, you're setting yourself up for failure, or worse— potentially serious injury. If your equipment is wrong for you, you will always be compensating for these maladjustments. Just as poorly fitted shoes force you to change your gait in order to walk, improperly fitted golf equipment forces you to compensate in ways that make a consistent, repeatable, balanced, natural swing impossible. If you have these problems, or any others arising out of neglecting the first five Spokes, all the technique in the world won't save your game.

In addition, when it comes to technique, I don't want you getting bogged down in what I see as one of the biggest problems pervading golf instruction today: overcomplication and a resulting unnecessary confusion. This is another way in which my approach to technique is different. I call it *technique made simple*.

This book covers all the basic fundamentals of technique you need to know, including drills to help you learn and internalize them, troubleshooting guides on how to handle most problems that might crop up, as well as illustrations to provide you with a clear visual reference. Aside from this, I take you through technique in a carefully chosen order, discussing shots from those closest to the hole to the ones farthest off, starting with smaller motor skills, which have fewer moving parts and less distance to cover. The reason for this is simple: The short-game swing is in fact a microcosm of the full swing. If you're having trouble with the short game, you have no hope of making a sound full swing, because it's a motion that is much faster, longer, and uses a greater number of moving parts.

Once your short game is well defined, we proceed to the full swing, which I teach in a somewhat unconventional way, but for very good reasons. I call this method the Bookends. We begin our look at the full swing with the preshot routine and launching pad (setup), then immediately proceed to the finish condition before heading to the in-between—the backswing, downswing, and follow-through. While at first glance this may surprise you, this approach to technique actually allows you to learn much more quickly and efficiently because it taps into the powerful mind–body connection. If your launching pad is perfect and leads you into a proper finish condition, a correct full swing is more likely to have occurred in between. In other words, if the Bookends are firmly in place, the rest of the swing tends to fall more naturally into place. This approach to the full swing is simple, yet revolutionary, and will save you a lot of time and frustration.

HOW TO USE THIS BOOK

Although the Six-Spoke Approach is a philosophy, or what I often refer to as a "blueprint for success," this does not mean I teach every student exactly the same way. It is not a cookie-cutter approach. On the contrary, I teach every student based on individual need. Not in the sense that the fundamentals are different—they are perhaps the single part of this game that has remained unchanged over centuries of play. I mean this in the sense that each student is starting from a different point, with different skills and problems, strengths and weaknesses. No two individuals' bodies or minds are exactly the same, nor do they react to information in the same way, or have exactly the same time constraints.

Read the chapters that follow carefully, and then allow yourself time to digest and understand the information presented and adapt it to yourself and your personal golf style. This part must be done *off* the course, both at leisure and on the practice range and putting green. A typical golf swing takes less than two seconds, often in excess of about 90 miles an hour, and involves many moving parts. How much can you think about with that much going on in such a short time? True learning cannot take place during the swing—a swing must be *felt and developed*. That is why you *must* devote enough time and attention to learning *off* the golf course.

Keep in mind, too, that the goal of the Six-Spoke Approach is the construction not of a pretty swing, but of an efficient golf game—something that will work for you, so that you can maintain a consistent level of play from which to grow and build and continually improve throughout your life.

I cannot teach you to play golf, but I can teach you how to *learn* to play golf. This book is intended to give you what you need to take with you to the practice area and short game area, to internalize, develop, and incorporate, until it is a part of you, and then take it to the course. If you do this, you will find that a few simple but essential guidelines and your own hard work have brought you great success.

The Six-Spoke Approach gives you the six essential building blocks you need to create a lifelong learning plan, in a manner intended to give you a greater understanding of yourself and your game as a whole. Please read and utilize this information in the order it is presented. Each Spoke builds upon the previous one, and all six Spokes are required for anyone to grow as a golfer.

I hope you will take the time to read the Six Spokes several times, taking with you each time another possible solution for each Spoke. Read the book first cover to cover, then highlight those parts that stand out most, that speak to you personally as a golfer. This way, you can easily refer to it again and again.

As you do so, you may notice that some concepts are restated in various chapters. This is in part because several concepts apply to various aspects of the game, which must be clarified. However, there's another, more profound reason for this seeming repetition. Some things are so fundamental and important that they need to be underscored, and I have tried, by means of restating these concepts in the text and by inserting related sidebars and charts throughout each chapter, to reinforce key concepts that might otherwise be forgotten as we move on to other fundamentals. The charts and sidebars are also meant to help you understand and quickly review, for future reference, these crucial fundamentals. Though this might seem redundant, it is my quite intentional way of emphasizing and reinforcing crucial points.

Finally, although golf is a sport that is largely self-taught, it is one that should be learned with periodic supervision. I strongly recommend that, if you do not already work with a golf coach on a regular basis, you seriously consider doing so. Every couple of weeks or so, or even once a month, is fine. In fact, when I taught at Westchester Country Club in Rye, New York, which has a regular membership (as opposed to Naples Grande Golf Club, a resort club where I teach now), I would not allow a student to take a lesson more often than every two weeks. You simply cannot properly digest, practice, and incorporate everything covered in an hour of instruction in less time than that.

Like life itself, the game of golf brings with it unexpected twists and turns, triumphs and hazards, bitter and sweet ironies. A sense of humor and, at times, a thick skin may be required. But in the end, please remember to have fun—it is, after all, a game meant to make life a little more pleasurable.

I hope you enjoy our time together. I also hope we meet someday in person. May you also find happiness and success in the Journey, and God Bless you!

Sincerely in golf,
TP

THE
SIX-SPOKE APPROACH **TO GOLF**

1 THERE'S NO SUCH THING AS "BUILT LIKE A GOLFER" **SPOKE 1: THE BODY**

The game of golf has witnessed more technological advances in the last 15 years than at any other time in its 600-year history. We've made significant improvements to clubs, balls, course conditions, teaching and coaching techniques, putting surfaces—you name it. So why isn't the average player's score going down?

The answer is deceptively simple. The one thing that hasn't changed in the history of golf is the human body, the most fundamental tool used to power the golf club. If you lack strength, speed, or flexibility, then the most expensive driver on the market won't help your game; it'd be like trying to race a Maserati with a lawn mower engine.

The next time you watch your favorite Tour players on television, take a close look. See how they make aggressive, athletic swings and stay in balance, or how they turn their shoulders so far and hit the ball great distances? Believe me, those people work on their bodies for hours a day, every day. When the prize money in professional golf tournaments started increasing dramatically, the sport began attracting world-class athletes in greater numbers.

This new allure and prestige—and the resulting attention to physical fitness and training—have changed the game forever, for amateurs and professionals alike. Proper physical training for golf has finally gained serious attention. Unlike their predecessors, today's competitors have personal trainers and a fitness van while they're on tour.

Most people view golf as a benign, even docile, activity; a hobby, not a sport. Think again: The golf swing generates up to 4 horsepower and reaches speeds of over 90—and sometimes more than 100—miles per hour. Golfers must have strength, speed, and an adequate range of motion to create that kind of power, not to mention the stamina to play for an average of four hours and to walk the equivalent of 4 to 6 miles, often on hilly terrain in often hot and humid conditions.

Golf is an athletic event—a true sport. As with any sport, to be good at it and to avoid injuries, you have to train properly. I'm not asking you to train for hours a day or to hire a fitness crew to follow you around, but I am suggesting you spend a few hours a week getting fit and staying in shape to play golf. The exercises provided at the end of this chapter will show you how.

Golf requires seven essential physical attributes: proper posture, a full range of motion, strength, stability, balance, speed, and coordination. Notice I didn't mention any immutable characteristics like height, body type, or bone structure. Unlike gymnasts, jockeys, ballerinas, and basketball players (who tend to share certain physical attributes), talented golfers come in all shapes, sizes, and ages. There's no such thing as "built like a golfer." While natural talent helps tremendously, any golfer can develop the necessary physical components.

Okay, so now you know that you need to do lots of work to reach your potential and prevent injury. Don't panic. Don't sweat the details. You can do it. Spoke 1 in my Six-Spoke Approach to golf was specifically designed to help you get your body ready to play your best golf ever.

This preparation stage is composed of two parts. Part one is the physical component, getting your body in shape to play golf by developing the necessary physical attributes. The exercises and drills in this chapter will get you there. Once you're fit enough to play great golf, you're ready to go on to part two of the Body Spoke: motor learning, or movement reeducation. You will educate your body to execute proper movement patterns. Once your body is capable of making a biomechanically correct golf swing, you're ready to learn what a biomechanically correct golf swing actually looks and feels like. We'll discuss all this in more detail at the end of this chapter.

> *Use the talents you possess; for the woods would be very silent if no birds sang there except the best.*
>
> —HENRY VAN DYKE

THE MODERN MIRACLE OF SPORT SCIENCE

Before we get to the drills and exercise routines, I'd like to introduce you to the man who designed them: Eanna Rushe, whose company is BioSport Technologies of Greenwich (Cos Cob), Connecticut. I call Eanna the golfer's best friend (aside from yours truly, of course). He's a sport scientist who is golf specific.

I sent many of my students for the numerous years I was at Westchester Country Club in New York to Eanna and recommend that everyone seek out someone in their geographic region of Eanna's quality. In Appendix A I have listed several people in various regions of the United States who are all excellent. Their hourly rates will vary. If cost is a factor, following the exercises designed by Eanna included in this chapter will get most golfers in the kind of shape they need to be in. Every student of golf should work with someone like him. Nothing replaces a hands-on relationship with an expert. In fact all golf coaches, to do their best work, should send their students to someone like Eanna. If your body can't make the correct movements, your swing will never improve, and both you and your coach will feel frustrated. If going to a golf specific trainer isn't possible, again, doing the exercises in this chapter will help you develop the necessary skills.

People have trouble with the physical requirements of golf for many reasons. The most common problem is a natural limitation such as a lack of strength or flexibility or an impeding injury. If physical problems are holding you back, consider working with a golf-specific sport scientist. The results will do wonders for your game.

You're probably thinking, *What the heck is a "sport scientist who is golf specific"?* Sport scientists use state-of-the-art technology, motion analysis, and expertise to evaluate your golf motion from a biomechanical and physical point of view. They can pinpoint specific weaknesses that are handicaps, analyzing your swing from a completely objective, scientific

Tom Patri (wearing cap) with Eanna Rushe.

point of view, with no guesswork or room for error. Sophisticated technology has made all of this possible. If you're considering a consultation with a sport scientist, here's an idea of what to expect.

When Eanna works with one of my students, the first session begins with an *intake*. He asks the player for a complete health history, including medical conditions and injuries, followed by a golf history (instruction taken, number of years playing, practice routines, and the amount of time spent practicing and playing).

Next, Eanna conducts a hands-on assessment. These are low-tech tests to determine the student's range of joint motion, posture, strength, and balance. Following this, Eanna does a video analysis of the golfer's motion to assess static and dynamic posture, rotational and lateral abilities, and stability. Finally, we will do a ZenoLINK evaluation. This is a 3-D biomechanical analysis of the golfer's motion. This is designed to assess athletic performance and efficiency during the golf swing. There are other companies that do similar evaluations, but ZenoLINK is the company Eanna prefers.

The ZenoLINK evaluation is a wonder of modern technology. Two high-speed cameras and a calibration frame are used to videotape the client from two different angles. One camera captures a "caddy view" (a player's chest on view); the other records a diagonal view from the side. Eanna sends the tapes to a biomechanist, who digitizes them, processes them, and posts a detailed report on the Internet within 24–48 hours.

The ZenoLINK report provides a three-dimensional representation of the golfer's swing. ZenoLINK enables a sport scientist to quantify a player's motion according to how fast each body segment (hips, shoulders, and arms) moves and the sequence of their movements. This allows the evaluator to assess attributes such as lower body stability— that is, the *lateral* or side-to-side movement relative to the rotational or pivotal movement during the swing. The analyst can also determine trunk stability, which indicates whether or not players lose their spine angle or bend too much to the right or left.

In addition, the ZenoLINK report provides detailed data about what's called the *kinetic link*, the physical process that transfers power during the golf swing. Ideally the chain of biomechanical events begins in the lower body, then moves to the torso, to the shoulders, to the arms, and finally to the club. In other words, the larger body components should create power, which is transferred to the smaller parts. This sequence occurs so fast that neither the naked eye nor a regular video camera can observe it accurately.

By using the ZenoLINK report, the analyst can see if the player has a problem. If the kinetic process fails to occur in the proper sequence during the downswing, then the golfer is likely to make a compensating motion. The typical result is a loss of power and probably accuracy. The analyst also knows that the kinetic link develops improperly for a number of reasons. Among them are instability, physical weakness, or inflexibility. Part of a sport scientist's job is to pinpoint the reason.

The hands-on evaluation, coupled with the ZenoLINK report, is a powerful combination of tools that enables a sport scientist to create a clear, accurate picture of the player's physical condition and to determine where the weaknesses are and how they affect the swing. His advice to me as a coach is invaluable.

The resulting data are reliable and objective. Separating opinion from fact is essential to this process, and the fastest way to discover what needs to be done to bring a player's movements into alignment. A sport scientist uses the ZenoLINK information to design drills and exercises to develop the motor patterns that the player needs. This program takes the golfer to the next physical level quickly, enabling both player and coach to use technique to reach peak performance.

An added benefit is an accelerated learning process. Using focused education to shorten the learning curve instead of trial and error or guesswork saves time and spares everyone from frustration as well as unnecessary expense.

The ZenoLINK evaluation is only one high-tech tool available to sport scientists. Here are other technical marvels that can work wonders for a player's golf motion:

TRUNK ROTATION MACHIINE

This machine helps with trunk range of motion and trunk strength. It can also help to develop better awareness of how to separate the shoulders from the hips in the golf swing.

GOLF SWING SIMULATOR

This machine helps the golfer with range of motion in the trunk and with strength in the shoulders, trunk, and hips. It can also be used to train the golfer to stabilize the lower body much earlier in the backswing to make the backswing more compact and efficient.

SPECIALIZED CABLE COLUMN

The cable column has a multitude of applications for the golfer. It can be used to break the golf swing down into component parts or can be used to train the entire motion.

WHO SHOULD CONSULT WITH A SPORT SCIENTIST?

I give about 1,500 hours of lessons and have conducted as many as 30 to 35 winter golf schools in a year. I have yet to meet someone on the lesson tee, regardless of skill level, age, or length of time playing golf, who couldn't benefit from working with a golf-specific sport scientist. Listen to this scenario, which occurs more frequently than common sense should allow:

"*I injured my shoulder in a car accident several years ago, but it has nothing to do with the problems in my golf swing,*" a student will tell me.

"*Then it's just a coincidence,*" I'll respond, "*that your right arm is out of plane, and then that causes the shaft to be out of plane in your golf motion.*"

I believe seeing a sport scientist or physical therapist is essential for anyone with an old or a recent injury. If you're in denial about the impact of an injury on your game, stop kidding yourself. Many injuries can haunt your game for years and prevent you from achieving the desired golf motion and ball flight patterns.

If students express reluctance about consulting with my friend Eanna, I warn them, "Then I can take you only so far." As for the effectiveness of their lessons, folks who don't consult with someone like Eanna are just making donations to my son's college fund by paying my hourly fees. They might as well save us both time by sending the check directly to my house.

If you've got a joint in your body that can predict the weather, you need to see someone like Eanna. No ifs, ands, or buts! If you really want to play your best, make an appointment with a golf-specific sport scientist so you can begin your journey to a fit golf body. That professional will work with you to minimize the limitations caused by the injury. Golf-specific trainers are often trained in sports science exercise physiology, athletic training, or physical therapy. Of course, it is always important to investigate their credentials before having them treat sports injuries or before following any of their advice.

I have many clients with golf fitness issues hobbling their progress. Many male clients may have adequate strength but are about as flexible as a 2x4. On the flip side, I have some female clients who have tremendous flexibility and are fit but lack the strength to support the club with an adequate amount of speed. If these men and women are serious about their game, they will go to someone like Eanna to resolve their physical limitations—all of which I feel, without help, make improvement physically impossible.

Finally, I'd like to mention something that eventually limits all of us—maybe you've heard of it. It's called the *aging process*. Many golfers sit on their butt on Wall Street, Madison Avenue, downtown Toledo, or wherever, for maybe 10 or 12 hours a day. Is this you? Then watch out! Age will bite you in that lazy backside if you don't work to counteract its effects. Do not grow old gracefully! On the golf course there's nothing graceful about it. Staying fit after age 40, when the biological bell goes off, is another excellent reason to see someone like Eanna. You don't want to lose strength, flexibility, and muscle tone. You need to work out to battle the aging process.

Even juniors can benefit from appointments with a golf-specific sport scientist. Don't get me wrong: Juniors have become especially good in the last few years. But if more of them had incorporated fitness training from the beginning, they would be much farther along, and they would have gotten there sooner.

After students have a few sessions with someone like Eanna, the light bulb comes on, and most of them realize why they weren't able to make a correct golf swing and why they finally feel something in their swing that they never felt before. That's a real eye-opener for them. Many have come back and thanked me and Eanna, but I consider it just part of our job.

All my students who followed Eanna's advice and did what I told them to do on the practice tee have succeeded. Every single one! Those who don't want to put the effort into it fall by the wayside. It's that black and white. Some people are searching for the Holy Grail. They think they can take a lesson or two from this or that coach or glean the right advice from an occasional magazine article. They think a perfect swing will fall out of the sky and onto their game. People like that are out there, all right. They're kidding themselves! With such an unrealistic approach, they'll never succeed at golf.

Enough said. If you're still with me, I'm assuming that you're not one of these people. I realize that not everyone can get to Greenwich, Connecticut, to see my friend Eanna. For those of you who can, I highly recommend it. For those of you living in other regions of the country, I've listed a few sports scientists I highly recommend in Appendix A. I've also listed some recommended reading on the subject of getting fit for golf. As I mentioned earlier, if going to someone like Eanna simply isn't possible, you can still improve your game tremendously by following the exercises designed by Eanna at the end of this chapter. I expect all of you to follow these routines faithfully, and when you reach stage three, you should do those exercises regularly. They are specifically designed to develop the seven key physical components required to play your best golf (which we'll go over in more detail now).

THE SEVEN KEY PHYSICAL COMPONENTS OF GOLF

I mentioned these components earlier, but let's go over them in detail so you understand your target. Eanna calls these seven ingredients the "essential physical components of golf." They are: posture, range of motion, strength, stability, balance, speed, and coordination.

1. **Posture**

   Posture presets your physical movement patterns. The correct posture brings your spine into optimum alignment, forming a 25- to 35-degree angle (depending on your body type) at the hips.

   If your posture is not correct at address, you'll be forced to make compensating motions to get the clubface to the ball. It's tough to launch the space shuttle from a 45-degree angle. You must be in a golf-ready (athletic) posture to launch that little white orb.

Many people sit at a desk all day, bringing their head forward and rounding their shoulders. Not surprisingly, they usually adopt this habitual posture on the range as well. This posture increases the strain on the tissues in the upper back and neck. Trunk rotation is limited, and the arms cannot move properly around the torso.

2. **Range of Motion**

To make a correct golf swing, you'll need a full range of motion in the neck, shoulders, and hips. Can you turn your head and see into the backseat of your car? If not, it's time to work on that neck. How about your torso? Can you make a full turn while keeping a consistent spine angle? Those hips of yours should also be able to pivot correctly.

If you have some physical shortcomings now, don't despair. Range-of-motion problems are common, especially in men. By using the specific exercises provided in this chapter, in time you'll be able to reach this range comfortably unless a physical limitation prevents you from doing so.

3. **Strength**

Golf is a sport of precision and power. The full swing is completed in fewer than two seconds at a high speed. Generating speed and power requires strength and flexibility. Remember, the energy transfer in the golf swing should start in the lower body and move to the torso, then to the shoulders and arms, and finally to the club. You need strong legs to create stability for the delivery of power, along with strong core (trunk) muscles to transfer the energy to your shoulders and arms. The core muscles are also important for maintaining a consistent axis of rotation (spine angle) and an on-plane motion. The shoulder muscles, especially the rotator cuff muscles, should be strong enough to help generate clubhead speed and maintain control of the motion.

4. **Stability**

For energy to be transferred efficiently, body segments have to be stable or anchored. Stabilizing the lower body requires strength, so we can say that stability and strength go hand in hand.

Let's use an analogy: Say you have a rubber band anchored around your left index finger and you want to shoot it at a target. Using the thumb and index finger of your right hand, you pull the rubber band back. If your left index finger won't remain stable (rigid) long enough for you to pull back and let go, what happens?

Your aim will be poor, or the rubber band won't fly very far. The left finger is your anchor. Similarly, your golf swing requires an anchor. Your lower body and trunk must be anchored so that energy can be transferred efficiently.

CHECK YOUR POSTURE

Here's a simple method to check your posture for potential problems. Have someone place a golf club down the length of your back and get into address position. Does the entire length of the club stay in contact with your back and head? If so, your posture is good. If it doesn't, you're rounding your upper back or shoulders too much, and your chin may be buried in your upper chest. Your spine rotates better from a neutral posture, so use the club regularly to get a feel for the proper posture (see page 26).

5. **Balance**

   I see balance problems all the time. Lack of balance often signals that you have poor core and leg strength. If these areas are weak, the body will compensate with other actions. This forces you into inappropriate mechanical positions, which disrupt balance and kill contact quality.

   If you don't start your swing in balance, you can't finish in balance. If you're not balanced, your swing will be inconsistent and unreliable.

   To coil and uncoil efficiently, which is essential to the golf swing, you need a solid base of support in your lower body. That's the only way to be able to finish in what I call a posted-up (level shoulders, vertical spine) or balanced position; most of your weight should post up over your forward leg.

6. **Speed**

   Remember that during an average golf swing, a clubhead travels more than 90 miles an hour and lasts fewer than two seconds. To produce such clubhead speed, each body segment must move quickly and in the proper sequence.

   Once you have developed the proper stability, strength, range of motion, and other physical properties, speed will follow eventually as a by-product of the work you have done. Practice the sequencing with ever-increasing speed.

7. **Coordination**

   This is the *kinetic link*, or transfer of energy, that creates a powerful golf swing. It requires a well-timed sequence of motion. The key is performing the actions in the

The kinetic link is the physical process where speed or momentum is transferred from the larger body segments (hips and trunk) to the smaller segments (arms and club). This process is initiated as the golfer transitions from the top of the backswing into the downswing. An ideal pattern would be the hips transferring speed to the trunk, the trunk transferring speed to the arms, and the arms transferring speed to the club shaft.

correct sequence. If you can do that, you will be able to drive the ball great distances in a relatively straight line. The lower body, torso, arms, and club must fire in sequence to produce a powerful shot. It is difficult to do this properly unless the previous six physical components are in place.

To play well you must possess all seven of the physical qualities discussed here. A correctly executed golf swing uses particular muscle groups, movements, and angles—elements that become repeatable with practice and development. A correct motion is essentially a finite product of physics, biomechanics, and other scientific principles. If you don't address your most fundamental tool, your body, you will have problems with distance, direction, and other crucial products of your golf motion. Your mechanics will suffer, and so will your score. That's a cold, hard fact of life in the game of golf.

Some golf coaches try to find ways to help you compensate for physical deficiencies. They might change your stance, grip, or ball position to counteract your limited range of motion. Although this medicates the symptoms (with varying degrees of success), it does not eliminate the problems. The result is an inconsistent golf motion, which will give you mixed results at best.

Our goal is a sound, biomechanically correct motion, not a manufactured motion tailored to compensate for your body's lack of strength, speed, range of motion, or other fitness problems. We want long-term, repeatable success! So let's get you headed in the right direction.

BODY SPOKE, PART ONE:
DEVELOPING THE KEY PHYSICAL COMPONENTS

The following pages cover exercises designed to develop the primary components needed to execute a sound golf swing. These exercises, provided by Eanna Rushe of BioSport Technologies, are divided into three groups and must be followed in sequence because each group builds upon the previous one. The first set of exercises focuses on strength, posture, stability, and range of motion. This stage lasts about six to eight weeks. The second stage incorporates fundamental movement skills and lasts another four to six weeks. The third stage centers on power, speed, and coordination because these are all by-products of the previous skills combined. You do not need to repeat the exercises from the previous stage; these are separate, progressive stages.

The exercises require a commitment of about 30 minutes, two or three times each week, but the more practice, the better. (Many Tour players I speak with are doing between one and three hours of physical work daily.) In addition to these exercises, Eanna has provided a five-minute warm-up stretching routine to follow before each practice session or round.

This program takes time, but the results are well worth it. Your swing may suffer before it gets better, but that's a good sign. As you develop new skills, your swing, along with your body, will undergo changes (or, as I like to say, great pains of growth).

After you have progressed through the exercises in this chapter and practiced a sound golf motion, you'll be playing better than ever. You'll add real, permanent improvements to your motion and, therefore, to your game—assuming, of course, you continue to practice these advanced exercises regularly. This is a lifestyle commitment, not a five-minute fix.

IMPORTANT NOTE: You should feel a mild stretching sensation in all stretches. Stop immediately if you feel pain. Never force your stretches. When you feel the muscle relax, you can increase the stretch a little more.

FIRST STAGE

TIME REQUIRED: 30 minutes, three to four times a week for six to eight weeks (to start). All stretches can be done daily.

A. Flexibility/Range of Motion

STRETCH: NECK

Start in standing position with good posture. Place left arm behind your back. Keep shoulders level and let head bend to right side until stretch is felt on left side of neck/upper shoulder area. You can place right hand on side of head and gently pull head to increase stretch. Don't force the stretch. Hold for at least 90 seconds. Repeat 1 time each side.

STRETCH: POSTERIOR SHOULDER

Start in standing position with good posture. Bring left arm across chest keeping arm straight. Using right arm, pull left arm across chest until stretch is felt in back of shoulder. Keep shoulders level and don't let trunk rotate. Hold at least 90 seconds. Repeat 1 time each side.

STRETCH: SHOULDER EXTERNAL ROTATION WITH CLUB

Stand with right arm at side with elbow bent to 90 degrees with palm facing up. Place club head into palm with the shaft on the thumb side. Rotate arm/shoulder to top of backswing position (approx.) with shaft hanging behind upper arm. Place left hand on shaft to rotate shoulder backwards. Don't force stretch. Hold 90–120 seconds. Repeat 1 time each side.

STRETCH: HAMSTRINGS

Lie on back and place right leg on wall and the left leg through the doorframe (if there is any low back discomfort keep left leg bent). Right knee can be slightly bent. To feel more of a stretch, move your body closer to the wall. Use pillow under head to decrease strain on neck. Hold 90–120 seconds. Repeat 1 time each side.

STRETCH: HIP FLEXORS

Kneel on left knee. Place towel or pillow under knee. Place right leg forward. With upper body straight gently lean forward until a stretch is felt in front of left hip/thigh. Don't let knee go out over toes of front leg. Hold 90 seconds. Repeat 1 time on each leg.

STRETCH: HIP EXTERNAL/INTERNAL ROTATION

External: Lie on back and place right foot on wall. Right leg should be bent. Cross left leg over right placing left ankle just underneath right kneecap. You should feel a stretch in the left hip/buttock area. As you move closer to the wall the stretch will increase. To increase stretch you can gently push left knee towards wall. Hold 90–120 seconds. Repeat 1 time each side.

Internal: Grasp outside of left knee with both hands and gently pull knee diagonally towards opposite shoulder. You should feel a stretch in buttock/hip of left leg. Hold for 90–120 seconds. Repeat 1 time each leg.

STRETCH: LATERAL HIP/THIGH

Lie on back and straighten left leg. Cross right leg over left trying to keep right buttock on floor. Grasp outside of right knee with left hand. You should feel a stretch on outside of right hip/thigh. Hold 90–120 seconds. Repeat 1 time each leg.

STRETCH: TRUNK

Lie on right side with knees pulled up towards chest. You can place a pillow or rolled up towel between knees. Try and have knees at least to hip level. Grasp knees with right hand to stabilize lower body. Rotate trunk and left arm to opposite side keeping lower body stable. Left hand should be about shoulder level. You may feel a stretch through the chest, rib cage, and hip area. Hold 90–120 seconds. Repeat 1 time each side.

STRETCH: CHEST

Sit on ball. Walk yourself forward letting the ball roll up your back. Have ball under upper back with the head supported on the ball. Keep body straight. Relax arms out to side with hands slightly behind shoulders. Hold for 90–120 seconds. Repeat 1 time.

STRETCH: BACK EXTENSION

Lie face down. Place hands on floor slightly wider than shoulder width apart and forward of shoulders. Keeping hips on floor slowly raise upper body off floor until a stretch is felt in lower back and abdominals. Go as far as is comfortable. Do not force end of range position. An alternative is to prop yourself onto your forearms if you are very limited in range of motion. Hold for 30 seconds. Repeat 2 times.

STRETCH: SIDE-LYING OVER PHYSIOBALL

Kneel on one leg beside ball. Lie on your side over ball and use other leg to push you onto ball. Use under hand to help support you. Legs should be in contact with floor and spread apart to help keep balance. Hold 90–120 seconds. Repeat 1 time each side.

B. Strength/Stability

BRIDGING WITH PHYSIOBALL
MUSCLES—TRUNK/LEGS

Lie on back with calves resting on ball. Extend arms straight up with palms together. Push hips toward ceiling keeping ball as stable as possible. Hold for 10 seconds. Do 10 repetitions. Work up to holding position for 60 seconds and repeat 3 times. Do 2–3 days per week.

STATIC LOWER ABDOMINALS
MUSCLES—LOWER ABDOMINALS & INTERNAL OBLIQUES

Lie on floor with legs bent and feet flat on floor. Perform a pelvic tilt by flattening lower back toward floor. This stabilizes pelvic area. Lift one leg about 2 inches off floor while keeping abdominals braced and lower back flat. Hold for 6 seconds then slowly return foot to the floor. Alternate legs. Don't hold your breath during exercise. Do 10–12 repetitions working up to 20 repetitions. Do 2–3 days per week.

MUSCLES—ABDOMINALS AND OBLIQUES

Lie on floor face up with legs bent and feet flat on floor. Feet should be about shoulder width apart. Perform slight pelvic tilt then curl upper body toward knees. The motion should be slightly diagonal with right shoulder going toward opposite knee and vice versa. Don't try to curl too far. A good guide is to have hands touch outside of knees. Do 2 sets of 10 repetitions, 2–3 times per week.

LUMBAR ROTATION WITH PHYSIOBALL
MUSCLES—ABDOMINALS AND OBLIQUES

Lie on floor face up with arms on floor about 90 degrees to body. Place legs over small to medium physioball. Legs should be bent approximately 90 degrees with calves resting on top of ball. Ball should be tucked into back of upper legs (hamstrings). Keeping shoulders square on floor rotate lower body about 45 degrees. Focus on core muscles doing the work. You can add a small medicine ball (4–6 lbs) between knees to increase difficulty. Do 2 sets of 10 repetitions, 2–3 times per week.

SHOULDER FLEXION WITH EXTERNAL ROTATION
MUSCLES—ROTATOR CUFF, SHOULDERS

In a standing position with good posture—slight knee flex with shoulder blades down and back, start with palms facing body with elbows slightly bent. Raise arms up and back so palms finish facing forward. Arms should not straighten during movement. Start with light dumbbells 2–3 lbs. Do 2 sets of 10 repetitions, 2–3 times per week.

ARM/LEG RAISE ON PHYSIOBALL
MUSCLES—UPPER/LOWER BACK

Lie face down on medium sized physioball with weight evenly distributed on hands and feet. Ball should be positioned on lower abdominal/pelvic area. Back should be straight. Raise opposite arm and leg so they form a straight line—don't arch lower back. Pause at top of range for 6 seconds. Repeat on opposite side. Keep ball as stable as possible during movement. Do 2 sets of 5 repetitions on each side, 2–3 days per week.

WALL SLIDES WITH PHYSIOBALL
MUSCLES—FRONT AND BACK OF THIGHS AND BUTTOCKS

Place ball against wall with ball positioned in lower back. Walk feet forward about 12–18 inches. Feet should be hip-width apart. Slowly lower body toward ground finishing with thighs parallel to floor. Don't let knees go out over toes. You might feel like you are sitting into a chair on the way down. Do 2 sets of 12–15 repetitions, 2–3 times per week.

SHOULDER RAISES
MUSCLES—ROTATOR CUFF/DELTOID

Stand with slight knee flex and shoulders down and back. Arms are at your sides with palms facing body. Raise dumbbells to shoulder height finishing with a thumb up position (arms rotate). Hands should finish slightly in front of body. Start with light dumbbells 2–3 lbs. Do 2 sets of 10 repetitions, 2–3 times per week.

ROWING WITH SPORTS CORD MUSCLES— MID–BACK

Sit on ball with back straight and shoulders down and back. Pull sports cord toward you by pinching shoulder blades together followed by the arms. Pause and return to start. Don't let cord snap back— keep it under control. Focus should be on pulling shoulder blades together. Start with a light sports cord. Do 2 sets of 12–15 repetitions, 2–3 days per week.

THREE-QUARTER BACK SWING ON HALF FOAM ROLL MUSCLES—LOWER BODY AND TRUNK

Stand on half foam roll with balls of feet. Feet should stay level with the ground. Assume golf posture. Club should be off the ground about 3 inches. Keeping lower body stable, swing club to three-quarter backswing position. Left arm should be approximately parallel with ground with shaft 90 degrees to arms. Hold for 10 seconds. Do 2 sets of 10 times, 2–3 days per week.

SEATED TRUNK ROTATION ON PHYSIOBALL WITH SPORTS CORD MUSCLES—CORE MUSCLES

Sit on ball with feet slightly wider than hips. Keep back straight. Grasp sports cord in both hands. Start with hands outside of right knee. Rotate to left side while arms move parallel to ground. Keep hands out and away from you. Arms should be fairly relaxed. Focus on recruiting core muscles to turn trunk and arms. Do 2 sets of 10 repetitions each side, 2–3 days per week.

TRICEPS EXTENSION

Grasp tubing and place elbows close to your side. Maintain an upright posture with knees slightly flexed. Straighten arms to full extension and return under control. Feel triceps (back of upper arms) doing the work. Do 2 sets of 10 repetitions, 2–3 times per week.

TRUNK TURN WITH PHYSIOBALL

Assume address position while holding ball. Stabilize lower body while rotating to top of backswing. Pause at top of swing for 2 seconds. Keep ball away from body with full extension in arms. Return to address. Focus on recruiting core muscles to turn trunk not just an arm lift. Maintain spine angle as you rotate. Do both sides of body. Do 2 sets of 10–12 repetitions, 2–3 days per week.

C. Posture Check

Note that flexibility and strength allow a golfer to adopt good posture.

- Hip hinge drill with club.

HIP HINGE DRILL WITH CLUB

Start in an upright position with feet about shoulder width apart. Place shaft of golf club in line with spine. Slightly flex your knees and hinge from your hips to assume your address position. Make sure the shaft does not leave the spine as you hinge from your hips and not from your upper back. You may feel like your buttocks go back as you get into your address position. Do 10 repetitions. This drill can be done daily.

SECOND STAGE

TIME REQUIRED: 30 minutes, two or three times a week for four to six weeks.

A. Core Movement Skills

TORSO SEPARATION DRILL WITH MEDICINE BALL.
FUNCTION—FEEL SEPARATION OF TRUNK FROM LOWER BODY

Assume address position while holding medicine ball. Arms can be bent with upper arms close to trunk throughout exercise—don't reach with arms. Keep lower body stable and separate upper body from lower body as if you were starting the backswing. Rotate trunk as far as range of motion will allow. Don't let lower body release. Focus on recruiting core muscles not pulling shoulders around with arms. You might feel a slight weight transfer to back leg. Use 6–8 lb medicine ball. Do 2 sets of 10 repetitions, 2–3 times per week.

WEIGHT TRANSFER DRILL WITH FORWARD PIVOT.
FUNCTION—TO FEEL A PROPER WEIGHT TRANSFER FROM BACK LEG TO FRONT LEG DURING TRANSITION FROM BACKSWING TO DOWNSWING

Set up in address position with arms across chest. Weight should be about 50/50 between both feet. Make sure the weight is on the balls of the feet (wide portion of foot). Without rotating your shoulders, shift your weight so it is about 75 percent on the front leg (left leg for right-handed golfer). Your left knee should be in line with the center of your left ankle. When you feel "posted up" on your front leg, rotate your body to a finish position. Do 2 sets of 10 reps, 2–3 times per week.

TORSO SEPARATION WITH WEIGHT TRANSFER AND FORWARD PIVOT.
FUNCTION—TO INTEGRATE CORE MOVEMENT PATTERNS SO THEY APPROXIMATE GOLF SWING

This drill is a combination of the above move. Assume address with arms across chest. Weight on the balls of the feet. Keeping lower body stable separate upper body from lower body. Focus on recruiting core muscles and turn your trunk as far as your range of motion will allow. Without rotating your shoulders back to the target, shift your weight so it is about 75 percent on the front leg (left leg for right-handed golfer). Your left knee should be in line with the center of your left ankle. When you feel "posted up" on your front leg rotate your body to a finish position. Do 2 sets of 10 repetitions, 2–3 times per week.

THIRD STAGE

TIME REQUIRED: 30 minutes two or three times a week. This should become a regular routine.

A. Power/Speed

COUNTER-MOVEMENT WITH STEP
FUNCTION—DYNAMIC STRETCHING THROUGH THE CORE WITH EMPHASIS ON GOOD
WEIGHT TRANSFER DURING TRANSITION FROM BACKSWING TO DOWNSWING

Assume stance width for medium to long iron. Mark the width of your stance with two golf balls or tees. Assume address position holding a medicine ball. Narrow your stance by bringing left leg close to right leg. Keep upper arms close to body throughout exercise. Simultaneously rotate into backswing while stepping in opposite direction (toward target). When you feel your weight transfer to your front leg, rotate to finish position. Step the width of your stance. Move as if you were going to release the ball by rotating your trunk, not by swinging arms. Start slowly and then increase speed of exercise. Use 6–8 lb medicine ball. Do 2 sets of 10 repetitions, 3 times per week.

MEDICINE BALL TOSS FUNCTION—UPPER BODY SPEED/POWER

Set up in front of a plyoback (mini-trampoline) or you can use a partner. Knees are slightly flexed with medicine ball held in front of chest. Chest pass medicine ball to partner or at plyoback by straightening arms. This exercise should be done quickly, but controlled. Start of with 4 lb medicine ball and progress to 6–8 lb ball. Do 2 sets of 10 repetitions, 3 times per week.

MEDICINE BALL TOSS WITH TRUNK ROTATION
FUNCTION—DYNAMIC STRETCHING AND SHORTENING OF THE TRUNK MUSCLES

Set up in front of plyoback (mini-trampoline) or you can use a part-ner. Knees are slightly flexed, trunk rotated with medicine ball held at side of body. Release ball by rotat-ing trunk muscles. Lower body should remain pretty stable through-out drill. Start off with 4 lb medicine ball and progress to 6–8 lb ball. Do 2 sets of 10 repetitions each side, 3 times per week.

SKIERS' JUMP
FUNCTION—SPEED/POWER IN LOWER BODY

Set up in address position with arms relaxed out to the side or placed across chest. Jump side to side along an imagi-nary target line. When you land on one leg make sure to let your hip and knee flex. Don't let knee go out over toes or leg buckle out from underneath you. Maintain your golf posture as much as possible. Try to change direction as quickly as possible. Do 2 sets of 10 repetitions, 2 times per week. Work up to 3 sets of 20–30 repetitions.

CHANGE OF DIRECTION DRILL WITH CLUB
FUNCTION—DYNAMIC STRETCHING/SHORTENING THROUGH CORE AND A BETTER CHANGE OF DIRECTION IN GOLF SWING

Set up in golf posture. Place a tee or golf club on ground approximating where the ball position would be. Start drill with club in post-impact position (shaft parallel to ground for right-handed golfer). Start swinging club into backswing position. As club passes over marker, change direction and swing to finish position. Start off slowly to get feel for drill then start to increase the speed. Do 2 sets of 10 repetitions, 3 times per week.

B. Impact Bag Drills

LONG RESPONSE
FUNCTION—MAINTAIN DYNAMIC POSTURE WHILE INITIATING MUSCLE STRETCH/SHORTENING EFFECT

Place one side of impact bag in line with ball position for medium to long iron. Set up in golf posture. Swing club into backswing position so left arm is approximately parallel with ground and shaft at 90 degrees to left arm. This is the start position. Pause in this position for 2 seconds before initiating downswing. Make sure that you don't come out of your spine angle as you move into the downswing. Swing club into bag as fast as possible. Make sure club releases fully on impact with bag. Return to start position and pause for two seconds before initiating downswing. Do 2 sets of 10 repetitions, 2 times per week.

SHORT RESPONSE
FUNCTION—ENHANCE THE MUSCLE STRETCH/SHORTENING EFFECT

Set up in golf posture. Place one side of impact bag in line with ball position for medium to long iron. Swing club from address back to impact. Start off slowly to get comfortable with drill and then increase to full speed. Make sure club releases fully into bag (do not try to push bag with club). Do 2 sets of 10 repetitions, 2 days per week.

C. Preplay Routine

TOTAL TIME REQUIRED: Five minutes before each practice session or round. OBJECTIVE: To increase tissue temperature and to stretch muscles.

- **Slow arm circles**: Start with knees slightly flexed and arms relaxed by sides. Slowly rotate arms in big circles. Repeat in both directions. Do 5 repetitions in both directions.
- **Rhythmic weight transfer drill with torso rotation**: Set up in golf posture with arms crossed over chest. Slowly transfer weight from right foot to left foot while you let the trunk rotate from side to side. Do 1 set of 20 repetitions.
- **Knee lifts**: March in place letting the arms swing freely. Bring knees to about hip height. Let trunk freely rotate from side to side. Do 1 set of 20 repetitions.
- **Rhythmic side bending**: Set up with knees slightly bent and arms stretched slightly wider than shoulder width overhead holding golf club. Slowly, bend from side to side keeping upper body in line with lower body. You should feel a stretch along waist/rib cage. Do 1 set of 10 repetitions.
- **Neck rotation stretch**: Set up with good posture. Slowly rotate head from side to side. You should feel stretch in neck. Do 1 set of 10 repetitions.
- **Shoulder/trunk rotation stretch with club**: Set up in golf posture with a club placed across your shoulders. Slowly rotate trunk from side to side keeping lower body stable. Do 1 set of 12 repetitions.
- **Hamstring stretch**: Place both hands on golf club for support. Bring one leg forward and place heel on ground with toe up. Both knees should be slightly flexed. Hinge forward from hips to feel stretch into hamstring and calf. Don't round upper back as you hinge forward. Hold stretch for 10–15 seconds on each leg.
- **Front of thigh stretch**: Use golf club for support. Lift one leg off ground and grasp ankle. Gently pull heel toward buttocks until you feel a stretch in the front of the thigh. Have a slight flex in the supporting leg. Try to keep your body fairly upright. Hold stretch for 10–15 seconds on each leg.
- **Rhythmic swing/step drill**: Set up in golf posture. Start with feet about 6 inches apart. Swing club into backswing while you step forward. As soon as lead leg touches the ground change direction and swing to finish. Start with slow pace and increase to full swing speed. Do 1 set of 12–15 repetitions.

SWING DIAGNOSIS 101

Swing flaws are sometimes symptoms of a particular underlying physical deficiency. Let's review some common swing faults among amateur players. The physical limitation that the fault may be indicating is listed after each one. Also listed are specific exercises to remedy each problem. This section will help you recognize particular swing flaws and provide ways for you to correct them. Incorporate into the routines outlined above any recommended exercises in this section that apply to you. Because the exercises illustrated here are fault specific, add them only if you or your coach have noted any of these problems in your motion. Like all the exercises and other information in this chapter, these exercises are provided courtesy of Eanna Rushe of BioSport Technologies, Cos Cob, Connecticut.

1. **Poor Posture at Address**
   Physical Cause of Problem: This is a flexibility problem (caused by tight chest muscles) and a strength problem (caused by weak upper back muscles).
   Physical Remedy for the Problem:
   - Chest stretch
   - Rowing with tubing
   - Hip hinge drill with club

2. **Right Leg Straightens During Backswing/Reverse Pivot**
   Physical Cause of Problem: Tight hip rotators and tight lateral hip/thigh muscles. Weak hip/thigh muscles are also a factor.
   Physical Remedy for the Problem:
   - Internal hip rotation stretch
   - Lateral hip stretch

3. **Flying Right Elbow/Disconnection of Arm Swing, Which Alters the Shaft Plane**
   Physical Cause of Problem: Tight internal shoulder rotator muscles and poor posture.
   Physical Remedy for the Problem:
   - External rotation stretch
   - Chest stretch

4. **Breakdown or Collapse of the Left Arm During the Backswing/Loss of Radius of Arm Swing**
   Physical Cause of Problem: Tight back (posterior) shoulder muscles and possibly weak triceps.
   Physical Remedy for the Problem:
   - Posterior shoulder stretch
   - Triceps extension (strength)

5. **Poor Trunk Turn/Poor Torso Rotation**
   Physical Cause of Problem: Tight trunk muscles.
   Physical Remedy for the Problem:
   - Trunk stretch

6. **Loss of Spine Angle**
   Physical Cause of Problem: Usually this signals a range-of-motion problem in the trunk area and poor trunk stability.
   Physical Remedy for the Problem:
   - Torso separation drill
   - Trunk turn with physioball
   - Trunk stretch

FOREWARNED IS FOREARMED: PREVENTING GOLF INJURIES

Proper training also helps to prevent injuries, which are common in golf. Professionals and nonprofessionals, both male and female, suffer different types of injuries. Male nonprofessional golfers most often sustain soft-tissue damage in the lower back, followed by injuries to the elbows, hands and wrists, and then shoulders and knees. Male professionals tend to injure the lower back, left wrist, and shoulders. Back injuries are the second most common problem in both professional and nonprofessional female golfers; the most common among professional women is injuries to the left wrist and among amateurs, the elbow.

The prevalence of lower back injuries is no mystery. The peak compressive forces of a golf swing on the lower back can be as much as eight times the body weight in both amateur and professional golfers. Ouch! In comparison, running produces peak compressive forces of only three times the body weight.

What causes different injuries among professionals and nonprofessionals is more significant than where the damage occurs. Amateurs tend to suffer injuries related to poor mechanics—they're trying to make athletic motions that exceed their fitness and flexibility levels. Professionals, who train regularly and warm up before every practice session and round, sustain repetitive sports injuries—caused by making the same motion over and over, not by failing to train their body properly to make those motions. Professionals by definition want and need to repeat their golf motions, but the injuries sustained by amateurs are highly preventable. Put another way: Be smart! Train your body properly and warm up regularly. You don't want to sponsor a vacation home for your chiropractor. You do not want to become a golf injury statistic. Golf injuries are not only painful, they usually mean missing several weeks of play.

Another way to avoid injuries is to resist the temptation to imitate the professionals you admire. Many golfers want to emulate Tiger Woods, for example. But if most amateurs reached the same position he does in his backswing, they'd need reconstructive surgery afterward. As they say on television (in fact, they should carry this warning when they televise professional tournaments): *Don't try this at home!*

GOLF INJURY STATISTICS: MOST COMMON GOLF INJURIES BY TYPE*
Professional Male Golfers
   Lower back
   Left wrist
   Shoulder

Amateur Male Golfers
   Lower back
   Elbow
   Hand or wrist
   Shoulder and knee

*Reference: *Clinics in Sports Medicine: Golf Injuries 1996.* Edited by Gary N. Guten, M.D.

Professional Female Golfers
Left wrist
Lower back
Left shoulder

Amateur Female Golfers
Elbow
Back
Shoulder
Hand or wrist

BODY SPOKE, PART TWO:
CREATING A BIOMECHANICALLY CORRECT SWING

If you've been faithfully putting in the time and effort to develop the seven physical components needed to execute a sound golf swing, congratulations! For those of you who are just skimming this chapter, casually making a mental note to try this exercise or that one or to do them once in a while (you know who you are), go back to the exercises and drills suggested here. If you want to improve your game without injury, you have no other choice. You can't take shortcuts! Perform these exercises faithfully, then come back and see me. I'll be waiting right here.

> *Letting go is ineffective unless it is proceeded by both physical conditioning and mental training. There is no substitute for the hard work and self-discipline that go into athletic training, but without the ability to let go, the discipline invested can actually be counterproductive.*
>
> —Dr. Gary Wiren

Once you complete your physical fitness program, you'll be ready to learn a new motion—a sound, mechanically correct one—because your body is ready to receive the motion. Then you'll be able to execute a sound golf motion without a visit to the orthopedic surgeon afterward. Your old motion is, in short, a bad habit, and golf habits, like any others, die hard. If you've been playing with a faulty motion for quite some time, swinging a club the right way is going to feel very different—at first. You'll need time, not only to incorporate the motion but also to sequence it properly.

Let me give you an analogy: Cross your arms as you would normally, then uncross them. Okay, now cross them again but in the opposite way. The movement feels strange, doesn't it? That's because your mind is used to sending your arms a particular signal, and they've been responding automatically. Crossing your arms in a certain way has become a habit. But if you keep practicing crossing them the new way, eventually that movement will feel comfortable to you. I don't know of any wrong way to cross your arms, but a fundamentally sound way (and many wrong ways) to make a golf motion definitely exists.

For those of you who like to watch professionals and imitate them, please be careful. You may not clobber yourself because of fitness issues (flexibility, for instance), but you could still sabotage your motion. Ironically, some touring pros use swings that are neither technically sound nor conventional. Nonetheless, they can play that way because they possess a preternatural amount of innate talent, such as exceptional hand–eye coordination or flexibility.

Now that your body is ready to play the best golf of your life and you've begun to learn what a biomechanically correct swing looks and feels like, you're ready for the next Spoke. So let's develop your mental abilities.

Note: Eanna Rushe would like to acknowledge Chris Welch for his assistance with biomechanics.

2 WHO LET THE MONKEYS OUT?
SPOKE 2: THE MIND

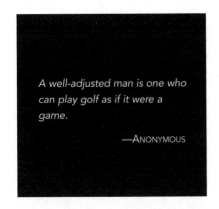

A well-adjusted man is one who can play golf as if it were a game.

—Anonymous

If I had told my golf students 15 or 20 years ago, "You need to spend some time with a sport psychologist," they would have thought I was calling them either mentally impaired or crazy. To say they'd be taken aback and probably insulted, too, would be puttiing it mildly. Yet the mind has always been critical to the game of golf. If you can't control your mind or your emotions, you can't play golf. Fortunately, we have recognized that much of the game is played on an optical and an emotional level. Today the mental side of golf is finally beginning to receive the attention it deserves.

Golf requires a training method that allows you to evaluate your objective in a logical fashion and then focus on that target before you even take a club from your bag. Countless times I've asked students, "How did you select that club?" The reply I hear most often is, "It just feels right." What the heck are they thinking? Was that feeling based on anything? Wind speed or direction? Position of the pin? Their lie? Their stance? Their daily horoscope? Who knows? On such occasions (after they've hit a lousy shot), I'll also hear, "I knew I shouldn't have used that club!" Brilliant. Then why did they choose it?

Such players lack an inner process that says, *Hey, pal, pay attention. Let's be logical here!* First, they're missing the critical importance of the preshot routine (which we'll talk about in detail in Chapter 13, "The Bookends: The Launching Pad and Finish Condition", page 158). They're also in a rush to get to what they believe is the meat and potatoes of the game— hitting the shot. They haven't learned that the mental routine that precedes the shot—and presets the odds for success—is even more fundamental. In fact, it is absolutely vital.

Although rushing to the shot is the wrong approach, I understand the tendency. I didn't learn this lesson overnight myself. Now I hope that my experience will save you time, cut your learning time in half, and lead to countless saved shots.

Years ago I worked with sport psychologist and author Dr. Richard (Dick) Coop of the University of North Carolina. Dr. Coop has worked with many top athletes, including Michael Jordan, Davis Love III, the late Payne Stewart, and Corey Pavin. He taught me the critical importance of having a trigger. When I approached the ball under his direction, I wasn't allowed even to pick a club until I had evaluated my lie, stance, wind conditions, pin position, and overall distance and had a clear mental picture of the type of shot I wanted to play. Then I could pick a club. That club selection was, and still is, my trigger.

Once I choose a club I become totally focused on my shot. (Sorry, folks. All of you become invisible to me.) For those next 15 seconds or so, everything else—birds chirping above, other players' voices, a playing partner standing a few feet away—just disappears. My attention is locked on to executing that shot—and nothing else.

Between shots, I relax. Golf courses are often located in beautiful settings, so I try to enjoy nature and (in most cases) the company of my playing partners. If I didn't stop to relax occasionally, my head would explode. No one should try to maintain that level of focus for more than four hours, because no one can. The game should be played with short periods of deep focus alternating with long stretches of enjoyment and relaxation.

How much attention am I asking of you? Let's say, just as an example, that the average round lasts about four and a half hours and requires approximately 90 shots, each of which lasts an average of 15 seconds, including the preshot routine. This means I'm asking you to pay close attention (i.e., focus) for about 23 minutes in all. The rest of that time, have fun! This approach makes the game much easier and certainly less stressful. If you choose to remain uptight the whole time, you'll make what should be an enjoyable time into a miserable experience.

Of course it's not always that easy just to focus and relax out there. Mental stumbling blocks can materialize and flatten your game. In this chapter I discuss the mental side of golf with my friend and adviser Dr. Rick Jensen, the president of the Performance Enhancement Center and the director of sport psychology at the PGA National Resort and Spa. Dr. Jensen has a doctorate in psychology with a specialization in sport psychology and exercise science.

The comments and advice included here come from Dr. Jensen as a sport psychologist, and from me as a professional golf coach. Both of us draw on our experience in working with thousands of golfers, including PGA and LPGA Tour professionals and some highly accomplished amateurs. After we discuss some general ideas about the mental aspects of golf, we'll concentrate on three key mental problems that golfers experience—anxiety, lack of focus, and anger management. We'll also discuss the relationship between the mind and an effective golf learning environment, along with the importance of having a positive attitude. So have a seat, relax, and listen up.

A CONVERSATION BETWEEN TOM PATRI AND DR. RICK JENSEN: ON THE MENTAL GAME

ARE YOU MENTAL? OR DO YOU JUST THINK YOU ARE?

RJ: It's good that the mental side of golf has begun to receive a lot of attention. But like any concept that comes into vogue, it's being taken too far by some people. Players too often assume that the problems with their game stem from something mental. Most of them need to take a breather and ask themselves honestly: *Am I mental? Or do I just think I am?*

Golfers commonly experience mental problems on the course such as anxiety, doubt, or lack of confidence. More often than not, the source of these symptoms isn't psychological. It's usually the result of a history of poor shots caused by faulty technique, ineffective practice habits, poor preparation, or other skill deficits. Players who suspect a problem with their game should determine first whether it's truly a psychological one or the consequence of a more fundamental problem.

TP: I agree, Rick. Many students I've worked with come to me thinking they're better mechanically than they really are, and that breeds unrealistic expectations. The physical limitations in their game may cause them mental anguish, but it's not mental mistakes that are driving up their handicap.

RJ: If that's the case, those players need to work on improving their skills or correcting some other flaw that's detracting from their game. Although some players may actually experience mental problems—anxiety, stress, and so on—these are conditions that can be resolved only by working on and improving technical skills, not by changing their mental attitude. Let's face the facts. If you chunk 15 out of 30 chips, you're going to be anxious. To use an analogy, if you were riding a bike that had a wheel that fell off half the time, you'd be scared, and for good reason. That response is not a mental problem, it's a normal reaction. When you're dealing with a similar situation in golf, you need to work on the physical problems in your game and stop blaming them on your mind.

Your Six Spokes, Tom, are valuable tools for determining where a player's weaknesses lie. I've encountered many golfers in my practice who don't play well because they're playing with the wrong equipment, they're out of shape, mismanaging their practice time, or they're technically flawed in certain areas. These problems are far more common causes for poor golf scores than a true mental issue. Before golfers decide that the problem is in their head, they should follow the guidelines in this book to determine whether it's psychological or physical.

This involves a lot of time and hard work, I know, so instead of doing this type of evaluation, people often prefer to think the game is somewhere around 90 percent mental, because it's an easy excuse to hang their hat on. It can dangle the hope of a quick fix in front of them. But the truth is, there are no quick fixes in golf.

REAL LEARNING TAKES TIME

TP: Unfortunately, this quick-fix mentality, though illogical, is extremely common. Take, for example, some of the students I send to you. Some of these players think a sport psychologist like yourself will see them for a session or two; then you'll locate the exact problem, and they'll get the miracle cure. They think that maybe you'll tell them, "Your family was dysfunctional, and your mother did this or your father did that, so just do this," and they're all done. But nothing could be farther from the truth.

Just as I can't watch students for an hour or two and then provide pointers that will cure their swing problems for good, I know that you can't locate the specific source of a problem and fix it on the spot. There's no simple prescription for getting better, and no magic wands, so players should get over that fantasy right now.

We can compare this situation with that of a student of mine who works in derivatives at a major brokerage house in Manhattan. Suppose she was heading to Hawaii for a month, and she sat down with me for three hours to teach me about derivatives. Would I be able to handle that portfolio while she was away? Of course not—no more than I could fix her swing with a few hours of instruction. She has to let me do my job, just as I let her do hers. They both take years of experience and a great deal of applied knowledge.

If players want help with their game from a professional, they shouldn't expect miracles. They aren't that skilled. No one is, not even Tour players who practice what they learn from coaches for hours on end before attempting to play in a competitive situation.

Instead of walking away with what you or I tell them and jumping onto that first tee and saying, "Okay, now I can do this," golfers need to take the time to understand and absorb new information completely. They have to practice and perfect what they've learned over time until it becomes part of their being.

As Bill "Coach" Strausbaugh used to say, "Golf is learned, earned, and acquired." Players simply cannot buy, borrow, or steal a golf swing. They have to comprehend each new skill, then earn the right to possess that skill through endless repetition and practice. This is a lifelong process. Golf is not a destination, it's a journey. There's a beginning and an end, but in between golfers have to keep going—learning, practicing, and refining their technique forever. They can't get off at a particular stop and find that they've "arrived."

I have presented the first five Spokes in this book before Technique (Spoke 6) for a reason. They're in the logical order required. Technique is something that all golfers, even professionals, work on for a lifetime. To achieve steady progress, however, players must continually attend to all six Spokes, not just technique, and incorporate them into their practice and play.

RJ: I sure hear that. Players need to change old habits, and that takes time, but repetition is the key to success. Sometimes, after a bit of practicing a newly learned skill, golfers begin to feel they're doing the right thing when they aren't. They think they've got it and then try to move on too soon. A coach who hasn't seen a student in a while will often see the same old problems crop up during a lesson. This poses a dilemma for guys like you, Tom. Should you tell the students they have the same problem they did a few months back, or should you throw in some new stuff so they feel they're getting more value for your fee? That's a tough situation. But somehow you have to show them that achieving genuine, lasting changes in the swing takes lots of practice and time spent with a coach on a regular basis.

TP: But I don't think that players need to see their coach daily or even weekly once they're beyond the initial consultation stage. I don't allow my students to come for lessons more than twice a month. Between lessons, I expect them to practice what we've worked on to the maximum extent their schedule allows, because that's when the real learning occurs. Otherwise, they're wasting our time and their money. Put another way: Golf isn't taught, it's learned.

RJ: I'm glad to hear you say that, Tom. I also think that when people go to the range to practice, they should skip the small bucket of balls. On every visit they should hit as many balls as they have time for and can hit before becoming mentally and/or physically fatigued. This last point recalls Spoke 1, The Body. If you hit just 30 balls before your back starts hurting, you're not going to get very far. To put things in perspective, some Tour professionals can hit 200 to 500 balls before they tire. A club player may not have that kind of time or stamina, but if you can't hit a lot of shots without fatiguing, you won't gain much in the way of skill. When you're working on a golf swing, 30 balls isn't much.

TP: Exactly. Real learning takes time. And it requires an environment that's conducive to learning. Let's talk about learning environments in more detail.

PROPER LEARNING ENVIRONMENTS

RJ: I think the key to an optimum golf learning environment is feedback. When I ask clients who have played team sports like baseball, soccer, and football how often they had supervision while practicing those sports, the answer is *always*. But with golf? The answer is *almost never*. Golf is a solo sport, I know, but golfers need regular feedback from a qualified coach. Many golfers don't realize this. Even the top professionals, the best golfers in the world, need this. David Leadbetter worked with Nick Faldo during Faldo's big run, Tiger Woods with Butch Harmon, the late Payne Stewart worked with Chuck Cook, and Phil Mickelson has worked steadily with Rick Smith. We could go on and on.

Of course, unlike team sports, where you pay a fee for the season, golfers usually have to pay a coach each time they show up for a lesson, and that can be expensive. The ideal scenario is to take regular one-on-one lessons. If the cost makes that option impractical, golfers can take supervised group lessons. During these sessions several players hit balls while the coach walks up and down the range, coaching each person. Also, some professionals offer packages of lessons for a lower fee that may include both individual and group instruction.

Golfers can also economize when hitting those many buckets of balls we talked about. Club members are usually allowed to hit an unlimited number of balls as part of their membership. Those who don't belong to a club can try taking another route. Some ranges, if you ask, will offer a membership fee or a range plan that allows you to hit any number of balls. This option is always worth inquiring about, because it can save a lot on practice fees.

TP: Good suggestions, Rick. Okay, we've talked about feedback in terms of coaching. How about explaining in more detail the other aspects of the learning environment that can contribute to a player's skill development?

RJ: Sure. In addition to players pursuing coaching regularly, they shouldn't forget to supplement this instruction time by practicing with a training aid, whether it's a specially designed device or drills your coach has given you. Let's say you're collapsing your right arm on your backswing. When your coach is present, he or she can verbally inform you of the error. However, when you're practicing on your own, you can use a right angle as a training aid, to ensure that you know whether your right arm is in fact in the correct position.

TP: By the way, the right angle is one of several excellent training devices I use often. I'd like to mention Appendix C in the back of the book, "Tom's Top 25," because there I describe what I think are the best devices for additional feedback during practice.

Okay, Rick, are there any other aspects of the learning environment that you would consider essential?

RJ: Players certainly would also benefit from what I refer to as *simulation training*. That is, practicing in such a way (or under such conditions) that enhances the likelihood that the skill being practiced will transfer to on-course conditions. Players should ask themselves, do my practice conditions simulate what I am likely to encounter on the golf course?

For example, simply hitting wedge shots to a pin placed in the center of a driving green is not going to be as useful as a condition in which a player can see the ball land on a green and watch it spin and release. Sometimes players don't have any control over this because they're limited by the type of facilities available. At other times golfers simply need to be aware of the kind of practice they should be doing and make an effort to practice shots like that. Whenever possible, all players should practice in conditions that simulate what they're likely to face on the golf course. If their short game is weak, for instance, they should practice regularly in the short-game practice area, not pounding drivers on the practice range. Their drives may look more impressive than their putting, but, while this may impress others at the range, it won't strengthen their game or improve their score. If a golf facility lacks a short-game practice area, players should try to find one that does. Otherwise, their learning environment is not meeting their needs. Additionally, players should come up with games that create pressure similar to that experienced on the course. Hit 8 out of 10 shots within a given distance from the pin! Hole out ten 5-foot putts in a row from around the hole! Simulation training means practicing in a way that allows skills and knowledge to be transferred directly to the golf course. The more practice simulates realistic conditions, the more players will take to the golf course.

Playing from the rough is an example of a common course condition that few players target in their learning environment. Higher-handicap players tend to be in the rough a lot. When I ask these golfers how often they practice playing shots like this, they'll say *never*. But they should practice them regularly and often. If their facility doesn't have a practice area with rough, they can get onto the course during slower times to practice hitting from that type of lie.

ANXIETY

TP: All right, we've talked about the learning process, where solid skills must be understood, practiced, and absorbed. But now, Rick, let's say a golfer has reached a level where his game is solid and consistent, but then he begins to experience true mental problems that are holding him back.

RJ: Okay, let's assume that the player has reviewed the other five Spokes and eliminated other possible causes of mental problems during play. His technique is solid and his ball control exceptional, but for some reason he just can't take it to the course. That's the time to take a hard look at his mental skills. Let's examine three common psychological concerns that can negatively affect a player's game—anxiety, attention control, and anger management. We can start with anxiety.

Those who have solid skills that disintegrate under pressure may be suffering from anxiety. Players often get anxious in particular situations—during competitive play such as a club championship or when playing with certain people like their boss or better players. Conditionally based anxiety can be resolved in three different ways—avoiding the situation, altering perspective, and managing physical reactions.

The first strategy is simply to avoid the situation that causes the anxiety. If this is possible, players should do so. Most golfers don't have to suffer needlessly if a viable alternative can be found. However, avoidance may not be a desired or even practical choice, because it may create a number of other problems. For example, a person who refuses to play with her boss at company outings may strain their work relationship, and that probably isn't worth the risk. If avoidance isn't practical, other solutions can still be found.

Changing perspective and viewing certain situations as opportunities, rather than threats, can improve a golfer's performance and bring greater enjoyment to the game. Anxiety may also be relieved by trying to keep the situation and the potential consequences in proper perspective. Analogous to this solution is the scenario of a gymnast who has to perform a routine on the balance beam. If she does the routine on a beam placed on the floor, she may fall, but at worst she'll just roll onto the mat. But if the balance beam is placed between two skyscrapers, the routine becomes a matter of life or death. The gymnast's perspective changes and so does the level of anxiety that she experiences. Although few people would attempt such a foolish stunt, many golfers, when faced with a playing situation of much less significance, similarly blow the situation out of proportion like this. They take a challenging but relatively safe floor routine and place it between two skyscrapers in their mind. Then the situation and the accompanying anxiety can be overpowering.

TP: That's a good analogy, Rick. To me the concept of controlling your perspective of a situation is an important one. As I see it, anxiety is a self-inflicted wound. When you play golf with others, if you get upset, then you're playing for the wrong reasons. The fear comes from your own expectations of yourself.

For instance, maybe you're setting unrealistic goals. Let's say you typically shoot a 90. If you're heading out with better players than you are and you tell yourself you're going to shoot 85, you're setting yourself up for disappointment and the anxiety that goes with it. Golfers typically experience their best-day play maybe once or twice a year. What makes them think their best game is going to happen on that particular day? They should stop putting unreasonable pressures on themselves.

Another common reason that people get anxious when playing with others is that they become self-conscious. But they should try not to see themselves as performing for others. They should be out there to have fun and get some exercise.

People often ask me if I'm anxious when I play, because I'm the club professional, as if I have to prove something. But I'm not a professional golfer. I'm a golf professional. I teach others for about 12 hours a day, and I also help to manage the activities of my golf school and teaching team. I'm lucky if I can get out to play once or twice a week. I have shot 64 twice in my life, but usually I shoot between 72 and 76. That's realistic, given my time constraints. When I play, I keep my expectations realistic. Otherwise, I wouldn't enjoy the game.

Let me tell you a story. In 1999, after the second day of practice rounds at the Buick Classic, held at the Westchester Country Club, where I served as Director of Golf Instruction for 11 years, Sergio Garcia asked if I wanted to play 9 holes with him and his father. I hesitated, because it was already five o'clock and I was getting ready to go home after a long day.

I hadn't hit a ball in about a week. This was a perfect opportunity to embarrass myself—tackling a difficult course under tournament conditions with a world-class player, when my game was rusty. And if I choked, I knew that I'd do it in front of a bunch of people who would be gathered at the first tee to watch Sergio play. That picture didn't thrill me, even if I would be just "that other guy playing with Sergio."

But moments later I headed off to get my clubs, because I decided it was a wonderful opportunity to see a great player up close and possibly learn something from him. As it turned out, Sergio was a great guy, and so was his dad, Victor. Did I impress Sergio with my impeccable game? I think not! He wasn't out there to see how I could play. He was there to have a good time. After all, golf is a game. If it becomes an uncomfortable, self-conscious endeavor that inspires anxiety, then you probably shouldn't play. Make a choice to enjoy it. Otherwise, why bother?

Remember Bob Rotella's famous adage: *Golf is not a game of perfect.* How true that is. It's really a series of misses. Your job is to turn those errors into something better by using the 14 clubs in your bag. In that sense, golf is a lot like poker, where you have to turn that crummy hand you've been dealt into a win by executing a series of strategic moves. If everyone held the same hand every time, would anyone bother playing?

All right, enough about perspective. Rick, you mentioned a third possible solution for the problem of anxiety.

RJ: Yes, I did. Players can also work on lessening anxiety at the physical level. We're all familiar with the body's reaction to stress—increased heart rate and blood flow marked by a pounding heartbeat, sweaty palms, and shakiness. Although the source of such symptoms is your perception of a situation, you can lessen the ill effects on performance if you can manage the physical symptoms.

Some people may actually play their best when they're a bit pumped up—a common characteristic of competitive athletes. But for some players, heightened levels of intensity interfere with their performance. When that's the case, it's time to do something.

RELAXATION TECHNIQUES

Relaxation techniques can be powerful tools for dealing with the physical reactions a player experiences when anxious. Relaxation techniques are best utilized when a player has practiced the technique to the point where he experiences a conditioned relaxation response. The more a player has trained his body to relax upon command, the more likely relaxation techniques will be effective during competition. If you try to use a relaxation method for the first time during the club championship, you are likely to pay more attention to your efforts to employ the technique than to trying to get the ball in the hole.

There are a number of practical and easy-to-learn relaxation techniques that golfers can use in competition. Such techniques include deep breathing, progressive relaxation, and self-hypnosis. Deep breathing is probably the most common technique used on-course. Players condition their body to relax through deep breathing practices. Deep breathing allows a player's heart rate to slow down and become more regular while also introducing more oxygen to the muscles through the bloodstream. (See sidebar, "Tom's Inhale/Exhale Drill," page 39.)

Some players utilize progressive relaxation, a technique in which a player focuses on the relaxation of specific body parts. A player may progress across a number of body parts—shoulders, arms, legs—consciously tightening the muscles and then immediately allowing them to relax. A player may apply progressive relaxation while walking down the fairway, waiting on a tee box, or standing on the putting green.

Lastly, some players utilize self-hypnosis, a technique designed to induce a state of relaxed focus. People often think of hypnosis as it is portrayed in the media or by entertainers in Vegas—putting a person in a trance and asking them to walk like a chicken. However, as a relaxation strategy, self-hypnosis training can provide significant benefits in training a player to induce a state of focused attention and relaxation. Self-hypnosis often involves the application of visualization as well, a skill that many golfers utilize in their preshot routines prior to each shot.

Whatever technique players employ, it must be used consistently during play. Otherwise, it won't be effective. Players must also rehearse the technique many times and train themselves thoroughly before they try to apply the new skill on the course. Those who do practice and apply any of these techniques consistently, however, will eventually add a powerful tool to their golf bag.

TOM'S INHALE/EXHALE DRILL

When working with students who have too much tension in their bodies or their golf swings, I'll have them inhale as deeply as they can and hold it for a few seconds, then exhale and let it all out. Then I'll ask them, Which of these states do you want to play from, the inhale or the exhale position? They'll answer, The exhale position. I'll ask them, Why? The answer is always, Because it's a lot freer and more relaxed. Darn right it is. So this is what I want you to do: When you're over the ball and you've assumed the address position, inhale as deeply as you can and hold it for a few seconds, then exhale slowly and fully release that breath. At the bottom of that exhale, start your backswing.

FOCUS (ATTENTION CONTROL)

TP: Okay, let's move on to another important issue in the psychology department. I call it *focus*, and I know you call it *attention control*, Rick.

Golf involves some relatively complex movements. To produce those movements, the mind has to be focused on the target (golf is in fact a target game, not a ball game, as many people think), and the body has to be a willing and ready participant.

RJ: That's what's supposed to happen, Tom, but distractions are always part of life on the links. You've probably had conversations with your partner where she realized you weren't really listening. You probably said, "I was, too, listening." And she came back with, "Okay, if you were listening, what did I just say?" Does that sound familiar, Tom?

TP: Ha! I'm afraid so, except the other way around. It also sounds like students of mine at the end of a lesson when I ask them to repeat what we worked on for the last hour.

RJ: Exactly. It happens to everybody. Despite all those perfectly timed nods and uh-huhs, you got busted. Maybe you meant to pay attention, but you were distracted.

The same thing occurs on the golf course. Players can be easily distracted during a typical round. Focusing attention on every shot is very challenging. That's why all players can benefit from improved focus. In golf we're concerned primarily with two types of focus problems—thinking about too many things while swinging the club ("having a cluttered mind") and the inability to remain focused in the present. Let's talk about the cluttered mind first.

Focus, Part One: The Cluttered Mind

TP: I think we can sum up this problem by saying, When you let the monkeys out of their cage, it can get pretty busy in the ol' head.

RJ: That's for sure. I'm not surprised that this problem is so common. Besides golfers, I also consult frequently with businessmen and -women. Business professionals are rewarded for their ability to manage several projects at the same time and to analyze situations and solve problems quickly. What they call multitasking or multilevel thinking is a valuable skill in business, but it can spell disaster on the golf course. Analyzing your swing and juggling multiple thoughts during competition are considered to be mental errors in golf. Players can strangle their athleticism on the course by trying to identify the faults and fixes for every bad shot hit during a round.

TP: Absolutely. Keeping a quiet mind during play is paramount. As I've said, a typical swing takes about two seconds from beginning to end and moves at 90 miles an hour or more. How much can you think about during that time and at that speed? How much can you focus on in those two seconds? Maybe one thing, and that's all. The movement must be an instinctual reaction.

You can't think and hit at the same time.

—YOGI BERRA, MAJOR-LEAGUE BASE-BALL PLAYER AND COACH

If you were Richard Petty racing into turn three of the Daytona 500 at 160 miles an hour, what would happen if you tried to think of all the instructions you had received from coaches, managers, sponsors, friends, relatives, your pharmacist, and the paper boy? Disaster! No one can process that much information in so little time, not even a computer. Like Petty in his prime, the action must be a thoroughly developed and trusted skill. If it isn't, you're not ready for the course, just as Petty wouldn't be ready for turn three.

Golf isn't a game of connect the dots. You can't take in all kinds of instruction while you're swinging, at each point, and say to yourself, *Tom said, Tom said, Tom said.* It's got to flow as one fluid motion, with your body and mind acting in concert like musicians in a symphony orchestra. Golf must be a spontaneous happening, for better or worse. That's why you have wedges and a putter—to recover when you miss a shot.

Thinking instead of acting is the number-one disease in golf.

—SAM SNEAD, MEMBER, WORLD GOLF HALL OF FAME

So, Rick, what can someone with a cluttered mind do for this problem?

RJ: The solution is an obvious one, though not as simple as it sounds. Players have to quiet the mind and focus their attention on the target.

TP: Oh, boy, there's that target thing again.

RJ: Yes, I know. This seemingly simple task will take practice—lots of it—but golfers will begin to feel their swing free up as the mind becomes less cluttered. Like other golf skills, mental skills require practice. Players may also want to seek coaching from a golf professional who can help them lock on to the target and make their swing with a quiet mind. For those who are working without a coach, the following drills may help, but they will never replace qualified coaching.

Mental Quieting Drill Number One (RJ's Drill)

Purpose: To enhance your ability to maintain your focused attention on each shot while executing each shot independent of:

- Thoughts of previous and/or upcoming shots.
- Swing mechanics.
- Body position.
- Negative feelings.
- Fear of a particular result.
- Awareness of the overall score.

On the Range

Using four clubs, mark out a box where you will stand while addressing the ball. Begin by using your preshot routine. This is an essential element of success. If you don't have one, develop one. (See Chapter 13, "The Bookends: The Launching Pad and Finish Condition," for detailed tips on developing an effective preshot routine.) Then, without thinking about various components of the swing (other than paying attention to the target or a general swing feeling), attempt to hit five balls without any thoughts entering your mind, from the moment you begin approaching the ball until the moment you strike it. If even the slightest thought enters your mind (say, *Keep* your knees flexed), then start over again with ball number one. Do not increase the challenge of the drill, move on to another task, or leave the range until you have successfully hit the number of balls that you have set as a goal (without thinking, of course). As your mental quieting skills improve, gradually increase the challenge of the drill by:

- Changing clubs after each shot.
- Hitting all draws or all fades.
- Alternating draws, fades, and straight shots.
- Alternating the above shots with knockdowns, three-quarter swings, and other shot variations that you might use during a round of golf.

Establish your goal for the number of balls to be hit successfully before beginning the drill. Monitor how many consecutive shots you can execute successfully while maintaining a mentally quiet state and track your improvement over time. This way you'll know if your thought control abilities are improving. Remember that all decisions about the type of shot you're hitting must be completed before approaching the ball.

Mental Quieting Drill Number Two (TP's Drill)

Here's another useful drill, which was taught to me years ago by Fred Shoemaker, the author of a terrific book called *Extraordinary Golf*. When Fred and I realized that I was getting too hung up with my swing mechanics, which were cluttering my mind, he sent me to the first tee. He told me I could play as long as I made a practice swing, got a feel for what I wanted to do in my swing, and then hit the shot. The moment I thought of a mechanical trigger or criticism, though, game over. I made one practice swing and had to stop because something jumped into my head. For the next several weeks I never got past the first or second tee without some criticism or command popping into my mind. I now often play 18 holes with very few mechanical occurrences. I really think this is one of the reasons I can play infrequently and yet still respectably well, given the little time I have to practice. Thanks Fred.

I continue to use this drill today, and now I'm pretty good at it, but my record is still only the 14th tee. I have never completed an 18-hole round without some mental chatter, though I always try. It's my goal. Like Rick's drill, you can't wear this one out. You should use it continually to improve your ability to quiet the mind.

Focus, Part Two: Staying in the Present

RJ: The second focus problem, which we mentioned earlier, is staying in the present. Golfers often can't stay focused on the shot at hand. Remember those times when you stewed over that easy putt you missed or that drive that wound up in the woods? That's a distraction that can make your other shots less than stellar because you're not focusing on what you should and staying in the here-and-now. Similarly, you may find yourself so pumped about that birdie you just made on 15 that you're thinking about just making par on the last few holes so you'll finally break 80. You've lost your focus, and instead you're focusing on what could happen shortly. Whether you're wallowing in grief over mistakes or gloating over potential future glories, you're playing holes without being present. To play your best, you must remain in the moment.

Some common reasons for losing focus are your awareness of the score, paying attention to others, outside stressors like family and business concerns, and the inability to let go of a bad shot.

Fortunately, you can train your mind to confirm when you're functioning completely in the present. Many players train outside of the golf course in disciplines such as meditation or yoga. Both of these disciplines are designed to train the mind to remain focused in the present while also in a physically relaxed condition. You can also train on the golf course to improve your ability to focus. The next time you play a round, take a series of five or six holes and rate how well you stayed in the moment and, when you were distracted, how quickly you came back. By making yourself aware of this necessity, you train your mind to concentrate. The following drill will help you to do this.

> *Hitting a golf ball is an act so precise that there is unlimited room for error. That error begins in the mind and finds expression in the swing.*
>
> —LORNE RUBENSTEIN, AUTHOR

ENHANCING YOUR FOCUS WITH A PRESHOT ROUTINE

Purpose: To improve your ability to focus your attention constantly and to replicate your golf swing by using a well-practiced, consistent preshot routine. (For additional information on developing such a routine, refer to Chapter 13, "The Bookends: The Launching Pad and Finish Condition.")

On the Range

Identify the specific procedure you use before striking the ball. Identify the order and manner in which you do everything, including: putting your hands on the club, visualizing the shot, selecting an intermediate target, walking toward the ball (including the number of steps you take), settling your alignment, the number of looks at the target, the number of waggles, and even the number of seconds you take to execute the entire routine. When you hit range balls, execute 12 consecutive routines. You should videotape this drill or have someone observe you to watch for variations that you may not be aware of. As your preshot routine becomes increasingly consistent, gradually increase the challenge of the drill by:

- Changing clubs after each shot.
- Changing targets after each shot.
- Establishing a desired result for each shot (draw, fade, within 10 yards of target).
- Having someone try to distract you during the routine.

TP: While we're on this drill I'd like to make a point, best illustrated by telling a story about something I observed some years ago. In the mid-'90s, when Nick Faldo was arguably the best player in the world, he was playing in the Buick Classic at Westchester Country Club. David Leadbetter, with whom I had worked on my own game in the early '80s, was gracious enough to allow me to watch Nick's practice session one afternoon (those are usually private). I was excited to see what Nick would be practicing and to observe a world-class player working with a world-class coach. The session lasted about two hours, and they were trying to reinforce Nick's preshot routine. During that time Nick never hit a single shot, because they both knew the importance of replicating the procedure exactly, so they couldn't stop until Nick had it down to a science. He never hit a single ball in two hours.

A consistent preshot routine puts you into a cocoon, a protective bubble, that allows you to eliminate all distractions. Players who want to reach their potential must understand the importance of this ritual. If they don't, they have no reason to move on. That day of observation with David and Nick made me a better coach overnight.

We've been talking about focus issues in terms of what players should not do. Now I'd like to mention some things that golfers should focus on. When a group of players hang around the tee, I'll ask, "What do you see?" They'll say things like, "I see a bunker, a lake, some trees." Then I'll say to them, "Let me ask you a question. When you take the parkway home, do you concentrate on the guardrail?" They say no, they concentrate on the road ahead. Why? Because if they focused on the guardrail, they'd crash into it. So why do they do just the opposite on the golf course? If players are thinking about the lake when they drive from the tee and the ball plunks into the lake, they've hit a perfect shot, because the ball hit the target they were focusing on.

We have to remember that we all have a guy sitting in the control tower of our brain who does his job perfectly, as long as he gets clear messages from us. Our conscius mind, on the other hand, is an idiot. It stumbles through life, always asking that guy in the control tower for the wrong things. If we give that man upstairs ambiguous signals, he'll throw our mind into a state of flux and confusion. He knows we don't want to hit into the lake, but we cue that action visually by focusing on it, which crosses some wires between the conscious and subconscious minds.

You have to paint a clear optical picture for that guy in the tower. If something like a lake or a bunker intimidates you, your mind dwells on it. Just as when you're driving a car, you must keep your mind focused ahead—and not on the guard rail. In golf, you need to focus on the hole, where you want the ball to go, not on that bunker or the woods, where you don't want it to go.

You need to behave logically on the golf course—that is, in an optically appropriate manner. Accomplished players always think and behave this way on the course, which is one behavior that's worth emulating. In other words, they focus on what they want, not on what they don't want to do. The quickest way to improve your handicap is to start thinking, seeing, and behaving like players on the next level. Doing so pushes the mechanics through the strainer.

Now let's move on to another important mental issue—anger management, also known as reality management. Rick, what can you tell us about anger management?

ANGER MANAGEMENT

RJ: We've all witnessed players on the course who need to learn higher levels of self-control. When they make a mistake, they whine, complain, curse, make excuses, and throw tantrums (as well as clubs). In short, they act like spoiled children when they are not getting their way. Use some imagination and you can picture what they were like on the playground.

Those who have this problem are rarely aware of it. They tend to blame problems with their game on others. Their pro stinks, their equipment stinks, the greens are bumpy, the dog ate their favorite golf book, and so on. If you know golfers who behave like this, chances are they won't be interested in this topic (or they may be blind to this behavior in themselves).

If you happen to see yourself in the description above, or if someone has pointed out this section and asked you to read it, then you have some good reasons do so. Most obviously, others will enjoy playing with you much more if you stop acting immaturely. After some improvement on your part, you may even find that those foursomes you have trouble putting together will suddenly become available again. Lo and behold, you might even enjoy playing golf more and score better.

TP: We should all remember that poor anger management skills makes us look like idiots out there. Trust me, I know. When I was playing in a competition that was televised on the local station, I lost my cool—on camera. I slammed my club onto the turf in a tantrum. Later, I saw myself on tape. I was never so embarrassed as when I watched myself acting like a raving lunatic. I think all those who act this way on the course should see themselves on video, acting like 3 year olds. That's a real wake-up call.

If you have trouble in this regard, you really should consider a plan to make improvements. Aside from being an unpopular golf mate and missing out on the pleasures of the game, if you can't manage your anger, you can't play well.

RJ: Absolutely. Overcoming this problem improves your game, because anger inhibits motor control. Even if you think your anger is justified, you're putting your body in a state where it doesn't function well.

Like anxiety, anger produces the old fight-or-flight response. That increases the heart rate, blood pressure, and adrenaline levels, which is counterproductive in golf. If you were a linebacker—someone who needs extra strength to tackle that 250-pound individual running at you at top speed—this response would be an asset. But in golf, being ready to rumble simply doesn't pay, because you need coordination and control. Without control, gently sinking that 12-foot slider or making that free, uninhibited full swing becomes difficult.

Anyone with an anger problem can strive for improvement, even though this is arguably the most difficult of mental problems to fix in golf, because the behavior is often deeply ingrained. Our responses to anger and/or disappointment began immediately after birth and have been profoundly influenced by our environment, personality, and other psychosocial factors. If you have this problem on the golf course, it probably affects other areas of your life as well. So why not seek help? The reward will be a happier and healthier personal and professional life, including a much better golf game.

TP: Thanks, Rick. Next, how about talking for a while about one ingredient of the mental game that affects all golfers at every skill level? You know the one I mean—attitude.

A POSITIVE ATTITUDE

RJ: You've brought up a biggie, Tom. In golf, as in all sports, you need a positive attitude. If you think you will fail, you probably will. Although I would encourage everyone to maintain a positive attitude on the golf course, I also want players to know that positive thinking does not compensate for the lack of technical skill. Golfers with poor technical skills will often shoot high scores whether they think positively or not.

The surest path to a positive attitude and a solid mental game is a technically sound game. If you practice and hone your skills and you see good things happening consistently, this in itself will build your confidence and improve your attitude.

TP: Good point, Rick. I think you can get a positive attitude in one of two ways. Either you're born with it or you develop it. I've been around people who are so positive that it's almost ridiculous. At first it seemed corny. I'd think, *How can anyone be so upbeat all the time?* John Elliott is like that. He teaches at the Golf Digest Schools, and I worked with him in the early 1980s. Buddy Alexander, who coached me in college, was that way, too. Buddy is now the head golf coach at the University of Florida and a former U.S. amateur champion. His teams have won two NCAA Championships. When I retired from playing and started teaching, I met Bill Strausbaugh, who inspired me in many ways, not just with golf. He was extremely upbeat. These guys were the kind of mentors who left you feeling as if you could take on anything, and that's what made them great. Buddy spent a great deal of time playing and practicing with me, and he was a real shot in the arm for my confidence. He made me feel as if I was the greatest golfer alive, even though I was probably just slightly above average then. By the time I competed at the NCAA II Championship I felt that it was all mine and that nobody was going to take it away from me—and no one did. I know that a positive attitude can be acquired. I'm living proof of that. I certainly wasn't born with it. Buddy helped me to create it.

Your environment—the people you gather around yourself—has a profound impact on your attitude. Take the analogy of a child who has been raised in a nurturing environment. If you place her in a stressful, non-nurturing environment for a year, she'll be feeling a lot less positive than when she went in. On the other hand, if you took a child out of negative, non-nurturing environment and put him in a comfortable, nurturing one for a year, you might well turn his life around. As adults, we have far more control over our environment, with whom we surround ourselves, and our lives in general. While it can sometimes be tough to make the necessary changes if we have slipped into a negative environment, in most cases, at least we have the power to do something about it.

When you get up every morning you have a decision to make. *You have a choice.* You can be a negative and a miserable, self-condemning slob, or you can decide that you're going to surround yourself with positive people and create a positive environment for

Never tell yourself you can't make a shot. Remember, we are what we think we are.

—GARY PLAYER, MEMBER, WORLD GOLF HALL OF FAME

yourself. And don't just pretend—take action to change your life for the better if necessary. That may sound simplistic, (and it is simple—it is a choice) but many key concepts of the mental side of golf are based on such simple logic.

As Bob Rotella once said to me under the famous oak tree at Augusta, "People call me a great sport psychologist. I think what I really do is teach logic." The principles are based on things people already know but don't remember when they play a sport. If you don't use logical thought processes when you play, your game will suffer.

RJ: You bet, Tom!

CONCLUSION

I'm a great believer in logic. It's a mental tool that serves all athletes well. That's why I speak so highly of people like Rick Jensen and Bob Rotella and Dick Coop, who can help players get regrounded in solid, logical thought patterns. This is a significant issue, I know, because I see how many of us act illogically on the golf course when we should be doing things that make sense if we step back and look at them. When you feel frustrated with your game, take a break, and ask yourself some important questions. For instance, *Am I taking risks that my skill level simply can't accommodate?* Of course, you may be too emotionally involved to ask the right questions—to see the situation objectively enough to help yourself. That's where professional coaches and sport psychologists come in.

Maybe you're still unsure about the value of hiring outside help. Okay, I hear you. Try looking at the situation like this. If you had trouble with your plumbing or telephone system or a toothache, you'd call in a specialist to help you solve the problem, wouldn't you? In golf you need to do the same thing. The specialist in this case, a sport psychologist (or a really talented coach), will help you figure out what the problem is and give you information and suggestions such as the proper drills to use for resolving it. Of course even a professional can't cure you overnight or without your help. You need to take the information that person gives you and apply it consistently over a period of time (in other words, *practice*). That's the only way you'll get better.

In Appendix B, I recommend sports psychologists who are leaders in their field. Also, I have recommended at the end of this chapter some excellent books that can help you with the mental aspects of golf. While these books are not a substitute for the personal one-on-one help of a sports psychologist, if you absolutely cannot avail yourself of a mind coach, the next best alternative would be to read books on the subject.

While you're making repairs to your game, try not to get too hung up with the nuts and bolts. I see too many people getting bogged down in the mechanics of the game. These are the players who always rush to the first tee just to work on their backswing. I sincerely believe that golf is being overtaught and undercoached today. I think you need to disengage from the mechanics of your swing when on the course and focus more on the process of playing golf. You need to get out there and create a score. And when you're on the course, you have to keep your mind out of the way. There should be a stable balance between mechanics and your mind.

As a golf coach, I ask you to do one main thing for your mental game—be logical. Just play your game, from preshot routine to follow-through, in a logical, sequential manner. I'm not asking you to be a Tiger Woods or an Annika Sorenstam. Just develop a routine where you can gather appropriate information, choose a club, and execute your shot. Do everything in a relaxed state, not in what I call a "tension convention," using logic as your guide. If you can do this, you'll not only play better and more consistent golf, you'll also have fun.

No one has ever said, *I wish I'd spent the day in the office instead of on the golf course.* But you can make things even better. See each round as an exciting challenge and an opportunity to be creative. After all, if you're not enjoying yourself out there, you might as well go to the clubhouse and play a little gin rummy—or go back to the office.

WHERE TO TAKE IT FROM HERE

Now that we've discussed the most common mental problems in golf, you probably have a good idea about the kind of work you need to do. Below are some excellent sources to get you started. Several of these books, in fact, make excellent reading and can be of help to almost anyone who is serious about golf.

Recommended Publications

- *Golf Is Not a Game of Perfect* by Bob Rotella with Bob Cullen (Simon & Schuster, 1995).
- *Golf Is a Game of Confidence* by Bob Rotella with Bob Cullen (Simon & Schuster Trade, 2001).
- *Mind Over Golf* by Richard H. Coop with Bill Fields (Hungry Minds, Inc., 1997).
- *Extraordinary Golf: The Art of the Possible* by Fred Shoemaker with Peter Shoemaker (Berkley Publishing Group, 1997).
- *Inner Golf* by Timothy Gallwey (Random House, Inc., 1997).
- *Golf: The Body, the Mind, the Game* by Dick E. Beach and Bob Ford (Random House, 1995).
- *The New Golf Mind* by Gary Wiren and Richard H. Coop (Simon & Schuster Trade, 1981).
- *Golf in the Kingdom* by Michael Murphy (Viking Penguin, 1997).

3 OPINION VERSUS REALITY (NUMBERS DON'T LIE) **SPOKE 3: ANALYSIS**

> It's far easier to improve upon weaknesses than upon strengths. When clearly identified, strengths become a source of confidence . . . while weaknesses serve as key opportunities for rapid improvement.
>
> —PETER SANDERS,
> PRESIDENT OF
> Shot by Shot

One of the most significant differences I have noted over the years between the way professionals and amateurs approach golf is how the pros plan and execute their practice time. Of course professionals spend far more time practicing—their livelihoods depend on it. Yet every player who is serious about improving would be wise to adopt a similar approach.

Professional golfers always have a very specific plan for how they will use their time in drills and specific shots, all relating to specific weaknesses in their game. They are much more organized in terms of their use of time and how it relates to the way golf is actually played and scored. They take their weakest links, combined with a keen awareness of statistics (which add up to the most crucial aspects of their scoring), and devote most of their practice time to these areas. Needless to say, PGA Tour players hit a lot of chips and putts during practice (due to the large percentage of every round that these shots entail), and they also hit a lot of shots in the weakest parts of their individual games. This is not only logical, but leads to better scores as well.

Adopting this approach involves two separate steps that go hand in hand: analysis (Spoke 3) and time management (Spoke 4). In order to manage your time most efficiently for your particular game, you need to do an ongoing analysis of your game—comprised of five distinct skills, which we'll discuss more in depth in the following pages—to understand exactly what your particular strengths and weaknesses are. In this chapter you will learn how to do this. Without doing this type of analysis, your practice time will be haphazard, and therefore inefficient. The time you spend practicing without a specific plan or direction will, quite frankly, be largely wasted. On the other hand, if you really know your game and concentrate on improving your individual weaknesses, your game will improve in the most efficient manner possible. Once you have learned how to analyze your own game, or have availed yourself of a service that will help you do this, we'll go on to Spoke 4—time management—which will show you how to translate your skills analysis into a solid practice plan based on logic and sound information about your specific combination of strengths and weaknesses.

Proper, perfect practice is a key to improving technique. Yet a golfer cannot practice in any meaningful way without detailed, objective analysis—analysis that reveals exactly which areas need improvement most. Improvement will not happen by accident, or even by the simple repetition of old habits, which many players consider to be "practice." Knowing which areas of your game need the most work, and then practicing in a logical fashion utilizing sound fundamentals, is the only way to improve your game significantly and quickly.

Once you get your results, of course, there's still plenty of work to be done—charts and readouts only tell you what you need to do the most work on, but they won't go out to the range and putting green for you.

OBJECTIVE ANALYSIS: TAKING HUMAN ERROR OUT OF THE MIX

I know what some of you are probably thinking: *The coach I've been working with for a while knows my game as well as anyone; that should be sufficient.* While a competent professional is an excellent source for spotting your weaknesses and providing valuable feedback on your game, the type of analysis we are talking about here is an empirical study based on numerical observations, using detailed measurements of performance and scores from several rounds. It eliminates guesswork and human error. Simply put, *it takes opinion out of the evaluation process.*

Although these statistics are certainly not a replacement for feedback and instruction from a professional coach, they are a tool that your coach and you can use for important insight into your scoring patterns. *This allows you to concentrate on areas that need the most time, attention, and practice.*

You may be thinking: *I know my handicap and average scores, and I've been tracking my rounds with a scorecard for years—I already know my game inside and out.*

To this I say: *You couldn't possibly.* Even golfers who track their rounds and know their average scores and handicap often do not realize where their weaknesses truly lie or exactly what those weaknesses mean. In fact, the results of an in-depth analysis are eye-opening. There's no substitute and no excuse not to do it.

Moreover, traditional golf statistics are a woefully inept way to track one's game. Despite the inexplicable persistence of these statistics, they won't help you pinpoint where you need the most improvement, and worse—they can be inaccurate and misleading.

That's why I'd like to introduce you to Peter Sanders, the president and developer of a company called Shot by Shot, which performs in-depth computer-assisted analysis for individuals. Peter is one of the only people I know who has made the analysis of golfers and their on-course performance his full-time job, and he has been involved in this field for more than 16 years. Given his knowledge and expertise in this area, I have enlisted his help with this chapter. He has been kind enough to share his knowledge as well as the charts and graphs in this chapter, all of which are from his extensive database.

Peter is an expert of golf statistical analysis bar none. He is therefore the most qualified person I know to discuss traditional statistics versus other more modern and objective forms of skills analysis and to explain why traditional statistics are a poor barometer of your golf skills.

A DISCUSSION BY PETER SANDERS OF TRADITIONAL STATISTICS

This outdated method of analysis consists of flat, one-dimensional indicators that cannot possibly accurately represent a three-dimensional game such as golf. These statistics are based on answers to some simple questions:

1. Did you hit the fairway with your drive?
2. Did you hit the green in regulation?
3. How many putts did you take?
4. Did you 1-putt following a sand shot?

These statistics are not only inaccurate, but in many cases can actually be misleading. Let's look at them one at a time to see what they can and cannot do.

1. **Fairways Hit**

   While the *fairways hit* category tells you whether you are driving the ball accurately, it doesn't tell you a thing about distance. More important, this statistic provides no insight into the character and severity of the missed shots. If you hit 13 of 14 fairways, for example, but missed the 14th out of bounds, the fairways hit statistic would be a very misleading indicator of performance. The fact is, *more strokes are lost due to mistakes off the tee, at every handicap level, than to any other problem in golf.* Among single-digit handicaps *almost 75 percent of all double bogeys follow a mistake off the tee.* Simply knowing how many times you hit the fairway does little to provide you with any informative analysis of your tee game. Golf is the only sport that does not recognize the importance of mistakes in its analysis. In football it is widely recognized that turnovers (fumbles and interceptions) play a major role in the outcome of every game. Baseball certainly tracks errors in the field and strikeouts. Of the 100-plus stats furnished to each player on the PGA Tour each week, however, not one refers to penalties incurred, balls hit out of play, or mistakes of any kind.

MEN'S SCORECARD											THE MID OCEAN GOLF COURSE • BERMUDA										
BLUE TEES	418	471	172	330	433	360	164	339	406	3093	404	487	437	238	357	496	376	203	421	3419	6512		
WHITE TEES	398	453	167	318	402	343	151	316	366	2914	389	451	396	214	332	466	353	184	396	3181	6095		
PAR	4	5	3	4	4	4	3	4	4	35	4	5	4	3	4	5	4	3	4	36	71		
HANDICAP	5	9	15	7	1	11	17	13	3		4	12	2	10	18	8	6	16	14				
SM 5/8/04	4	6	3	5	5	4	3	4	6	40	4	5	5	4	4	5	5	3	4	39	79		
Fairways hit	✓					✓		✓		3	✓	✓			✓				✓	5	8		
GIRs	✓		✓			✓				3	✓	✓		✗✓		✓		✓	✓	6	9		
Putts	2	2	2	3	2	2	2	2	2	19	2	2	1	2	1	2	2	2	2	16	35		
HOLES	1	2	3	4	5	6	7	8	9	OUT	10	11	12	13	14	15	16	17	18	IN	TOTAL	H'CAP	NET
Sand saves								8 B					Sand	Miss									
Other		Chip												Chip									
W/L																							
W/L																							
POINTS																							

Mid Ocean Course was designed by Charles Blair MacDonald in 1921 and was revised in 1963 by Robert Trent Jones.

COURSE/SLOPE RATINGS: BLUE 72.0 / 138   WHITE 70.1 / 132   SENIOR 69.5 / 128   Date _____ Scorer _____ Attest _____

2. Greens Hit in Regulation (GIRs)

This is the most relevant of all the traditional statistics. For golfers at a higher level, it provides an excellent overview of the efficiency of their entire long game. First, you can rarely hit the green in regulation after a mistake off the tee. Second, because it also represents a birdie opportunity on the green, this statistic bears a very strong correlation with the PGA Tour's money list. The problem, however, is that this statistic provides little value to the average golfer. For example, a 15- to 19-handicap golfer (the "average" nonprofessional) hits only four greens in regulation per round—hardly worth noting. Further, if you aren't hitting enough GIRs, *this statistic provides no indication as to why.* The problem could be many things: a lack of length or accuracy off the tee, problems with approach shot accuracy, or a combination of the two.

3. Number of Putts

Counting putts is easy but can be very misleading, because the distance of each putt is critical. Evaluating your putting based solely upon the number of putts, *without including the distances*, is like trying to balance your checkbook based only on the number of checks written without the amounts.

Furthermore, average 15- to 19-handicap golfers will face 12 short-game opportunities each round (10 chip or pitch shots, and 2 sand shots). Their relative skill level in this area will dramatically affect the putting distances faced and therefore the number of putts per round. Also, without knowing putt distances, it is impossible to determine where your true problem lies. If your lag putts leave long second putts, obviously you need to pay attention to distance control. If lags regularly leave you 2 or 3 feet from the hole, then short putts are the issue. The Shot by Shot Putting Analysis program (currently available online at www.shotbyshot.com) is a simple and inexpensive way to monitor your putting skills with this kind of accuracy.

4. Sand Saves

While keeping track of the number of times you successfully got up and down is relevant, it can be misleading because it involves two skills—sand shots and putting. Merely tracking successful sand saves gives no indication as to the cause of the failed saves—say, whether the sand shot left too long a putt, or whether you missed a makeable putt. As with the tee game, it is mistakes from the sand that do more to separate every handicap level than do saves. A mistake is the failure to successfully hit the green from a greenside bunker, and average 15- to 19-handicaps will make a mistake from the sand almost three times as often as they will save the opportunity (mistakes occur 33 percent of the time; saves, 13 percent). Tracking putting distances following an attempt from the sand as well as the mistakes provides a complete picture of your real skill level.

NEWER, BETTER METHODS

Now that you understand why traditional statistics are woefully lacking when it comes to accurate and objective analysis, you may be thinking, *So what is a better, more accurate way to view my game?*

As Peter Sanders explains, "There are five distinct skills involved in playing golf: tee and advancement shots, approach shots, chip/pitch shots, sand shots, and putting." Each player's score is made up of a combination of these shots. "Strengths, and every player has them, can be an instant source of confidence. A weakness, when properly identified, can be a source of rapid improvement."

While there are several services available to you, which run the gamut from computer-fed analysis to Web sites to handheld devices (such as Palm Pilots), I personally recommend Shot by Shot, which I have found to be by far the best. I strongly recommend it to all my students, from Tour professionals to my serious amateurs—all are characterized simply by a real desire to improve. In fact, I first discovered Shot by Shot because my student (LPGA Tour member) Missie Berteotti introduced me to it many years ago. Her analysis, which turned out to be a great time-saver and a wonderful learning tool, allowed us to hone right in on her individual weaknesses. After seeing the results with Missie and then learning more about the company and what they do, as well as the subsequent successes of my other students who have used their service, I now consider such analysis an essential part of the process of learning to play for golfers who are serious about their game.

In the 10-plus years since that I have been working with Shot by Shot, and investigating other such products and services, I have found it to be by far the best. Not only is the company's database the most extensive and their analyses most thorough, they have the best hands-on personal service I have seen. I have consistently referred my students to this company, and my students have had tremendously positive results with their services.

Shot by Shot's online putting analysis service runs $35 a year, and their in-depth paper-based game analysis program costs $500 a year. For more information on these services and contact information, please go to the sidebar on Shot by Shot located on page 55.

Although I strongly feel this professional computer-assisted analysis is by far the best option, if you simply cannot avail yourself of this service, there are a couple of other options available to you. One is to track your rounds on your computer using a spreadsheet (using a program such as Excel). Make sure you develop detailed spreadsheets that track your statistics in clear, black and white terms. Track every round you play, listing exactly how many of each type of shot you took. Don't rush this process; it will take several rounds (at least 8–10) before clear patterns begin to emerge. If you do not have a computer you can use to track your rounds, your other option is to track each of your rounds in detail using a golfer's notebook. There are commercial notebook products available to help you track your game, or you can simply use a loose-leaf notebook and organize your game into various skill areas. Track your rounds faithfully, apply some basic math skills, and see what patterns emerge. Similarly, it will take several rounds, but eventually a very distinctive and obvious shot pattern will emerge which will allow you to hone in on exactly which types of shots are costing you the most each round.

These latter two options are of course far superior to not tracking and analyzing your game. However, with a professional computer-assisted analysis, aside from convenience and proven accuracy, comes the additional bonus of receiving data from a vast database that compares your game with others in your handicap level, or those slightly above and below your handicap. This can be quite useful in helping you develop realistic goals for improvement.

COMPUTER ANALYSIS: A REAL EYE-OPENER

For those of you who opt for computer-assisted analysis (which I hope is all of you), I'd like to walk you through the process a bit so you know what to expect. In addition, going through these steps will help those of you who do your own analysis using your computers or a notebook, since you will need to follow similar steps.

First, Shot by Shot provides a three-dimensional analysis of your game. The firm's computer program will analyze your game in light of the five types of shots discussed previously, and convert this information to easy-to-read charts. These charts show you the relative strength of each of the five skills in your game, and exactly which types of shots are costing you the most strokes with the greatest frequency. They also reveal the distances at which your approaches generally lose their accuracy. Again, with this information you can concentrate on working on your precise areas of weakness.

The chart on page 54 uses Bob, an actual student, to provide vivid examples of how Shot by Shot can provide valuable insights into your game.

REAL PLAYERS, REAL IMPROVEMENT

Bob, a student of mine, swore the key problem with his game was his putting. I took him out to the putting greens to work with him and found that his putting was indeed not perfect, but—despite his protests—it also didn't look much like the way he'd described it. I decided to ask him how he'd fared in the game he'd played the previous Saturday with the usual foursome, and he produced a scorecard for me.

As he recounted the game, it became clear that after 16 holes he'd had a good score going. Then, on the 17th green, he missed a short, easy putt. He knew it was a shot he shouldn't have missed, but he blew it. His buddies had chided him over it, in addition to his kicking himself. The truth of the matter was, however, that his putting had been solid up until then; his real problem was with getting off the tee, which left him scrambling from the rough all day, and with approach shots that missed the green. His putting, it turned out, had actually saved his behind from what could otherwise have been a much higher score.

The bottom line is, Bob didn't realize what was really costing him the most strokes each round. Like all of us, he's only human. While I would never tell a student that time spent on the practice green is time wasted (goodness knows none of you spend close to enough time there!), it turned out that Bob had other issues with his game, and his practice and lesson time were better spent elsewhere.

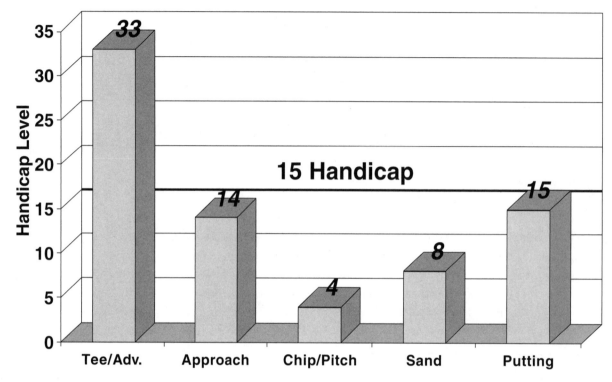

Bob - 15 Handicap
Relative Handicap Profile

Handicap Level

35 — **33**

30

25

20

15 — **15 Handicap** — **14** — **15**

10 — **8**

5 — **4**

0

Tee/Adv.   Approach   Chip/Pitch   Sand   Putting

First, I recommended that he collect more data on his golf game and get computer-assisted analysis from Shot by Shot. He did, and the results were not only surprising to him, but also extremely valuable, as they were to his coach (yours truly).

I've included charts to illustrate what we found out about Bob's game, which will help you see how to interpret the results of your own computer-assisted analysis.

You'll see from the chart above that Bob, who's a 15 handicap, has some fairly obvious strengths and one fairly dramatic weakness. Once Bob understood how good his short game is, and particularly his chip/pitch and sand shots, he could start playing to these strengths. Furthermore, the understanding of how much his tee and advancement game are affecting his performance has enabled him to mitigate the problem. In this case length is not an issue, so while Bob is working with me on swing mechanics to cure his wild tee shots, he can realize immediate improvement by choosing to avoid the driver on tight holes (in other words, proper course management, which we discuss in Chapter 15, "Golf Versus the Golf Swing").

Moreover, once we had the hard data we needed, we were able to set up a blueprint for practice time that quickly zeroed in on the areas that needed the most improvement. The progress Bob has made since learning what he really needs to be working on has been astounding.

HOW TO UTILIZE THE RESULTS

In addition to providing the readouts with specifics on which shots are costing you the most, Shot by Shot has compiled a database of more than 25,000 rounds, so they can compare your game to others at your handicap level or just above it to show how you stack up. They can also show you your game in relation to a touring professional's. This comparative data can be quite revealing in analyzing your game.

Different players use this type of analysis in different ways. Many will simply adopt this discipline as a normal part of their routine by recording every round. Others may choose to record and analyze only competitive rounds, while still others may choose to record 5- to 10-round snapshots of their game periodically. I prefer that students choose competitive rounds, since that's when the heat is on. However you choose to use it, this process and the feedback can be very beneficial. In brief, it allows you and your coach to:

- Identify strengths and weaknesses.
- Establish specific, realistic improvement priorities and goals—that is, a "blueprint" (see Chapter 4, "Time Management," for related information).
- Monitor progress.
- Establish new improvement priorities as goals are reached.

Once you have your analysis in hand, and you've thoroughly reviewed it on your own and with your coach, you're ready for the next step: Time Management.

SHOT BY SHOT

Shot by Shot provide two types of analysis: either a paper hard-copy analysis, or a Net-based computer service. To obtain the hard-copy analysis, you fill out detailed scorecards provided by Shot by Shot over a minimum of three rounds and send them back. However, I feel you need a minimum of a dozen rounds of stats to really get solid feedback and make accurate determinations about your trends. The company will send you a detailed spiral-bound report with easy-to-understand charts that show exactly where your strengths and weaknesses lie. A five-round trial is $100. The service costs $500 a year; you receive a report after every 5 rounds for your first 20, and after every 10 rounds thereafter.

The Net-based service is an Online Putting Analysis, for which you enter your own data. For $35.00 per year, you can run analysis on as many rounds as you wish. The Web site is pretty cool—check it out at www.shotbyshot.com.

For further information, you can contact Shot by Shot by calling (800) 628–4481 or by writing to:

Peter Sanders
President, Golf Research Associates
P.O. Box 16837
Stamford, CT 06903

4 IT'S NOT HOW *MUCH* YOU SPEND, IT'S *HOW* YOU SPEND IT **SPOKE 4: TIME MANAGEMENT**

If you always do what you've always done, you'll always get what you've always got.

—POPULAR SAYING

Everything we discuss in this book places demands on your time, from the areas we covered previously on the body, mind, and analysis, to equipment and technique. The same is true in all aspects of your life. Whatever it is—whether it's your children, marriage, career, or golf game—it requires your attention and effort. If you want to be successful at those things you consider important, you need to devote time to them.

Sadly, many people spend a lot of time and energy pursuing various endeavors but never actually accomplish what they set out to do. They don't fully realize that they have a *choice* in how they spend their time. The key to accomplishing what you want in the time you have is management of that time. Efficiency is refined with proper time usage. This is as true of golf as it is of life.

The key to successful time management is planning, which involves setting goals. Without having a clear goal and planning an exact strategy for how you will accomplish it, whether your goal is to get a higher-paying job or to shave shots off your score, you will likely waste valuable time in the short term. In the long term you will fail to achieve that goal, or at least fail to reach it fully. If you wish to lower your scores, but you either devote little or no time to practice, or the practice time is haphazard and not specifically targeted to your weaknesses, you will defeat your purpose. In fact, you will fail. Later on, when you're playing on the course and you've achieved little or no significant improvement (meaning no change in ball flight or short-game skills and, as a result, no change in your bottom-line score), you'll be disappointed. Remember the adage, *If you fail to plan, you're planning to fail*. This applies no less to learning golf than anything else.

You are likely reading this book because improving your game is important to you. To reach this goal, there are two important questions you must ask yourself.

1. **Where Do I Want to Go?**
   This question is personal to each player. Your goal may be to change your ball flight, the shape of your shots, the quality of contact, or your consistency. If you are a high handicap—say, 25 or above—your goal may be to break 100 regularly. If you're a midhandicap, your goal may be to break 90, and so on, all the way to the scratch player who wants to compete in local and regional amateur events, then go on to win championships.

Each of these goals is highly worthwhile and a fine achievement, if reached. But remember, as another old saying goes: *Be careful what you wish for*. As each goal is achieved and each score surpassed, a new goal replaces it. The human animal is rarely satisfied. Of course, this is what we coaches are here for and what my job is all about—helping you to continue surpassing your personal bests, and guiding you on your golf journey. We could literally spend the rest of this book discussing this issue, but we have too much other ground to cover. Still, I'd like to touch on it briefly; it has everything to do with setting and reaching goals pertaining to your golf game.

Lowering your score will not necessarily bring happiness or enhance your appreciation of the game. Golf is an extremely difficult game that is seldom, if ever, mastered, even by the most gifted of players. Therefore, keeping scores in perspective and remembering why you play is critical. You may play because of the challenge, the camaraderie, the fresh air, the pleasure of watching the ball in flight, the prospect of winning a particular event, or whatever. *Don't lose sight of these things*. Always remember and consider the importance of maintaining your overall enjoyment of the game when setting your goals. Have fun on the journey. (And remember . . . golf is a journey, not a destination.)

2. **How Do I Get There?**

Once you've identified your goals, planning how to reach them is equally important. I can help guide you in this area, but you will need to put some effort into the process and establish a well-thought-out, organized plan. Developing this plan is the key to time management.

Telling yourself you want to spend more time practicing is merely a desire—part of a wish list. Telling yourself you will practice at least two hours each week and see your coach for an hour once every two weeks is a goal. In order to achieve what you want, you need to make a regular appointment with yourself and stick to it.

First you must decide: How much time in your life do you have for golf, and of that time, how much can you devote to developing your game? Whether you're a student or a retiree with plenty of time for golf, or a married 40-year-old with three kids and a demanding job, these questions must be asked and answered. People often set goals that their available time won't allow them to achieve. Your goals must match the time you have, and you must be willing to devote time to doing the work required to accomplish those goals.

If you only have time to slip out once a week for an hour, you may as well spend that time chasing a golf ball around a course. Try to have fun and manage your expectations accordingly. If you have more time and want to improve your scores, you'll have to set aside a percentage of that time for what I call *effective practice*. This is a crucial step in golf time management. Finding and making time for effective practice is critical because learning the golf swing rarely occurs on the course. Most often, it occurs during practice. After that, reinforcing those skills requires practice time on the course. This is the time when you are transitioning from the range to the course and not necessarily looking to shoot a particular score.

> *Awareness of our strong points brings confidence, inspiration, motivation, and satisfaction. Only awareness of our weaknesses, however, allows us to strengthen our weak links and improve consistently.*
>
> —DAN MILLMAN

PRACTICE: CONCEPT VERSUS REALITY

Let's discuss what effective practice is. Chances are you know folks who are out at the range all the time, seemingly working hard, because you see them there for hours, beating bucket after bucket of balls. Yet when the weekend comes along, you invariably find yourself surprised at their deficiencies despite the numerous hours spent practicing. Maybe you're one of these people yourself. Even those who religiously set aside regular practice time should not simply grab their clubs, run out to the practice range, and start beating balls blindly.

When I head out to the range at Naples Grande Golf Club I see most players lined up, attempting one reckless shot after another. They stand there, pausing a moment to admire (or frown at) their shot before hitting another, and another, occasionally looking around to see if anyone else is looking on. Meanwhile they hide ugly secrets in their bag: Maybe they haven't hit a solid wedge shot onto a green in years.

This problem runs deep—it's rooted in human nature. People tend to show off their best stuff on the driving range, practicing what they are best at. Crazy? Yes, although understandable. No one wants to openly practice their weakest link, but they should do *exactly that.* Given that you're out in the open, with others watching, it's tempting not to practice your weakest shots. Do me a favor: *Don't fall into this pattern. Concentrate on your weakest areas when practicing, no matter who is watching.* Otherwise, you're wasting your time. In golf, greater progress is always made when improving weaknesses than in maintaining strengths, or at least in establishing some sort of balance between them. I'm not saying you should never practice shots you are comfortable with or enjoy. But any more than a few in any practice session is taking your game nowhere. Your best shots may be more impressive in the practice areas, but ultimately you'll shine more brightly on the course by concentrating on what really needs the most work. After all, you're only as strong as your weakest link.

One final note on practice here. Those of you who consider warm-up time before a round to be practice, listen closely: *Warming up before a round does not count as practice time!* Hitting a few shots before heading to the course won't give you the adequate amount of time or frame of mind to work on your fundamentals. You would never see a concert violinist tune up her instrument, play a few notes, and expect to learn a piece immediately prior to a performance, let alone play it well. The same is true of golf. Golf is a motor skill, just as playing a musical instrument is. To borrow further from the musician analogy, the most efficient way to achieve improvement when you practice your shots is to go over the parts that are giving you the most trouble. Good musicians may practice the easy parts, but they will definitely spend lots of time playing the parts they're having trouble with. In the long run it's the only way they can play the whole piece perfectly and with confidence.

SHORT-GAME SKILLS: THE KEY TO LOWER SCORES

Because the short game makes up more than half of golf, common sense tells you that, for the vast majority of golfers, half of practice time should be spent on the short game—more if it's a particularly weak area.

Over the 20-plus years I've been teaching, I've never seen anyone improve in their bottom-line full-swing scoring within a year by more than a stroke or two (which, I must note, is a significant feat). I have, however, had many students reduce their score by 10 shots or more in a single season simply by improving their short game.

This is not because I am an ineffective full-swing coach. These results are virtually universal. It pertains to what can realistically be accomplished within the constructs of the game given one's time availability. Generally speaking, the short game not only constitutes a large percentage of the game—arguably about 50 to 60 percent of it (and thus a large part of the overall score)—but it is largely *undertaught*, *underlearned*, *undercoached*, and *extremely underpracticed*.

Part of the reason for this is that golf teaching professionals don't spend enough time developing their skills as coaches in this area. The industry in general has become so

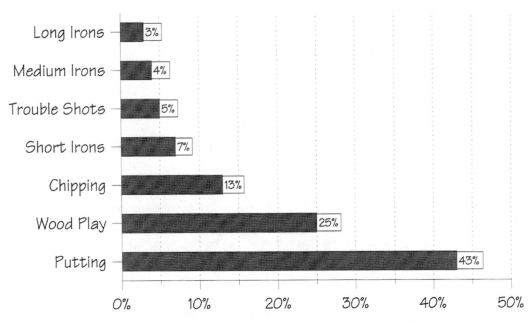

The Game of Golf is

A lot of people are shocked when they see this chart for the first time. For example, they can't believe that medium irons make up only 4 percent of the game, or that chipping and putting combined make up approximately 56 percent. These statistics speak volumes, and they underscore the fact that time management—especially time management based on understanding how the game of golf is played—is crucial.

enamored with the complexity of the full swing that too little attention is spent on the short game.

Of course, that doesn't entirely explain the unwarranted neglect of the short game. Westchester Country Club has one of the greatest practice facilities available in golf. There's a huge driving range and a 12-acre short-game area, which includes two practice greens, five practice bunkers, and a nine-hole par-3 golf course. When I first arrived there, I quickly learned that if I wanted to hide from the membership, the short-game area was the perfect place to go. It was a virtual ghost town. I imagined that if I ever broke my leg, I wouldn't be found for days. Of the 1,200 hours of lessons I taught there per year, fewer than 10 percent were short-game lessons—not because I didn't encourage them, but because my students were not agreeable to the idea. (As I developed relationships and people began to trust my judgment, more and more began to go down to the short-game area, and it became fairly active over time.) It's the same story everywhere you go: crowded driving ranges, empty short-game practice areas.

I've found that, in general, most golfers don't realize how many shots they take from 30 yards and in. In the three-day golf schools I teach now at Naples Grande, I give students a stat book on the first day, and ask them to keep score and stats from 30 yards and in. They give me a look as if to say, *What the heck are you doing?* I repeat my instructions: Count the strokes from 30 yards and in—putts, chips, pitches, and bunker shots—and how often they're successful versus unsuccessful.

On the morning of day two, my students are horrified at how many shots they actually take from 30 yards and in. That's when I tell them, "In the next three days, I can't cure you, but I *can* show you how it's possible to reduce the number of putts you take by 15 to 20 percent and to change your save percentage around the perimeter of the green by 15 percent or more." This is as true for you as it is for them, and it involves developing a practice plan based on sound time management principles.

PRACTICE TIPS FROM THE PROS

When I observe players on any professional tour, it always strikes me as interesting to note how the professionals play the game of golf, and how their statistics play out. The leader in the greens-in-regulation stat on the PGA Tour is usually at around 71 percent. This means that almost 30-odd percent of the time, the leader is missing greens. That's the *leader*. All 125 pros on the PGA Tour money list have a scoring average of under par. Obviously, number 125 on that list isn't hitting 71 percent of the greens; many are hitting less than that, and yet still manage to shoot a score under par. These players obviously possess a wonderful ability to get the golf ball in the hole from on or around the greens.

That being said, when I watch these Tour players practice (versus the amateurs), I see the professionals spending a great deal more time in the short-game area. They are also much more organized in terms of their time usage and how it relates to the way golf is actually played and scored.

DEVELOPING A PRACTICE PLAN

As discussed in Spoke 3 (Chapter 3, "Analysis"), uncovering your individual strengths and weaknesses is relatively simple in this computer age. If you track your game with accuracy, the analysis you receive will be a totally accurate, objective readout of where your weaknesses lie. What the computer can't tell you, however, is what to do with those results. In Spoke 3 our friend Bob learned that the chief weakness in his game wasn't his putting, as he'd thought; rather, his drives and approach shots were the real culprit in hurting his scores. Equipping yourself with self-knowledge, as Bob did, is half the battle. The next step, no less important, is utilizing that information to bring your game to the next level as efficiently and quickly as possible. That's where Spoke 4, Time Management, comes in. This means developing with a coach (an objective, knowledgeable observer) a solid practice plan for *every time* you practice. These plans will help you take specific, tangible steps toward lasting improvement.

Keep in mind that time management also goes hand in hand with Spoke 6, Technique. Once you know which areas of your game need the most work, you are ready to create a practice plan, employing the sound fundamentals for those areas that need improvement. Your coach can give you drills or a plan to follow, or you can apply the drills in this book, which are designed to help you develop all the sound fundamentals of technique. In the long run these drills and this plan will allow you to significantly lower your scores.

Improving your game requires a steady plan of attack on your weakest areas in a logical, step-by-step manner, based on prioritizing your goals and then tackling them one at a time. Several small steps will add up to giant results, but you must be patient and methodical in your approach. Pick one or two things at a time to work on, continue to work on them until you've perfected them, and *only then* move on to the next step. All it takes is dedication, commitment, and a bit of good old-fashioned discipline. The results will be remarkable, satisfying, and—even more important—*lasting*.

THINGS GET WORSE BEFORE THEY GET BETTER

It takes time and discipline to learn a motor skill. Remember the analogy we made in Spoke 1, The Body, about the difficulty of relearning motor skills? We discussed folding your arms across your chest as you usually would, then trying to fold them the opposite way. At first, folding them a different way feels very strange, but as you continue to practice, relearning the skill by performing it in a different manner, eventually it feels right. The same goes for relearning the correct fundamentals of the golf swing. You start by learning and working on the correct fundamentals, which feel awkward at first. Your swing will likely get worse before it gets better. After the awkward phase comes a new comfort level and your swing will improve, as will your scores.

What we're basically talking about here is changing behavior. While you can improve your game by learning new golf skills and correcting errors in your old golf habits, the process will not always be an easy one. Change has a psychological impact that, if you are aware of it and understand it, can help you during this learning process.

When people try to change their golf swing or golf motion, they react to the change in a variety of ways. Their experience and how they react to it will either allow the change to be long lasting, or not. When people learn a new grip for the first time, they'll say it feels awkward. Of course it does. Your hands are very feel sensitive, so when you place them on the club in a new way it feels very different to you. In time, however, it will become more comfortable, and you need to realize this in order to stick with it long enough to create a lasting improvement.

One other issue we need to address is whether you're ready to make changes in your game. Some people come to me ready, willing, and able, while others have a tough time permitting change. Some students allow me to sneak changes in, while a certain percentage will go back to their old habits regardless of what I do. Often those people want instant gratification, and if they can't get it, they return to what they're comfortable with. As a coach, I can only wish them good luck and send them on their way; they don't understand that motor skills take time to change, and that the more the old habits are ingrained, the more effort it will take to change them.

DON'T BITE OFF MORE THAN YOU CAN CHEW

Another important point to make is this: When setting your personal goals and translating those goals into a detailed practice schedule, you must avoid the all-too-human tendency to try to fix everything all at once. There is only one way to successfully approach golf: one step at a time. To do otherwise will lead only to frustration and, likely, to poor results. Soon you'll get discouraged and revert to the bad habits you set out to improve.

If a coach tries to give you four or five things to work on in a one-hour lesson, *run away*. The brain can only decipher and assimilate one or two motor-skill changes at a time. I like to believe it's one at a time. Sometimes it might be two things—for example, one forward-swing issue and one backswing issue, and they may still need to be practiced in separate sessions. It's best to isolate one item at a time so there is clarity and comfort in the brain in handling the information. Trying to overload your brain with too many things at once will only frustrate you and likely lead you to self-defeat.

SETTING REASONABLE GOALS

When setting goals or determining their priority, you need to proceed in a very specific manner and have your information clearly defined. As you go through and decide which areas to attack first, you want to set goals that you can attain but are not necessarily easy. The idea is to push you to your limit without setting unrealistic, and thus self-defeating, goals. I recently had a student who came to me and said his goal was to swing like Tiger Woods. Since he was about 5 foot 5 and 195 pounds, I didn't think that was quite possible. I see people on both sides of the spectrum. Some people have more talent than they give themselves credit for, and they have the time to devote to their golf. These people often don't realize where they can really take their game. They never set their goals high enough because they've never had solid coaching. Then I see those who set their goals through the ceiling and either don't have the time to attain them, or are simply not physically talented enough to get where they expect to go in the time frame they have mapped out.

I think a reality check is an important part of a coach's job, and students also need to be willing to adjust their expectations accordingly. We need to match up your goals with your time and talent and come up with something you can actually accomplish in, for example, six months, without getting discouraged in the interim.

DIFFERENT STROKES

I try not to dictate goals to people; rather, I try to let people tell me what their goals are and how they conceptually track improvement. Some people have scoring goals, others handicap goals, while still others are more interested in changing their ball flight in terms of shape and trajectory and/or quality of contact. Some have performance goals, such as wanting to win the club championship or make the college team. A few even come to me with the general goal of simply enjoying the game more. While many of these goals translate back to the ability to score, the player's head is on other things, such as performance or handicap. It's important to understand how you conceptualize your goals so that you can measure your success in terms that will motivate and satisfy you.

Different types of goals affect how you will track your progress in the short term, midterm, and long term. In certain instances, such as the goal of simply enjoying the game more, there are no short-term versus long-term goals. On the other hand, if you're looking to win the U.S. Amateur you'll need some short-, mid-, and long-term goals because by definition you're looking to see where you are now and where you'll be a year from now, three years from now, and five years from now.

CREATING A BLUEPRINT FOR SUCCESS

Prioritizing your activities will assure that the most important things get done. Working on the most crucial weaknesses in a preset order of priority—a blueprint for success, if you will—leads to more dramatic results than either scattered efforts or those aimed at the stronger areas of your game.

Many times when students come to me they have no concrete goals. They don't really know where they're trying to go. They also lack a "game plan" or anything in their heads that would make sense on paper. If people ran their businesses the way they run their golf games, they'd be bankrupt. After I observe them in a first session, we'll sit down and I'll give them an overview of their golf game in terms of what's going on mechanically. We often do a similar thing in later sessions in which I take them out on the golf course for actual play. In most cases, we supplement these observations with a Shot by Shot computer analysis of several rounds. After we gather all the information I'll sit them down, go over how they're managing their game, and help them create a conceptual game plan including short-, mid-, and long-term goals. Once we can see what's wrong from both a golf-swing standpoint and a golf-game standpoint, we can develop these areas together in a cohesive blueprint for creating their best score.

> The greater danger for most of us is not that our aim is too high and we miss it, but that it is too low and we reach it.
>
> —MICHELANGELO (1475–1564)

> In my opinion, the average golfer underestimates himself.
>
> —BEN HOGAN

HOW TO CONSTRUCT A BLUEPRINT: AN EXAMPLE

Let's go back to Bob (whom you met in Spoke 3, Analysis) as an example, applying a logical system of priorities in order to see exactly how computer analysis can translate into concrete practice goals. Using this approach will help you maximize your time management and bring you to the next level as quickly as is humanly possible.

Bob's handicap is a 15, and his average score is between 85 and 90. As for his specifics, we can see from the chart on page 54 that Bob's greatest weaknesses, costing him by far the most strokes, are his tee shots and advancement shots. These are followed by his approach shots and putting. We can also surmise that Bob's chip and pitch shots and his sand shots are in pretty good shape. This gives us a pretty solid picture of where Bob's game is at.

The next step is to take this information and use it to develop some specific, achievable goals for Bob, as well as a specific practice plan designed to help him reach those goals. By laying out specific steps designed to accomplish your goals, and a practice plan that effectively conquers each of those steps in order of priority, your goals become more tangible, and your practice time more purposeful.

Let's go over how you would go about doing this, using Bob's chart as a starting point.

Step One: Create a Goal Statement

In Bob's case, a reasonable long-term goal would be to break 85 consistently and lower his handicap to 12. With the amount of time and attention he has to devote to practice and his level of commitment, we figured six months was a reasonable time period for Bob to reach this goal (keep in mind that these are like due dates—they're an approximation, not etched in stone; by getting hung up on exact dates, you can drive yourself nuts).

Step Two: Develop a Master Plan

This involves writing down the individual steps Bob needs to take, in order of priority, to reach his goal. Using your analysis as a guide, this is where you will likely want a coach to observe the areas you're having the most trouble with and diagnose the specific fundamentals of technique you need to work on. *This is a crucial step.* If Bob, for example, simply took the fact that he needs to work the most on his tee and advancement shots, and then blindly hit tons of drives all day, he'd wind up in the same place as before and probably more frustrated than ever. If anything, this would only reinforce his poor swing. Bob's analysis was key to narrowing down his biggest problem to the full swing, yet he has *specific issues* in his full swing that must be addressed in order to solve his problem.

With regard to Bob's full swing, I recommended that he devote most of his time to practicing hitting shots between a pitching wedge and 7-iron while he developed a fundamentally sound swing, because these clubs are easier to hit and learn with. As he progressed, he could then translate those sound fundamentals to longer clubs such as a 5-iron, 3-iron, and woods. Bob's specific problems that he needed to correct were his grip, problems with his alignment and posture (both of which are setup conditions), and his finish condition was not balanced because the pace of his swing was too fast and his head didn't remain level. (By the way, if any of these things are unclear to you, don't worry—we will cover the fundamentals of technique in later chapters. These are only listed here for purposes of illustrating how to develop a sound practice regimen using the time management principles discussed here.)

As for Bob's second most urgent issue, his putting, I noticed he had trouble getting his eyes over the ball (another setup condition). His left wrist kept breaking down, and his stroke was not symmetrical; rather, it was longer in the back motion than the forward.

Bob needed to remember our rule of thumb: You cannot work on more than two things at a time; otherwise, your mind will become overwhelmed. If Bob tried to tackle all these issues at once, it wouldn't work. Instead, he must address these issues *one at a time*, *in order of priority*, devoting the most practice time to the areas that need the most work.

Step Three: Create a Practice Plan

Let's go over what Bob's initial practice plan looked like to see how we do this. First, he decided how much time he had available to practice—a goal he could stick with, not a fantasy. In his case he was able, realistically, to devote two hours a week to practice. (This was in addition to his usual two rounds of golf a week. Remember, playing a round does *not* count as practice time!)

Given the relative weaknesses of his full swing and putting compared with his stronger pitching, chipping, and sand shots, we assigned percentages of time to each area. A reasonable plan here is to devote about 55 percent of practice time to the full swing, 35 percent to putting, and 10 percent to pitching, chipping, and sand shots.

Therefore, of his two hours, Bob is going to devote about 55 percent—or a little more than an hour—to his full swing, and more specifically to his grip and alignment. He will need to check his grip *every time* he prepares to hit a ball during practice. Of course, he can also sneak some additional practice time at home or work if he uses a training aid known as a form grip during his free time. With regard to his alignment, Bob will use a training aid every time he sets up a shot to make sure his alignment is absolutely correct. (For information on these and other recommended training aids, see Appendix C, "Tom's Top 25".)

Because Bob wants to concentrate on just these few things for now, he does not attempt to fix his posture or finish condition at this time. Only after he has mastered grip and alignment will he tackle the next two issues on his list.

I'd like to stress that what's most important is that you get the fundamentals absolutely correct and practice them repeatedly until they are ingrained. During practice time you might hit a few dozen balls, or maybe none. The key is to focus on the *fundamentals, not* on the ball. (See the story about Nick Faldo and David Leadbetter in Spoke 2, The Mind on page 43.)

As for Bob's putting, he'll spend another 35 percent of his time—about 40 minutes—there. Because they're the two most crucial weak links in his putting, he will work on getting his eyes over the ball and preventing his wrist from breaking down. He was given specific drills to monitor these issues. From these drills he would obtain clear feedback when the coach was not present. Later on, when he's fixed these problems, he'll move on to making his stroke more symmetrical. He will practice the drills for these two areas (which we'll cover later on, under Spoke 6, Technique) until he has mastered them. Again, taking on more than this at the same time would be self-defeating.

Finally, to keep up his areas of strength, Bob will spend the final 10 percent of his time—10 to 15 minutes—practicing his chipping, putting, and sand shots. He doesn't want to lose ground in those areas while he refines his full swing and putting; still, devoting longer than this will yield less improvement than would devoting the extra time to his weakest areas.

Step Four: Regularly Evaluate Your Progress

When you practice, taking notes, both mentally and physically, is a must, because it's a way to actively track your progress. Working quickly and/or without thinking—going through the motions—will not yield positive results. Practice as if you are playing a shot during an actual round. See and plan it, go through the preshot routine, execute the shot, then analyze your success. *Make your practice time real*. You need to plug away at it and not give up until you've either reached the goal you've set for yourself that day, or you've exhausted yourself and the sun has set, whichever occurs first.

Every time Bob practiced, he made notes regarding the time spent in each area and a bit about what happened, such as what he was feeling and any problems that arose. It's a good idea to get into this habit. He simply jotted notes using a loose-leaf notebook, but I have other students who use pre-printed golf journals. Whatever works best for you will do. The journal is like a diary that documents your practice and, over time, your progress. Recording each practice session was also very helpful to me at the next lesson, and it allowed Bob to remember important details he would have otherwise forgotten. Seeing steady improvement over time bolstered his confidence and kept him motivated.

The bottom line is, you need to stay focused and organized as you set goals, and manage your time to enable yourself to achieve those goals.

SOMETIMES THEY SURPRISE YOU

A good friend and student of mine, Tom Chiusano, who works in radio in New York, is a pretty talented and highly motivated golfer. When Tom first came to me as a student, he hadn't accomplished a whole lot in his golf game. He was about a 9 or 10 handicap, and he wanted to win his club championship and play some high-level amateur golf within about a year's time. Frankly, I didn't know if that was really possible. In my estimate, Tom could perhaps win his club championship in about two years. Yet sure enough, within a year's time he had won his club championship *and* had qualified for the U.S. Mid-Amateur. Tom is very strong in the motivation category and he was willing to take the information I gave him and work his backside off, doing whatever he needed to do to get to the next level. He is gifted at time management and dedicated to playing better golf. Given his motivation and personality, Tom was able not only to meet, but even to exceed several of his goals within his designated time frame. Way to go T.C.

The moral of the story is: No one but you really knows what kind of motivation is inside you, and no one can do it for you. As a coach, my job is to steer you toward realistic, reachable goals, but in the long run you're the one who has to stick to the plan and do the work required to get there.

BOB'S SAMPLE JOURNAL ENTRY

Date:	April 8th
Total Time Spent:	2 hrs. 15 min.

Areas Worked On:

1. Full Swing:
Grip
Alignment

Time Spent on This Area:
About 1 hr., 15 min.

Specific Drills/Areas Worked On:
Checked grip repeatedly; used grip aid; used alignment aids on ground

Observations:
Realized when I put the alignment aid down that I've been aiming far right. Felt it was easier to aim toward target. Path to target felt more natural, less out of whack. Getting more comfortable with grip.

Problems:
When I'm properly aligned (and checked grip) and hitting the ball, I'm hitting it left of target.

Additional Notes:
Used pitching wedge and 7 iron

2. Short Game:
Putting—Eyes over the ball; wrist breakdown

Time Spent on This Area:
About 45 min.

Specific Drills/Areas Worked On:
Eyes over the ball drill; left and right hand only drills

Observations:
Once my eyes are over the ball, it's easier to see the line of putt. When not breaking down my wrist, ball striking is more solid.

Problems:
Problems with reverting back to wrist breakdown. Need to be very disciplined in not permitting breakdown.

Additional Notes:
Spent remainder of session on sand shots and chip shots.

Above all, do not make the mistake of preparing a practice plan, doing it once, and think you've got something mastered. Golf rarely, if ever, works that way. Put in some real time, and it will be mastered. Do not rush to the next thing. Real learning takes time.

When you take a shot and you do not get the results you are looking for, always remember: It's not the fundamental information that has changed; it's your execution of that information. Do *not* abandon the fundamentals you have been taught. Instead, figure out why and how you are not translating those fundamentals into a solid swing.

If you're looking for instant gratification, try a TV dinner, not golf. That's a sure formula for failure, so don't fall into that foolish pattern. Don't ever leave solid fundamental information your coach has taught you until you've developed it, learned it, and ingrained it.

While on this subject, I'd like to relate a story to you. Back in 1986 when Jack Nicklaus won his last Masters at Augusta, you may recall that it all came down to the final hole, where Greg Norman had a chance to force a play-off if he made par. Greg drove the ball beautifully down the center of the fairway. With a mid-iron in his hand and a birdie and a victory a definite possibility, Greg hit his shot far right of the green. He failed to get up and down, made bogey, and finished a shot back, handing the championship to Jack. I am told that Greg, who was ranked number one in the world at the time, went to his then-coach, Butch Harmon, to figure out why he sometimes hit that type of shot dead right. His coach identified the problem, which was caused by one very specific area in his swing; Greg, who is an enormously talented athlete, then went to work on that one aspect for some 18 months straight. The best player in the world, who was working with one of the finest coaches in the world, working on one thing for 18 months. Amazing focus and single-minded dedication. Even if it's just a story, it's a good one.

Given Norman's approach to learning, you can understand why I am floored when students come to me and say, "I want to take a lesson to improve my golf game," and they mean just that: taking a *single* lesson and improving their game, in about an hour. You might be able to get a new pair of glasses in that time, but not a new golf swing.

As for Bob, he worked on those few yet crucial things for the entire month between lessons. He made real progress in that time, and he earned it.

STAYING MOTIVATED

It's human nature to become gung-ho and want to accomplish everything all at once, but as we've talked about, that's a mistake. Given that improving your golf game is a long-term, gradual process, it's important to stay motivated to accomplish your goals. By physically writing down a plan and keeping track of your progress on a weekly basis, you will see your progress as it happens.

Of course, your coach can help encourage you to stay motivated. But in the end, it's up to you. If you are seeing a coach for the wrong reasons—you want to hang out with the pro, say, or all your friends are doing it—you are not likely to be really motivated by a desire to improve. If motivation is a persistent problem for you, you might want to rethink whether you want to spend any more money on golf instruction at all.

On the other hand, if you're willing to put in steady time and effort and follow your blueprint faithfully, you will reach a higher, more satisfying level of golf.

Remember, too, to give yourself positive reinforcement and understanding. No one gets things right the first time, and it takes encouragement to persevere. A father who wishes to teach his daughter to ride a bike applauds the successful aspects of her efforts rather than simply criticizing her each time she doesn't do it exactly right. To do otherwise would discourage her and undermine her confidence and efforts. Think of yourself as the child and your inner monologue—that voice inside that praises and carefully criticizes you—as the parent.

Equally important is that you keep a positive attitude and stay focused on your goals, even when the results you get that day, or that week, aren't what you hoped for. Don't waste your time getting angry at or feeling sorry for yourself. Golf takes time, and change takes time.

CONCLUSION

If this chapter seems too commonsensical to you, it's because it should and is. Often when people come to me, they're not making much sense. They're very efficient in other areas of their lives—maybe they run a successful business, they've raised wonderful children, and they generally have their affairs in a clear and concise routine—but they approach their golf game very differently. They have no game plan; they come to me with reckless abandon, poor time use, and no understanding of where they want to go or how to get there. What they're missing is a blueprint, a system of guidance so they can take their golf game where they want it to go instead of fumbling in the dark.

Mastering time management is really learning to run your golf game as you would your business or household: with an organized system of concrete goals and a plan to attack to accomplish those goals one by one. Time management is a realistic, commonsense goal that can be applied to your golf game.

Okay, so now that you've developed a solid practice plan tailored to your particular areas of weakness, what are you sitting around here reading a book for? Get out there and practice!

5 ONE SIZE DOESN'T FIT ALL
SPOKE 5: EQUIPMENT

During his career, Arnold Palmer tested literally thousands of clubs, mainly putters and drivers, in search of the perfect ones. Top players constantly change the clubs they use, looking for just the right fit. In fact, they use very specific parameters for testing various aspects of their clubs.

Compare this relentless, even scientific search for perfect equipment with the approach taken by most amateurs. On countless occasions I've had students show up with a shiny new driver—or worse, an entire new set of clubs—and when I ask them how they decided on this particular model, they reply "I liked the look of it," or "Someone told me it's a terrific club."

Invariably, this response makes me cringe. Even with a new $600 driver or a $2,000 set of irons, they are doomed to disappointment. Like Cinderella's sisters trying to make the wrong shoe fit, no matter how hard they try those clubs simply are not going to work for them.

All too often, players pick the wrong clubs off the rack—and for the wrong reasons. The odds against you randomly picking clubs that match your specific needs and specifications are staggering. Professional players would never even consider using such ill-chosen, ill-fitting equipment. They use only tools that are precisely right for them. In the same way, *if your clubs are not exactly right for you, they are working against you: Every swing will require a type of compensation that will be difficult to repeat, at best, and will severely limit the potential of your game.* There are a lot of issues that make the game of golf a difficult one, so do yourself a huge favor: Eliminate those issues you *can* control. The time and cost are relatively small, and the benefits are immediate—and well worth it.

DISPELLING SOME MYTHS ABOUT FITTED CLUBS

MYTH ONE: "IT'S NOT THE CLUBS, IT'S ME."

While this may be true enough—your swing may indeed need some work—if your clubs aren't right for you, the game has just gotten a whole lot more difficult. For example, if you're a young, strong, flexible player who creates a fair amount of speed in your swing, a shaft flex of "regular" will kill you. It will be impossible for you to square the clubface with any consistency, not necessarily because of your swing, but because the shaft is too soft for your swing speed. On some shots, the club may release early and result in an ugly hook. On others, the clubhead may lag, causing a big flameout to the right. Club flex, from soft to hard, from very flexible to very stiff, is one of the critical factors in selecting the right equipment. Many of my female students benefit from a more flexible shaft, which actually increases their clubhead speed. So, too, with many seniors. In contrast, a hard-swinging junior doesn't necessarily need clubhead speed, but rather control. Such control is found in using a stiffer flex.

Not only is the flex of the shaft important, but so are the weight and length of the shaft as well. Similarly, the angle on which the club sits flat and square on the ground, its *lie angle*, is crucial. The proper lie angle depends on your height and posture when addressing the ball, as well as other factors such as hand position. Lie angles should be evaluated dynamically (in motion), not statically, from the fingertips to the ground (as one well-known company suggests). Golf is played in motion—not at a standstill. I'll talk more about all these topics throughout this chapter.

> *Every player should be fitted for clubs and not assume that he or she needs a standard set. Would a baseball player use a bat that was too short and didn't reach the outside half of the plate? No. Then why would a golfer use a club that once he got in a good athletic setup, didn't reach the ball, golf strike zone?*
>
> —SAM SNEAD, *THE GAME I LOVE*

MYTH TWO: "I CAN ADJUST TO THE CLUBS."

You might be able to, assuming you have loads of time on your hands and are blessed with world-class skill. Otherwise, you are very wrong. The Gene Sarazens, Walter Hagens, and Sam Sneads of this world were so extraordinarily talented they could probably have played golf well using a tree branch. The same goes for Tiger Woods and Fred Couples today—but not you and me. The older players I just mentioned also grew up in a time when they would mess around with their swings and figure out what worked and why. (The Old School Way = Trial and Error + Talent.) Today, we are better equipped to evaluate your individual needs. However, if you look at footage of these older players' swings, you can see that each swing is highly individualistic, but functional. Talent was the overriding force.

Fortunately for us, we have the benefit of much of these pioneers' explorations. We have distilled the fundamentals of golf from their swings—fundamentals that are available to any player today. Practicing and really learning these fundamentals is what I'd like you to focus on. To do this, you must take out the counterproductive maladjustments caused by your clubs. They'll only work against your efforts to learn the fundamentals.

MYTH THREE: "WHAT'S THE BIG DEAL? IT'S ONLY OFF BY HALF AN INCH OF LENGTH OR A DEGREE OF LIE ANGLE."

A very big deal, my friend. While it's true that club weight, length, loft, and lie are measured in small increments (club weight is measured in mere grams, for instance, and lie in units of 1 degree), each of these increments can make a huge difference in your swing. For every 1 degree your club is open at impact for a shot of 200 yards, the ball will fly 33 yards offline. If a club is too long, it will be difficult for you to control the quality of contact or square the face on a consistent basis. Similarly, if a club is too heavy, amateur players tend to try to manipulate it with their hands. Often they'll attempt to lift the golf club with their small muscles—hands, wrists, and forearms—failing to make a powerful windup using their torsos. This problem occurs frequently with poorly fitted junior players, and it leads to bad habits that are difficult to correct later on. As with all players, it's very important to fit junior players correctly to ensure that they get off to a good start in their golf careers.

MYTH FOUR: "HAVING MY CLUBS FITTED WILL BE EXPENSIVE AND TIME CONSUMING."

Wrong again. Actually, the *opposite* is true. Having the clubs properly fitted is often built into their price tag, meaning the place you're buying them from will do the fitting at no extra cost. If you use professionals to do the fitting for you, they will charge their normal hourly fee. Thus the cost would normally run between nada and about $100.

Failing to obtain properly fitted clubs, on the other hand, will end up costing you more money and time than you can imagine. First, there is the frustration with the shiny new club and the search for and cost of the replacement (then there's the cost of gas, credit card interest, marriage counseling . . .). Second, there's the cost of taking lessons with a club intended for another's swing. Next, there's the time wasted trying to learn to swing with the ill-fitted club. Additionally, there's the possible costs of the doctor and/or chiropractor whose job it is to fix your back and other problems resulting from making an unnatural swing with the wrong instrument. So much for the *fitting* being expensive and time consuming.

Seriously, though, the entire club-fitting process will take up no more time than does a lesson, and often less. A PGA professional who is a certified fitter (and please make sure the fitter you choose has gone through some type of certified club-fitting course) will bring you to the range. There, fitters follow a system that allows them to create a variety of configurations in a golf club—changing the length of the club, the lie angle of the club, the shaft flex (whether the deflection point on the shaft is low, medium, or medium high), the grip size, and so forth. Fitters will have a number of clubs and a lie board, and will use both face tape and lie tape to make marks that they've been trained to read, and that tell a story about the equipment. While the fitters feed you clubs that have a variety of specification configurations, they watch your ball flight, quality of contact, and reaction to balance; using this information, they alter the club again and again until they have marks on both the lie angle side and the face side that allow you to achieve a gratifying ball flight. When you're finished, fitters provide you with a set of specifications that you can then take to your favorite golf shop to order your clubs.

The goal of club fitting is simple: You should be swinging the club, not the club swinging you. To accomplish this, the club needs to be fitted to your individual size, strength, height, posture, and dynamic swing motion.

Many people who are taking golf lessons express a concern that their swing could change. That is a possibility. However, most fits are done to what we call a *neutral position*. A qualified, competent fitter understands that they are not fitting to create a compensation by means of tweaking the equipment; rather, they are fitting the clubs in concert with a teaching professional and thus fitting you with your long-term developmental goals in mind. In fact, the fit will aid the teaching professional in moving you in the direction you want to go. It is vital to discuss clubs with your coach before placing your order.

For *some* of the clubs already in your bag, it could be possible to have relatively minor adjustments in lie and length made. The process of lie adjustment is done using a lie angle machine. Most club repair shops and some golf clubs have one available and will be able to assist you with this. Remember, though, that if your club isn't easily adjustable (for instance, if the steel alloy will snap when it's bent more than a degree or two), or requires major adjustments in the shaft length, this will not be an option.

CUSTOM BUILT FOR: **Peter Harris**

CUSTOM SERIAL NUMBER: **BAB3633**

RH Titleist 704.CB Irons
1/2" over standard length
standard lie angle
Dynamic Gold 8300
Titleist Tour Velvet Cord Round -
Standard

FINAL INSPECTION BY:

___LC___

The manufacturing team at Titleist takes great pride in producing quality golf equipment. Every set of Irons is manufactured to exacting tolerances and inspected for conformance to strict specifications. Thank you for putting your confidence in Titleist golf clubs . . . the number one choice of serious golfers everywhere.

John Worster, Executive Vice President
Titleist Golf Club Operations

Pat Donnegan, Director
Titleist Golf Club Manufacturing

CUSTOM SPECIFICATIONS

IRONS	LENGTH	LIE	LOFT	OFFSET	SWING WT
704.CB					
3-iron	39.50"	60.0°	22.0°	.160"	D2
4-iron	39.00"	61.0°	25.0°	.145"	D2
5-iron	38.50"	62.0°	28.0°	.130"	D2
6-iron	38.00"	62.5°	31.0°	.120"	D2
7-iron	37.50"	63.0°	35.0°	.110"	D2
8-iron	37.00"	63.5°	39.0°	.105"	D2
9-iron	36.50"	64.0°	43.0°	.100"	D2
PW	36.25"	64.0°	47.0°	.100"	D2

Here are sample specifications that were made for a male amateur golfer. The entire process took less than half an hour.

I'd also like to add a word of caution here. Please be aware that if you go to a golf club repair shop to get your clubs adjusted, just as there are good doctors and bad doctors, good lawyers and bad ones, and good golf teaching professionals and bad ones, there are some highly competent club repair people out there—and also some who are definitely not qualified. Changing the length of a golf club can really affect the shaft flex, and the swing weight, depending on how the length is changed. If someone cuts an inch off the club's butt end, understand that it's going to affect the club's shaft flex and swing weight. You can't simply cut an inch off a golf club and expect it to perform exactly the way you want it to. These increments must be closely monitored in accordance with your individual needs.

MYTH FIVE: "I WON'T BE ABLE TO GET THE CLUBS I LIKE IN THAT SPECIFICATION— AND EVEN IF I CAN, THEY'LL TAKE FOREVER TO GET HERE."

Now you're reaching. But I've heard this complaint enough times to realize the need to address it. With the specs you obtained from a club-fitting professional, as discussed in myth four, you will be able to order clubs from any major manufacturer—Titleist, Callaway, Taylor Made, and so on. All these companies are capable and highly receptive to custom club orders. The best news is, the cost for spec clubs is no greater than that for clubs bought off the rack. Moreover, the time period between ordering the clubs and receipt is usually four weeks or less, or up to a maximum of eight weeks—and in any case, it's a short time to wait for the clubs that will be right for a lifetime. The difference in your swing once you receive and begin working with them will be remarkable and well worth the wait.

When I discuss the issue of club fitting at my golf seminars, invariably someone still balks. At that point, I pick out someone in the audience, and ask, for example, "Sir, what size shoe do you wear?" That person might say, "Size 10." I'll then ask, "Would you consider wearing a size 7?" to which he'll answer, "Of course not." "Why?" I'll ask. The reply? "That would be pretty painful."

Exactly. A painful experience, not unlike your experiences on the course when you're playing with the wrong clubs. In the 15 or 20 minutes it takes you to find the right pair of shoes, or maybe a fraction more, you can get clubs fitted to your exact specifications. And like a well-made, properly fitted pair of shoes, these clubs can last you a lifetime—not to mention that you gain significant quality of life on the golf course.

FINDING A QUALIFIED CLUB FITTER

There are two simple ways to find qualified club fitters: by talking to the folks at your local PGA section office, or by calling the manufacturer of the clubs you have chosen. Most golf club manufacturers can recommend someone in your area equipped with an appropriate club-fitting system and trained to fit its brand of clubs. Contact information for several major club manufacturers is provided in Appendix D.

MYTH SIX: "I DON'T KNOW WHO TO SEE TO GET FITTED."

Agh! A very large percentage of PGA professionals are certified to fit players. See the sidebar called "Finding a Qualified Club Fitter" for information on finding a qualified PGA member in your area.

Aside from carefully examining fitters' qualifications, you need to make sure that they have an appropriate setting available to fit you properly. I consider anything less than an outdoor practice range to be inadequate. Only actually seeing your ball in flight will permit a proper fitting with accurate shaft length and lie angle configurations. Being fitted indoors in a cage or netted area is not the best scenario. Can it be done? Yes, it is possible, but it's not the optimum environment.

MYTH SEVEN: "I CAN ALTER MY CLUBS MYSELF."

Yeah, like giving yourself a haircut . . .

Enough said. Next myth!

MYTH EIGHT: "THESE NEW CLUBS FEEL FUNNY AND MY SWING IS WORSE, NOT BETTER."

True, there's a brief, awkward adjustment phase when you're getting used to new clubs. Hang in there. The same would be true of trying to get used to a proper grip after using the wrong one for years: weird at first, comfortable in no time. Repetition is the key to learning. The same goes for fitted clubs—they will start to feel much better, and for the first time you'll be able to make a swing without unnecessary adjustments. Work with your coach more frequently during this time period.

NOW WHAT?: HOW TO SELECT THE RIGHT CLUBS

Now that you understand the importance of having fitted clubs, and now that you've obtained your specifications, the next step is identifying clubs that are right for you and your game.

We could probably spend quite a bit of time on this topic. The variety of clubs now available is remarkable, and the process of locating "your" clubs can be overwhelming. The best thing is to take your time. You are making an important and expensive decision—ranging from hundreds up to thousands of dollars. Never, ever buy a club before you've had the chance to try it. For example, demos from the pro shop are a great way to at least get a feel for different brands. Avoid sticking to first impressions. Some clubs can look a little funny at first, but when you hit them long, high, and straight, the funny part fades away quickly. What you're seeking are clubs that are good for you. Please, folks, I urge you to lean toward performance—not looks—when selecting clubs.

CONCLUSION: SO WHAT ARE YOU WAITING FOR?

As you can see, I'm quite passionate about properly fitted clubs. (If you were to meet me, you would see I'm like that about quite a few things.) It makes no sense not to address this issue. Getting your clubs properly fitted to your individual skills is relatively painless, takes little time, isn't expensive, and is one of those things that, if *not* done, will directly interfere with your swing and sabotage your efforts to improve your score. This is one obstacle that is totally unnecessary, yet also simple to remove. Of all the six Spokes you need to address to enable your game to reach new heights, this is one of the very few that *doesn't* take any real time or effort on your part. Consider it a gift, get it done, and move on to more important matters, such as getting your body and mind in shape for golf and learning and perfecting your technique.

SOME CLUB-SELECTION POINTERS

Here are a few tips to keep in mind:

- Eight-degree drivers are tough to hit—don't be afraid to go with a 9- to 12-degree model.
- Cast cavity back irons are forgiving, while forged muscle backs—although they can feel great and provide clear feedback—are much less so.
- Whatever type you choose, a lob wedge is critical.
- Putters come in a gazillion types and sizes—go with the prettiest one, and start the lifelong process of collecting putters (and remember, putters should almost always be kept, because sometimes the old ones work best). *Just kidding, folks.* Take several that appeal to you out to the practice green and narrow your choices down over hundreds of practice putts. Consider feel, visual appeal, loft (yes, putters have loft) and length of shaft. Then have the putter fitted, too (yes, there is a fitting process for putters).
- Your chances of hitting a successful bunker shot are often gone before you ever set foot in a bunker. When I examine the sand wedges that come with stock sets, I find that they're often poorly designed. These so-called sand wedges are often no more than weak pitching wedges, good for lofted pitches but useless for bunker play. Please make sure your sand club has enough bounce and enough loft on it to produce the type of explosion you need to hit a good sand shot. To be safe, ask your local PGA professional to examine your sand wedge.

INTRODUCTION TO TECHNIQUE AND THE LEARNING PROCESS: **THE FINAL SPOKE**

6 THE LAST PIECE OF THE PUZZLE
SPOKE 6: TECHNIQUE

At last, we've reached the point where I can finally do my job as a golf coach. However, without the first five Spokes solidly in place, in the order they're presented, a Tom Patri or any other golf teacher or coach is pretty useless.

Your golf game is like a six-cylinder engine: If the first five cylinders (or, in this case, Spokes) aren't firing correctly, the sixth can't do its job. If you've gotten this far, it means you've understood and addressed the first five Spokes in your golf journey, and are now ready to proceed to the sixth and final Spoke, which is Technique. For those of you who have rushed through the previous Spokes to get here (and you know who you are!), please go back, and return to this Spoke when you're ready.

Go on. We'll wait.

For those of you who have put in the time and the effort to develop these Spokes, you are to be congratulated for your efforts. Give yourself a quick pat on the back, then get ready to do some more work, because now you are finally ready to improve your technique significantly. You are now mine—lucky you!

Up till now, chances are excellent that you were not properly physically trained for golf, your mind was not fully prepared, and your equipment didn't fit you. In addition, until you understood and knew how to address the issues in your game, you could not address your weakest links by developing a logically laid-out practice regimen. Now that these five major factors have been improved, for the first time ever in your golf life all aspects of your game are working in harmony with one another. You're ready to develop your technique and bring your game to your personal highest potential.

THE BEST WAY TO PROCEED WITH YOUR TECHNICAL DEVELOPMENT

Technique must be developed in stages. Trying to master a complete motion all at once is like trying to swallow a cake whole. You'll choke—and it won't be pretty.

Not only must technique be broken down and learned in smaller, more manageable steps, but it must be approached in a clear, logical order: from short game to full swing.

Let me give you an illustration of the perfect way to learn the game. Back in 1991, I had a student from Japan named Yoshino Numata. His employer had transferred him to West-chester County, New York, for a couple of years. He had seen me featured in a magazine article and sought out my help with his swing. He possessed slightly above-average athletic ability, and although interested in golf, he had played for less than a year and had no prior formal instruction. When I asked him to warm up, he took out a pitching wedge. Given his limited experience, I was happily surprised by his quality of contact. His grip was quite good, and his posture and positioning were well above average. Not all of his shots were perfect, but they were quite reasonable and impressive considering the amount of time he had been playing golf.

When I asked him to take out a club that was a little longer than the pitching wedge, he took out a 9-iron, which surprised me again, as most students would have jumped to a 7- or 5-iron. He'd only gone down one club. He then hit a few shots. Again, I asked him to take out an even longer club. He chose an 8-iron. We continued, as he demonstrated above-average ability with each of his clubs until we reached the 6-iron. "I can't," he said when I asked him to take it out.

His words startled me. He then explained, "A 7-iron is as far as I've gotten. I don't feel I can go on to the next one until I've mastered a club." I asked him if he'd tried a wood. His reply was, "Why would I hit a wood if I haven't mastered a 6-iron yet?" When I asked him how he had gotten this far without any formal instruction, he told me he had simply used illustrations of technique from a book as a guide. The verbiage he found less useful, but the pictures made it possible for him to imitate the fundamentals with precision.

Numata passionately wanted to learn the game, and he was endowed with a seemingly ungodly amount of patience, at least in comparison to most players from the West that I have known. What I'd encountered purely by chance was the perfect student. I gave him advice on his swing—not a lot, but enough to keep him busy working to the next level. Off he went, but for how long, I wasn't sure.

A full year later, he returned for his second lesson. He had finally gotten through the balance of his clubs, including the driver, and had been on a course. I asked him how it went. "It was a nice experience," he told me, "but I expected more from myself." I asked him if he minded telling me what he shot. "An 84," he calmly replied. His first time out. (Wow!) I told him that was actually quite good—astoundingly so. After all, most people never break 100, and even fewer ever break 90.

While I realize it is unrealistic to expect average players to spend a year or more perfecting their technique solely off the golf course, as Numata did, a lot can be learned from his approach. He didn't make the mistake of jumping around from one thing to the next, or quickly heading on to the next thing before really working on and perfecting the previous one.

In short, it's not unreasonable to expect all those golfers who truly want to improve their game to spend a significant amount of time between rounds developing their technique, one manageable step at a time, moving on to the next aspect of their technique *only* after developing the previous one, and then practicing and reinforcing these skills regularly. Expecting any less of yourself is a recipe for mediocrity and frustration.

If you're reading this, clearly, you want more from your game. But please, be patient with the process. If you put in the work and time, you will eventually find that you have left the competition far behind (or at least your former, less-than-spectacular game). That, my friends, is the pride of accomplishment.

TAKE TIME TO LEARN IT RIGHT

Remember Yoshino Numata, my student from Japan? The way he learned to play, one club at a time, is the ideal way to learn golf, yet few Westerners have the patience to swing with one club at a time hundreds of times to develop their skills. In a world of instant gratification—microwaves, instant oatmeal, instant communication—we have come to expect that our successes in all areas should be rapid, including the progress in our golf game. But to really learn to play well requires a lot of time and repetitions in a structured, detailed environment with periodic coaching. There are no instant results in this game. Anyone who tells you differently is lying to you and probably trying to sell you something.

There are actually four steps to the learning process:

1. The lesson.
2. Practice time (repetitions at a practice facility).
3. Bridge time (practice on the golf course).
4. Golf course time (trying to create a score).

Too many students take a lesson, maybe take a few practice shots of whatever they've learned (or maybe not), then to head to the course to play. This is ridiculous—they can't possibly have learned and developed a new motor skill in little more than an hour. All they have done is cover the first of the four steps—taking a lesson, or beginning to develop a new fundamental. Skipping over practice time is foolish; without it, the time and money for that lesson are wasted.

The third step, bridge time, is one that I think many golfers neglect altogether, but it is as important to the learning process as the other three. Bridge time happens when you go out onto the golf course, but not under the real pressure of regular play or trying to create a good score. Around five o'clock or so, or whenever the course is quiet, head out to practice whatever shot you're working on under real course conditions. Of course, this step should not be done until the first two have been covered: All four steps need to be followed in order.

A NOTE ON SOUTH PAWS

Because most of my students play right-handed, I (as do most of my colleagues) usually describe techniques as though I am working with a right-handed player. Left-handed professional tour players Phil Mickelson and Mike Weir may hopefully someday make this politically incorrect. In the meantime, for you lefties out there, anything I say about setup, position, arm or hand angle, and the like, should be reversed.

Back in 1957 Ben Hogan declared, "The average golfer is entirely capable of building a repeating swing and breaking 80." That is as true now as it was half a century ago—perhaps even more so, given the amazing technological advances we enjoy. Yet these advances cannot and will never replace the need for good old-fashioned hard work learning the few, yet crucial, fundamentals of the game.

THE PRESHOT ROUTINE, PROPER SETUP, AND OPTICS

The vast majority of amateurs do not devote enough time and attention to two key fundamentals of technique: the preshot routine and setup. Their significance is often altogether lost on the club player.

I've frequently been accused of being a "setup" teacher, as though this is a slight. I take it instead as a compliment, because the fact is, without proper setup you'll never play better golf than you're playing right now.

In the 20,000 lessons I've taught a year over the past 20-plus years, I've never had a professional student (PGA, Nationwide, LPGA, or Senior Tour) who didn't ask me to check setup conditions and preshot routine first. Conversely, I have not once had an amateur player ask me to check these first. This ought to tell you something about the importance to your success of learning proper setup and continually checking it. How many times have you or anyone you know spent a lesson, let alone a reasonable amount of time, working solely on perfecting the preshot routine? (Don't answer that—I already know!)

Please understand that the preshot routine and setup conditions are crucial to *every shot*. If you don't build a successful setup condition, the execution of the motion will be difficult and the correct optical relationship to your target will be missing.

We humans are particularly ill built for this game we love, which is why we need to make a conscious effort to overcome problems inherent in the learning process due to our basic build. We're binocular, vertical animals who stand erect and use both eyes. In golf, on the other hand, we're in an inclined vertical position rotating our heads down parallel line while looking at a target 200 yards away. We simply can't function naturally within this setting. From a physiological standpoint, we're in big trouble—*unless we learn a process that allows us to understand what we're seeing and trying to develop an appropriate approach*. Otherwise we don't have a chance—we'll be constantly in self-correct mode, and most of us are not athletically gifted enough to pull that off without a well-defined process.

If, for example, you unknowingly aim too much to the right, the club will likely get too far behind you in the backswing and then come up over the top in the downswing. It's a simple cause-and-effect relationship: the brain tries to compensate during the swing for poor setup conditions. This optical relationship is something you need to be aware of, because if you ignore it or try to fight it, you will never play well. Let me give you an example of how this optical relationship works.

There's a constant conversation going on between your eyes and your subconscious. You say to yourself consciously: *I want to go from point A to point B*. But let's suppose you unknowingly aim to the right. Now your eyes say to your subconscious, *Didn't he just ask me to go from point A to point B? Then why is he aiming 30 yards to the right? All right, let's try to help him out here*. Your mind then goes into a kind of self-correct mode—also known as compensation. But the golf swing happens in less than two seconds and at speeds of up to 100 miles an hour. Unless you have the rare athletic ability

> *The golf swing is 98 percent setup, 2 percent start, and the rest is in the Lord's hands.*
>
> —BILL "COACH" STRAUSBAUGH

> *If all you ever do for the rest of your career is teach short game and preshot, you'll be doing a real service to the industry.*
>
> —JIM FLICK, TO AN AUDIENCE OF TEACHING PROFESSIONALS

RESPECTING THE CLUBFACE

If I shook your hand while looking the other way, you'd probably think I was a jerk. I make eye contact (meaning I face you) as I shake your hand, out of respect.

Most amateurs don't respect the clubface, overlooking it entirely. When amateur players go to set up, they usually place their feet down and then work the clubface into the equation. Conversely, all professionals begin by meticulously tweaking the clubface until it faces the target (that's why it's called a club*face*, folks—the face respects the target) and then building their bodies around the clubface until they are in a parallel position. As such, they never create what we call *bisecting lines*—when the club is facing to the left of the target and the body to the right. While as individuals they might have a few quirks, they all wind up with the same, perfect result. That's because professionals realize something most amateurs don't: The address position of the clubface is most vital!

of a Michael Jordan, a Derek Jeter, or an Olga Korbut, you simply can't recover that quickly. Instead, you create inconsistencies in your swing.

Ironically, most of my students express a desire to hit the ball not only farther, but also more *consistently*, yet I'd wager that about 99 percent of the amateur students who come to me initially do not set up properly—*99 percent*. Because they're not positioned correctly in relation to the target, they're constantly in that self-correct mode. By creating and consistently applying a sound preshot routine and proper setup, they begin to develop a process that triggers their mind and body to get them into a desired position on a consistent basis.

Unless and until you build a sound fundamental preshot routine that leads to a sound fundamental setup, understand the optical relationship to the target, and have a way of getting into the same position each time, you will never, ever play golf at the next level. You're done. It's over. Go home. This is true whether you're putting 2 feet from the hole or driving a golf ball 320 yards—either way, your game will be filled with compensations.

If you want to get to the next level, you need to start *seeing* things at the next level. A preshot routine is the fastest way to bring a 25 handicap down to a 20, a 20 down to a 15, and so on. Your thought processes and optical references have to be advanced before your swing can become more advanced. In other words, you have to start seeing the world a bit differently.

As with other aspects of technique, the preshot routine and setup are an essential part of the timeless fundamentals of the game. These fundamentals are key to the learning process, so take time to learn them well and check them regularly.

SPEAKING OF FUNDAMENTALS

In the past 25 years much has changed in the world of golf. Course design has changed, equipment has become more sophisticated as technology has advanced, and more teaching aids and instructional resources are available to golfers than ever before.

TAKE REHEARSAL SWINGS, NOT PRACTICE SWINGS

You may notice that among Tour players, there are two kinds of animals when it comes to practice swings: those who take a real, thorough practice swing (for a perfect example, have a look at PGA touring professional Scott Simpson), and those who do not take any practice swings at all during their preshot routine. There are a few pros who arguably do take a casual or mini practice swing, but only for a warm-up.

Practice swings should occur immediately prior to beginning your preshot routine. However, whenever you do take a swing prior to the "real" one, I want you to think of it as a rehearsal swing, not a practice swing. Here's why:

Practice swing is too casual a term. You need to take a more serious approach. Think about a full-dress rehearsal the night before a Broadway premiere. When the actors go through this rehearsal, they use full makeup and costumes; there's no ad-libbing, and no stopping. They perform the play exactly as they would if the audience were sitting in front of them.

When you take a rehearsal swing, I want you to do the same thing. People who take casual rehearsal swings are setting up for disaster. The reason is when you take a rehearsal swing, you are saying to your brain, *This is exactly what I want*. Your mind says, *Okay, so if I do that, we're in business*. You want to take your rehearsal swing behind the golf ball, down the exact same target line, so that you see the same optical reference to the line you're playing on. If it's a full swing you're rehearsing, for example, you want to make a full motion, hold your finish, check your balance . . . Give this swing the same length, pace, and intensity that you are about to play with. Make it real!

What hasn't changed are the fundamentals of the game. Odds are, these will never change. Forty years ago the term *strong* was used to describe a grip position. It means the same thing today. When describing club conditions as *square*, *open* or *shut*, *too inside* or *too outside*—these terms are the same as they always were. Today's fancy equipment and all the bells and whistles money can buy won't give you a sound, repeatable swing if you don't take the time to learn the fundamentals thoroughly, one at a time.

Learning these fundamentals requires time, effort, and patience on your part. However, while technique takes time and effort, and is honed and mastered over a lifetime, learning the fundamentals shouldn't be complicated.

TECHNIQUE MADE SIMPLE

Unfortunately for many of you, up until now learning the fundamentals of the game has been made unnecessarily complex. The following chapters will cover technique in a way that will make the learning process easier, more straightforward, and less intimidating. This book will serve not only as a primer for learning these fundamentals, but also as a guide you can refer back to throughout your golf career.

The terminology has been simplified to make the illustrations and drills easier to follow and the techniques simpler to understand and visualize.

Moreover, technique has been laid out in the order it should be learned—from the smallest swing closest to the hole to the longest swing on the tee box. The reason is basic, yet profound: In many cases, the skills utilized in the short game swing are a smaller version of those in the full swing. Nearer the hole, the swing is at its shortest and least complex. The full swing is much more complex, with many more moving parts at a higher rate of speed. Heading to full swing first is like trying to gallop on the horse before you've figured out how to climb on. Once you can do the latter, the former technique is a natural outgrowth, and you're ready for it.

Additionally, I teach students the full swing in a way that cuts out a lot of time and confusion but makes sense if you stop and think about the methodology. You will notice I begin teaching the full swing with what I refer to as *Bookends*. Much like those devices that encase books, these Bookends are the two parts of the swing that sandwich the rest: the launching pad (you may call it the setup) and the finish condition. Just as bookends provide a structure holding books in place, the launching pad and finish condition provide a solid foundation that shapes the swing. I have found in my experience as a golf coach that, if the launching pad and the finish condition are perfectly sound, the mechanics of the in-between part of the swing most often fall naturally into place. You cannot begin with sound fundamentals and end in a proper finish condition without much of the rest of your swing falling reasonably into place. Capitalizing on this principle, the Bookends method will help save a lot of time and effort in developing a mechanically sound, repeatable swing.

The rest of the full-swing chapters cover the in-between (takeaway, top of the swing, transition, starting down, starting forward, impact, follow-through, and finish). Any thorough discussion of the full swing would of course be incomplete without them.

All that said, let's move on to the fundamentals of the short game.

7 INTRODUCTION TO THE SHORT GAME
THE MICROCOSM OF THE FULL SWING

The best way to learn golf is to start near the hole. In the ideal world (of patient people) we would start from 2 feet and work to 200-plus yards. The short game, which causes so much anguish and is enshrouded with mystery so out of proportion to the actual physical mechanics involved, is really just a microcosm of the full swing. It's a shorter, simplified version of the golf motion. The truth is, if you can't coordinate a putting stroke at a rate of 1 mile an hour and ranging from 18 to 24 inches, how can you expect to control a 5-iron off a sidehill lie with a swing speed of 90 mph or more that takes less than two seconds, with a vast distance to cover and a much greater number of moving parts? The answer is, you *can't*. If you can't avoid 3-putting or can't occasionally hole a putt to save par or bogey, what reason is there to go any farther? Why hit the 5-iron or driver if you can't pitch the ball competently onto the green from 30 yards? The short game is a building block for the full swing. On the other hand, a player who masters the short game—the microcosm—will be ready and quite able to build a sound, repeatable full swing.

SHORT-GAME SYMPTOMS, FULL-SWING ILLS

The same may be said of *problems* you are experiencing in your short swing: The weaknesses that occur in your short game are mirrored in your full swing. For example, a player who comes out of posture during a full swing tends to do the same on the putting green and mis-hit putts. Those who are reverse pivoters in their full swings have similar problems during pitch shots. No instructor would be remiss in examining students' short game to identify clues on what ills befall their full swing.

Aside from being the best way to progress, the importance of a solid short game for improving your overall score cannot be overestimated. Remember our discussion in Spoke 4, Time Management: The short game makes up more than half the game of golf. In fact, if a student walked up to me right now and said, "Tell me, bottom line, how to improve," I would reply: "For this *entire season*, spend *all* your instructional time and dollars, as well as *all* your practice time, on pitching, chipping, sand play, and putting." I guarantee that this individual would achieve significant, noticeable, bottom-line scoring improvement, and would also probably hit more solid, consistent full shots. This individual could be you.

BECOMING A COMPLETE GOLFER

As you begin to remedy short-game problems, you will learn to be a better scorer—which is what it's all about, really—and you'll begin to introduce and develop, through short-game drills, the *feelings* you should have when practicing the full swing and, later, when taking that full swing to the golf course. The sensations you experience when making a properly executed short swing—pivots, hinging, cocking, swinging—are all applicable to a correctly executed full swing.

This is all part of the process of seeing yourself as a complete golfer, developing both a sound short game and a reliable full swing, and specifically learning to use these different skills to adapt to a wide range of course conditions.

BRINGING IT TO THE COURSE

Aside from developing these feelings, it's important that golfers learn to develop better decision-making skills around the greens. As with the full swing, many golfers find it difficult to translate their short-game skills to actual course conditions and situations.

I try to spend about a third of the time with my students on the practice tee, a third of the time in the short-game area, and a third of our time on the golf course. This latter part is key to developing short-game skills, because I spend time talking and walking them through actual short-game situations as they arise. Too often, students will pick up the wrong club or hit the wrong type of shot around the greens. Once this is pointed out and the student begins to think about short-term strategies properly, meaningful improvement is achieved.

Part of developing this skill is becoming creative with your short-game shots. Very often there is more than one shot that can be hit and more than one club that can be used in each situation. When on the course, ask yourself the following questions: *What type of shot does this situation require? How many different ways can I play this particular shot?* And finally, and most important, ask yourself: *Which shot offers the best chance for successful execution?* Though the following chapters will offer solid guidelines on how to execute each and every shot, you need to bring your own creativity to the game as well.

THE SHORT GAME PRESHOT ROUTINE

We discuss optics and the importance of the preshot routine in Chapter 6, "Technique." Remember in the short game that your preshot routine is as important as it is in the full swing, so carefully develop a preshot routine for every shot, whether that be a 2-foot putt, a chip, or a full swing.

In addition, as you move closer to the hole, golf gets a lot more demanding. For example, if you're standing on a tee box on a par-4 hole, the fairway may be 40 yards wide. Your second shot might be to a green that's about 40 feet wide, and then you're putting to a hole that's 4 inches wide. The demands on the face of the club are more intense, because the margin of error is much smaller. For this reason, it's all the more important that you develop a routine that will train you optically in the short game.

ONE FINAL THOUGHT

In order for your game to reach the next level, you need to perceive things at the next level. This is no less true of the short game than of the long one. A solid preshot routine (and of course, sound setup conditions) is essential for developing this perception. Precise shots to exact locations furthers this perception. Employing solid thinking, imaginative practice, and perseverance will help you develop and refine this perception.

On that note, let's move on to the fundamentals of short-game technique.

Tom's Short Game Lesson Notes

I. Putting

A. Grip Style (circle one):

Conventional
Cross-Handed
Claw
Langor
Long/Belly Putter

Grip Notes: ______________________________

____

B. Posture

1. Upper Body: ______________________________

2. Lower Body: ______________________________

C. Alignment/Ball Position: ______________________________

D. Face/Path: ______________________________

E. Length/Pace: ______________________________

F. Pre-Putt Routine: ______________________________

Drills: ______________________________

II. Chipping/Pitching/Sand Play

A. Grip: ______________________________

B. Posture: ______________________________

1. Upper Body: ______________________________

2. Lower Body: ______________________________

C. Alignment/Ball Position: ______________________________

D. Mechanics: ______________________________

E. Distance Control: ______________________________

F. Pre-Shot Routine: ______________________________

Drills: ______________________________

III. Mental Conditioning/Optics: ______________________________

____

This is the form I use to provide lesson notes to students after a short-game lesson. You should prepare and keep similar notes after every short-game lesson.

8 ROLLING THE PILL (IS YOUR FEEL REAL?) **PUTTING**

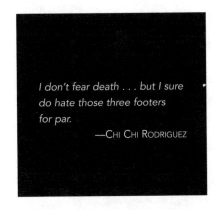

Year after year Loren Roberts has been one of the shorter drivers on the PGA Tour. Yet he has survived quite nicely on the circuit more than two decades because he is a great putter. His putting prowess not only keeps his career going, but has led him to win a fair number of tournaments and make a wonderful living. While putting is a proven survival tactic for Loren Roberts, for you it's a crucial skill you need to develop. Simply stated: *If you can't putt, you ultimately can't play—at least not very well.* Allow me to explain.

There are all kinds of statistics out there about how much of the game putting occupies. The number most commonly tossed around is 43 percent. However, one thing is certain: A player is expected to reach the par-3s in one shot, par-4s in two, and par-5s in three. Each regulation figure allows two strokes on the putting surfaces. Two times 18 holes is 36, and if par is 72, then *50 percent* of all shots in a regulation round of golf are spent on putting. If a teacher told his students that tomorrow's test would count for at least 40 percent, and possibly 50 percent, of their total grade, do you think it would be wise for them to study? You bet!

Similarly, if you want to play golf well, putting warrants a *significant amount of your time and attention.* Do you spend 50 percent of your practice time putting? I see the opposite tendencies in club-level players all the time. Many have adequate skills on the tees and fairways in terms of ball striking, but they putt like a drunken monkey—and can't figure out why. The reason is obvious: They're the same people I never see out at the short-game practice area.

Fortunately, learning to putt well is not the impossible task a lot of players seem to make it. Although it strikes fear in many a player's heart, with a solid time commitment devoted to developing the feel and technique, you will give yourself the ability to make more than your share of putts—certainly a high number inside 6 feet and a few more inside 15 feet. Moreover, *you will not 3-putt any green—ever!* (Yes, this is a realistic goal!)

THE PUTTER: YOUR MOST OFTEN-USED CLUB

Fact: During an 18-hole round, typical amateurs take 35 or more shots with a putter, which means they take more swings using a putter than any other club! Looking at it another way: there are 14 clubs in the bag. If one club is utilized at least 43 percent of the time—and sometimes close to 50 percent—isn't that the club you want to pay the most attention to?

One thing I love about putting, from an athletic standpoint, is that it leaves nobody on the bench. A player need not be athletic, flexible, fast, or particularly dexterous. World-class talent is not required. The putting stroke covers, at most, 36 inches on either side of the golf ball (and that's for a monster-length putt on a giant green), although more often the stroke is a lot shorter. In fact, the longest putt is usually in the area of 30 feet (that's feet, not yards, and 30 feet, as opposed to 300 yards). With such a short stroke, there should not be a lot of moving parts or a lot going on, so *anyone* can improve by focusing on the fundamentals necessary for the stroke.

Before we get into the nuts and bolts of putting and practice drills, let's start with a brief discussion about what putting is and the basic skills putting mastery requires.

OVERVIEW OF PUTTING

PUTTING 101: WHAT IS PUTTING?

In the broadest sense, the goal of putting is to achieve consistent solid contact, which results in speed control as well as sending the ball in a prescribed direction. In the narrowest sense, the goal of putting is to get the ball in the hole in as few shots as possible. It usually occurs on a green, though not always, as it may be used anytime you are confident the ball will roll truly. During the stroke itself, the putter face makes contact with the ball as the putter begins to ascend (during the upstroke). This in turn makes the ball turn down (top spin) and roll toward the target. Although your ultimate target is the hole, because of a green's contour, the direction in which you start the ball will often differ.

SHOULD YOU ALTER YOUR PUTTING TECHNIQUE?

I want to make clear as we proceed through our discussion of the fundamentals of putting that I am not necessarily asking you to change your putting style, which may be ingrained by years of play. In putting, far more so than in the full swing, there are a tremendous variety of styles, even among professionals. Your style really boils down to your personal preferences. Whether your style works on a day-to-day basis depends on whether it is fundamentally sound. First, you must clearly understand your style; then you can choose, based on facts, whether change is needed. If your style results in a successful, repeatable stroke, then by all means leave it alone. If it's not mechanically sound and/or shots are lost each round on the greens, you will need to modify your putting stroke in order to achieve lasting success. *Preferences should not take precedence over success.* Remember: In putting, as in all aspects of the short game, there is less room for error than in the long game, because the hole is only a little over 4 inches wide.

FINDING YOUR PUTTER'S SWEET SPOT

A golf club's sweet spot is the place where, if struck squarely, it will deliver maximum energy to the ball, giving the ball the best chance of staying on its intended line. Most putters mark the sweet spot with a line painted or engraved at the top. (But do not trust that the manufacturer's mark is in fact correct. Always test it for yourself.) Any putter that is not so marked can be marked by hand using a piece of tape after locating the sweet spot. To do this, simply hold the putter lightly by the shaft, using two fingers, while the putter is dangling from your grip. With the face of the club pointing skyward, gently bounce a ball on the face of the club toward the center of the club. The point where the putter stops vibrating and contact feels solid is the sweet spot.

Before you decide whether your style should remain unchanged or be scrapped, let's examine and define carefully what I consider *successful* when determining whether your style works for you.

There are a number of methods to measure success. In putting, some suggest that success or competence is achieved if the number of putts in a round averages less than 30. But because this number depends on several things, such as the accuracy of your approach shots and the efficiency of your chips, pitches, and bunker play, I believe success should rather be defined as your ability to hole a high percentage of putts inside 5 feet and a decent percentage of the putts inside 10 to 15 feet, as well as your ability to get long putts (outside 15 feet) to a makeable distance on a consistent basis.

THE SKILLS REQUIRED FOR PUTTING

As mentioned previously, no extraordinary talents are required to putt well—good putting is based on developing and applying motor skills all of us possess, such as hand–eye coordination, the ability to judge distances (you drive a car, right?), and a few others.

READING GREENS: UNLOCKING THE MYSTERY

Reading putts is truly what makes putting an art form—sadly, a largely forgotten one. It requires developing the ability to analyze the various green conditions you encounter, and then visualizing, at an appropriate speed, the proper line of the putt, and creating a strategy to overcome those obstacles. This critical skill comes with practice and experience.

You will encounter different conditions on the greens you play, including varying slopes, grass textures, grass lengths, surface firmness, ridges, hollows, and hogbacks. Of course, your job is to visualize how all these conditions will influence the ball's behavior based on your observations.

While reading greens is the kind of skill you will develop with experience, the greatest assets you can bring to a putting green are your eyes, your awareness, and your attentiveness. To help guide you in developing this skill, let me give you an example of how I advise you to read a green.

Let's assume you're riding in a cart. As the cart gets within 30 yards of the green, you should already begin to survey the surface and location of your golf ball, gathering information about the overall topography of the green and lay of the land. For example, the green may be slanted overall in one direction or another, showing some kind of tendency in the terrain. As you get closer to the ball and to the putting surface, you may wish to note which sector of the green your ball would be in if it were divided into a four-piece pie. If the ball and pin are in the same quarter of this imaginary pie, things become relatively easy—you can focus on just that one sector of the green. If the pin and ball are in different quarters, you may have a putt with more than one directional move depending on the complexity of the green design.

For now, let's keep our example simple by focusing on that one quarter of the pie. What you would do next is survey that quarter regarding its overall basic movement. Is

Reading a green is like reading the small type in a contract. If you don't read it with painstaking care, you are likely to be in trouble.

—Claude Hamilton

it slanted toward you or away from you? Is it slanted left to right or right to left? Where is your ball positioned relative to the pin?

You should get into the practice of surveying the putt from *two, and sometimes three, distinct sides: behind the ball, from the low side of the slope, and from behind the hole.* When you survey from behind the golf ball, think in terms of water. If it started to rain, where would the water go in relation to the line you are looking at? Let's say you determine from this analogy that the water would go from left to right. You would then proceed to a midpoint on the low side of the putt and then to a point a good 10 or 15 feet away from the line in order to confirm that the slope is actually moving toward you. If what you see confirms this, then you're done reading your putt in terms of break. You're now going to survey, from the same position, the overall length of the putt to get a visual feel for the distance. If for some reason you don't get confirmation at this second point, you move to the third point from which to survey: behind the hole, meaning on the opposite side of the hole looking back toward the ball. Generally you won't need to go to that third point because if you've made a good read, the second position will confirm the first one, and at that point you'll have a pretty good handle on what the ball is going to do.

The next step is to go back to position one—behind the ball—and, taking into account the break pattern you have already determined, figure out how much speed will be required. Is it uphill or downhill? How much length and pace must you apply to the stroke to make the ball travel in that line, then die and move off the intended line and toward the hole, your ultimate target?

Grain: A Consideration When Reading Greens

The high quality of maintenance of the bent-grass greens often found in the northeastern United States has reached an excellent standard. Given the positive changes in turf grass in Florida, the southeastern U.S., and any Bermuda-type grass areas, and the new grass that's being planted and maintained today, grain in these places and its effects have also been greatly reduced, based on past history. Reduced, but not eliminated.

However, you're still more likely to encounter some grain effects in Bermuda-type grass areas, such as the Southeast and Southwest (more so than in the Northeast or Northwest). Bermuda grass tends to grow toward large bodies of water, even ones you can't see. For example, in Naples, Florida, where I teach, the Gulf of Mexico isn't visible, but it's only a couple of miles away, so you better believe it has an impact on the putting surface there.

Bermuda grass also tends to grow toward the setting sun. Late in the day, remember that those blades of grass are growing toward the sun.

In bent-grass or mountainous areas, the green will run away from the mountain, because in most cases that's the way water runoff travels during rainfall. Bermuda grass will also be influenced over days, weeks, or years toward water runoff.

Another good habit to get into is to observe every inch of your playing partners' putts to analyze how each ball reacts on the slopes and other conditions of the green. This information is highly relevant and will help you understand the green's influence on balls when it's your turn to putt.

The practice drills that follow in this chapter will help you develop the ability to read greens and visualize the correct shot.

PRE-PUTTING ROUTINE

Remember our discussion of the preshot routine back in Spoke 2, The Mind? This information applies no less to putting. A solid preshot routine is vital to your success—*vital!* Without it, the mechanics that follow will not matter.

Let's go through the putting preshot routine I use, with the understanding that I am not telling you to adopt my routine, but rather to use it as a springboard toward developing one that works for you.

I begin directly behind the ball in the line I'm about to putt on after having read the green. I stand facing the putt, looking at the ball; I trace an imaginary line from the ball down the intended line, seeing the ball break off the line as it loses speed and falls into the hole on exactly the side and point of the hole where I want it to enter. I imagine the scene very graphically in my mind, down to the last detail. I take several looks from the ball back to the hole and from the hole back to the ball, visualizing this.

Then I walk into the putt in a slight semicircle, get set up in a putting position alongside the golf ball, and make two practice strokes while looking at the hole (not down at the ball), allowing myself to see and feel the stroke that's about to happen. Thus, these are realistic rehearsal strokes in terms of length and pace, and in terms of what I'm seeing and feeling. I then slide the putter head in behind the golf ball on the intended line and tweak the face until it is facing on the exact line where I want the ball to start. I do not build my grip or stance until I feel as though the face is absolutely perfect. Next, I move in my right foot, then my left, building my stance. I fix my grip to the club. At this point I might take one more look at the hole (which is a *preference*, not a *principle*), set, and then make the stroke. This entire process takes about 10 to 12 seconds, and is fairly spontaneous and done by feel. I don't think it, I feel it.

THE LAUNCHING PAD: PROPER SETUP CONDITIONS

There is no shot clock in golf and no delay-of-game penalty (although at a certain point, you'll start to annoy those around you). Therefore, there is no reason to pull the trigger without a proper, perfect launching pad condition. Take your time and do it right—*every time.*

TRAINING YOUR EYES TO PUTT

I call the area 2 feet from the hole the danger zone, *because most players expect to make a 2-foot putt—so much so that they are often too casual when putting their clubface behind the ball or sighting their target line. What you should do every time, even with putts you assume you can make, is develop a preshot routine when you place the putter down, using a series of checks and tweaks with your eyes that allow you to develop your optical skills with great precision—respect the placement of the face of your putter. Then when you pull the trigger, so to speak, it will be almost impossible to miss, even if you make a slight error on the stroke.*

As with the full swing launching pad, the putting launching pad should be balanced. Keep your shoulders and forearms level. The ball should be positioned under your left breast (and therefore is slightly forward), and your eyes should be over the ball and positioned *parallel* to the target line. Your feet should be placed shoulder-width apart (from the insteps), square, and solidly balanced.

The proper setup conditions for putting are as follows:

- **Grip.** Although there are several ways to grip the club, the grip I recommend is a neutral one. Your thumbs should point straight down the shaft. The forefinger of your left hand should run along the outside of the fingers of your right hand on the outside of the left side of the shaft, in a kind of trigger, or neutral, position. This is called a reverse overlap grip and I should say it's a preference of mine, not a principle.

    People have found success putting split-handed, cross-handed, with a standard conventional, a double reverse overlap, and other grips. Great putters have made these various personal preferences part of their putting setup routine, and that is fine with me. The bottom line is, you should grip the club in such a way that your hands don't oppose one other, and that they do work in a swinging motion agreeable with the clubface—meaning that it doesn't cause a rotation in the clubface or let the clubface deviate radically offline in any way.

Neutral Grip: A putting grip should have the palms of each hand face each other. In this position, they will work with one another in a linear manner.

- **Alignment.** Square to slightly open, but not closed. For many golfers, aligning shoulders, hips, forearms, feet, and eyes parallel with the target line is best.
- **Posture.** Stand comfortably, bent at the hips, allowing your arms to hang from your shoulders without any restriction or tension. Your knees should be slightly bent.
- **Weight Distribution.** Centered, meaning balanced equally between the feet.
- **Ball Position.** Slightly forward of center under the left breast. I usually line up the logo of the ball perpendicular to the clubface, using it as an aid for the starting putting line.

Ball Position: The ball should be forward in your stance. Two checkpoints that may help are to: (1) position the ball just inside the left heel and (2) under your left breast. A forward position encourages topspin roll—aiding the ball to hold its intended line.

- **Stance.** Feet are shoulder-width apart. (Insteps = shoulders)
- **Eyes.** Your eyes should be directly over the ball, or behind the ball over the line of the stroke. In fact, all other putting setup conditions, if done properly, will allow this vital eye position to occur.

SLIGHTLY MEANS JUST THAT—*SLIGHTLY*

> *When I ask you to take an aspirin, please don't take the whole bottle.*
>
> —HARVEY PENICK, FROM HIS *LITTLE RED BOOK*

I want to clarify the word *slightly*, which is used throughout Spoke 6, Technique. It means just that: slightly. Most of my students come to me with an exaggerated version, to varying degrees, of all these setup conditions; it often takes me a few lessons to get them right. They do this because they read somewhere, for example, that there were "four easy steps" to the chipping launching pad, and they didn't take any of it in moderation. So we often spend our first lesson trying to remedy the lack of proper setup conditions, using the concept of *slightly* as our guide; the second is usually spent correcting the exaggeration from not taking me literally enough about the word *slightly* after the first lesson; and the third is spent getting back on middle ground (eureka!).

EXERCISES TO CHECK EYE POSITION

When you set up the ball, you can easily check yourself to see if your eyes are squarely over the ball. Take a second ball and hold it against the bridge of your nose, right between your eyes. Drop it straight down from there. If it lands on the ball or on the target line behind the ball, *bingo!* If not, fix it by playing with your posture and the position of your setup.

Another method for reinforcing proper eye position is to check yourself in front of a mirror to see where your eyes are in reference to the golf ball.

One important point to be made here is that, if your putter is too long for you, you will not be able to properly position yourself. If the putter is incorrect with respect to lie angle and length, you will be unable to get in the proper eye line position as well. See Spoke 5, Equipment, on properly fitting your clubs.

When your eyes are positioned over the ball path, you should see an instant improvement in your putting by virtue of your body position.

MAKING THE STROKE

SYMMETRY IS ESSENTIAL

The most important aspect of putting is to be sure your putter does the same thing on both sides of the ball. This means the *length* and *pace* of the stroke are equal on the backswing and the follow-through: They're *symmetrical*. This is why the putting stroke has often been characterized as a "pendulum" motion. Imagine a pendulum clock—what would happen to its speed, timing, and accuracy if the lengths of the pendulum began to vary on either side? (However, beware of taking the clock analogy too far—unlike a clock, your motion should be *rhythmical, meaning it should have a tempo to it, and not be mechanical.*)

I believe that a symmetrical and rhythmic action is superior for the vast majority of players because it is the easiest to coordinate and the most effective for controlling the distance a ball rolls, which is a cornerstone of putting. Other approaches make it very difficult to calculate and control distance on both sides of the stroke with accuracy and repeatability.

As for the speed of a ball, I'm a big proponent of the ball dying at the hole. Because the ball is a circle rolling toward a larger circle (the hole), at the right speed (which we discuss in greater detail below) all the edges are in play, meaning a ball can topple into the hole on all sides. Contrast a putt that will stop rolling 2 or 3 feet past the hole. Only the dead or very near dead center putt will drop. All others will likely either roll over the edge or simply catch the edge and lip out. I want all the edges of the hole to be your friend as a result of your properly controlled speed.

A FLUID STROKE (CONSISTENT TEMPO)

Hand in hand with the concept of maintaining a symmetrical stroke is a fluid stroke—one with a consistent tempo back and through. Tempo is a highly individual matter. If you're the type that does everything quickly, the tempo of your stroke will likely be quick. The reverse applies if you tend to saunter or do things at a more leisurely pace. All that's important for you to recognize is that you should match your tempo with the length of your symmetrical stroke, and keep that stroke rhythmic.

CONSISTENT GRIP PRESSURE

In addition, grip pressure should remain consistent throughout the stroke. There have always been preferences for various grip pressures—light, medium, and firm. I believe a medium to firm grip pressure is best, as it allows the player to maintain control of the putter. I think amateurs often greatly overdo light pressure, leading them to lose this control.

THE DIFFERENT THEORIES OF PUTTING

There are quite a few putting theories out there. Two of these theories include the hot stroke *theory and the* longer follow-through *theories. The hot stroke theory, embraced by Gary Player, involves swinging the putter back and then popping the ball at impact, stopping the putter at that point. The longer follow-through theory involves the player taking the club back a short distance and then really accelerating through the ball to a longer follow-through. However, I feel the symmetrical, rhythmic approach to putting is best for most players, because it offers the easiest way to coordinate distance and control consistently.*

TEMPO AND ITS RELATION TO DISTANCE

Tempo should be directly related to distance, and employed on a consistent, predictable, repeatable basis. For example, if you're taking the club back to distance A and then forward to distance A, you should use pace A. If you're putting from B to B, use pace B, and so on. Length and pace must be symmetrical. Again, be careful to make it rhythmical, *not* mechanical.

TAMING YOUR WRISTS

The single biggest source of putting problems is the breaking down of the left wrist joint (if you're a right-handed player; lefties should of course reverse these directions). When this happens in the impact area, deviations of the face and path of the putter occur. It's essential to keep your left wrist in a relatively flat condition, or the same condition as it started in the address, throughout the stroke.

The key to preventing this problem is checking during your setup to make sure you have as flat a wrist condition as possible. Then maintain that condition throughout the stroke.

Some people feel that the back of their left wrist is staying flat, while others feel their right wrist is staying concave or bent. You can't keep both wrists flat. It doesn't matter which wrist you choose to "feel" as your anchor, but one of those conditions must exist and be maintained in a good putting stroke to make quality contact, meaning to control distance, and to keep the face square while maintaining the path of the putter.

Preventing Left Wrist Breakdown: Right-Hand-Only and Left-Hand-Only Drills

Two excellent drills to help prevent or fix this problem are the right-hand-only and left-hand-only drills. To do these, first hold the putter in your right hand only and put a golf ball between your right wrist and the putter shaft. Put pressure up against the shaft to keep the ball in place and make some strokes using your right hand only. Then try this with the left hand only: Put the ball on the top of your left wrist against the putter shaft and putt with the left hand only. Alternate using the right hand only and left hand only, placing the ball between the wrist joint and putter to feel those conditions (left wrist flat or right wrist concave) being maintained throughout the course of the stroke. Do not allow the ball to fall out.

KEEP THE HEAD AND BODY STILL THROUGHOUT

Once you have your arms and body properly aligned for the putt, your body and head should stay quiet throughout the stroke. *I cannot overemphasize the importance of this point.* Where many students go awry is at the moment the putter strikes the ball, when

Flat Left Wrist at Impact: Delivering a flat left wrist at impact when putting is essential to both quality of contact (distance control) as well as face and path (direction). Thus, every degree of variation causes you to lose, to a degree, your ability to control distance and direction.

Left Wrist Breakdown: The number one flaw in putting.

there is a tendency to chase the ball and putter with the eyes, head, and upper body. Most golfers are not even aware they're doing it. *This habit must be broken.*

When you putt, your body should stay centered, and you should feel as though it's still or quiet from the waist down. Because all the movement in your stroke is generated from the arm swing, your arms are the only part moving throughout the entire stroke. By staying centered, you'll ensure improved center-face contact, better direction, and, as a result, truer roll.

Similarly, you must guard against moving your head and upper body during the stroke. This is not the same as keeping the head *down*; I'm asking you to keep your head *still* (or, as I like to say, *Keep your coconut quiet*). You can putt just as well looking out at the horizon after properly addressing the ball as you can looking at the ball itself as long as you stay still during the stroke. You don't have to see the ball to putt it well. Similarly, you can putt just as well with your eyes closed if you have properly addressed the ball. Movement of your head deviates your shoulder line, which will cause a path and face change during the course of the stroke. This interrupts the quality of contact or center-face contact, which in turn negatively affects the speed of your stroke as well as the direction of your putt.

TWO DRILLS TO REINFORCE KEEPING THE HEAD AND BODY STILL DURING PUTTING

If you find that movement is a problem for you, the following drills can help:

- Practice putting with your head against a wall to eliminate head movement.
- Practice with your buttocks against the wall to eliminate body movement.

These two drills are really self-explanatory. One is placing your forehead against the same wall to keep your head still throughout the stroke. The second is designed to detect body movement by placing your backside against a wall to stabilize and keep the lower body still.

When you do turn to check your distance and line, simply pivot your head to the side to avoid lifting either your head or upper body. Lifting or altering your upper body region will increase the probability of poor contact or direction.

HOLD THAT POSE

I strongly encourage all my students to hold their finish position, then observe what happened and take mental notes. What you should see is a wrist condition that is identical to setup (no breakdown or hinge) and no change in your posture or lower body from your setup position.

The formula to ingrain this is: **Stroke** (make the motion)—**Hold** (the finish condition)—**Look** (pivot, don't lift your head, to look).

THE TWO KEYS TO PUTTING:
DISTANCE AND DIRECTION

In a nutshell, putting requires two basic skills: the ability to control (1) distance (that is, speed), and (2) direction.

DISTANCE CONTROL

(Putting Stroke) Length + Pace = (Ball) Distance

Distance or speed control gives you the ability to use more of the edges of the hole, which become your friend by thus increasing your chances of holing putts.

In putting, speed has to be perfect. In fact, if I had to choose between direction or speed in terms of importance, *I'd choose speed every time.* If you're on the right line but have the wrong speed, the putt will likely be short of the hole, will not take the break and pass beyond the hole, or, if it's online, will lip out unless it's dead center of the hole. Conversely, if the speed is good but the direction is off, you'll still end up relatively close to the hole; on occasion you'll catch an edge and the ball will fall into the hole.

To control speed, you will need to make *quality* center-face contact. Almost every concept discussed in this chapter is intended to give you the opportunity to make solid contact every time.

EASY DOES IT

When you're working on speed control, realize that one revolution of the golf ball is equal to 5.28 inches. That's how precise your control of speed should be when you roll the ball down an intended line, especially on a breaking putt.

DIRECTION CONTROL

Face + Path = Direction

The second component of putting is direction. *Your clubface and the path of your stroke determine the direction the ball will travel.* In putting, you're aiming down a specific, straight line toward a target. With the proper setup conditions and a square face (along a path that is perpendicular to the line of the putt), you will roll the ball right online.

With the proper set-up conditions and a square stroke (along a path that is perpendicular to the line of the putt), you will roll the ball right online. The two most relevant factors in allowing the ball to start on the desired target line and maintain a consistent roll are (1) the path of the putter which should be along the target line, and (2) the condition of the face, which should be square.

PUTTING IT ALL TOGETHER:
A CORRECT, CLASSIC PUTTING STROKE

Study the following photos closely to see what it is you're targeting.

To enable you to put it all together and master putting, let's work on the drills that follow.

PUTTING DRILLS

1. **Putt with Eyes Closed**

   This is one of my favorite putting "feel" drills; I've used it with my students for years. It's great for gauging whether you can control distance by feel alone. The beauty of this drill is that putting blindly, without the benefit of your eyes to guide you, allows you to really feel the length and pace of your stroke and how it relates to the distance the ball will travel. Simply set up to your target, get ready to putt, and then, just as you're ready to start your stroke, close your eyes. Ask yourself: *Is the tempo good? Is it symmetrical? Am I making any body movements (other than my arms and shoulders)? Does the clubface feel square at impact? Are my wrists hinging?*

Correct, Classic Putting Stroke: Observe the square lines—of the feet, knees, hips, forearms, and shoulders, with the eyes are over the ball. Control distance with a symmetrical stroke in terms of length and pace. Also, the stroke should be an arm swing with a quiet coconut (*i.e.*, your head and eyes must remain *still!*).

After you've struck the ball and before you open your eyes, call out to yourself where you think the ball went—long left, short right, long center, in the hole, whatever.

After the ball is long gone and you are holding the finish position, look to see where it went. Was your prediction accurate? Initially you will find you've made a lot of bad calls, because what you feel and perceive and what actually happened don't go together. In time you will reach the point where what you actually feel and what actually happened are consistent. At that point, you will be in control of the ball.

2. **Putt While Watching the Hole**

   This drill will help you develop a focus on the target rather than the ball. Golf is a target game, not a ball game. This drill also aids speed control through the use of optics. As I like to say: *Trust your eyes—they will teach you.*

3. **Putt While Adding Numbers**

   Remember my telling you earlier that putting is a feel stroke? This terrific drill, which was shown to me by Dr. Craig Farnsworth (whose book *See It and Sink It*, by the way, is great stuff), is intended to get you to stop thinking about your stroke and permit your body to feel it, leading to a more normal, natural stroke.

4. **Around-the-Clock Drill**

   In this drill you rotate around the hole, placing balls at various points along the circumference of an imaginary clock face. As you travel the 360 degrees around the hole, you putt at all different breaks, just as you would encounter during a round of golf. Start at 2 feet from the hole; make all the putts, then move back to 3 feet, and so on. If you miss one, start again. This exercise helps you concentrate, not just go through the motions, and to feel some of the pressure you encounter during a round of golf.

5. **2 × 4 Drill**

   A simple yet valuable training aid can be made from a 2 × 4 piece of wood. Cut it down to a 3-foot length, and make sure it isn't warped. Sand each side until it is extremely smooth and apply linseed oil or varnish. (If you are really ambitious, you can also polyurethane it for smoother gliding and weatherproofing.) You want the putting heel to glide very smoothly. To use it for putting practice, lay the board on the ground just inside the line of putt (so that it's 4 inches tall), then place the heel of your putter against it and use it as a linear putting track. This device will also come in handy later as a training device for aim, alignment, and setup conditions when you chip or take a full swing. Personally, the 2 × 4 is my all-time favorite teaching aid. (What can I say? I'm a cheap date.)

   For putting practice, this device will help you improve the linear conditioning of your stroke's path; as you do so, it allows you to continue to check the face and finish condition each time you take a stroke. Over time, you will definitely notice that the path of your stroke is improving. As you make practice strokes with your heel affixed to the board, monitor yourself visually to make sure your putter face does not deviate off a

Lag Drill Using 2 x 4: To do this drill, use the board as your guide and focus on a perfect stroke with a square setup, keeping your eyes over the ball, make a symmetrical stroke, with a flat wrist at impact, and hold your finish.

square condition (that is, you don't want it to fan open in the backstroke or fan close in a forward stroke). As you practice, you will retrain your arms and hands and how they work in relation to your putting stroke. As long and as often as possible, you want to feel as though the putter face is at a right angle to the intended line.

On longer putting strokes—outside 10 or 15 feet—there will be some deviation of face and path (arcing). The putter will arc slightly as the length of the stroke increases. When you first do these drills, I'd like you to putt from inside 10 feet, working on the face and path; at this distance there should be little path deviation. If such deviation is minimal or nonexistent here, then at 15 or 25 feet you'll experience less than you used to, and you'll have a better chance of staying on the intended line during all your putts.

6. **3-, 4-, 5-Foot Drill on a Relatively Straight Uphill Putt**

Start making putts close to the hole, and each time you make 20 in a row, move back in 1-foot increments. Anytime you miss, go back to zero and start over again. This drill not only gives you necessary repetitions, as in the around-the-clock drill, but also gets you focused and comfortable with pressure. These 3-, 4-, and 5-foot putts are the ones that keep your round alive.

7. **Hole Reducer**

Many golfers fear the dreaded 4-footer. A large part of this is expectation—you expect to make a 4-foot putt. Yet a lot of these same people never practice these putts, thinking right up until they actually have to make them that they're "no problem." View your 4-foot putts the way NBA players see foul shots. They do expect to make them, but they also practice them regularly. You should, too. A 4-foot putt is just as valuable as a 300-yard drive: both are worth one stroke.

One way to help develop your confidence as well as your visual skills as they relate to the line of the putt is to use a hole reducer. It's designed so that you're putting to a reduced-size hole, which requires you to be very precise—any putt that is just a little off center or traveling at the wrong speed will not go in.

When people see the hole reducer for the first time, they often freak out. Interestingly, however, they also get into an automatic self-correcting routine in which they try to be more precise in their aim—even before I've begun to give them any instruction. They simply realize that the demand on their skills is greater. (Remember, golf isn't taught, it's learned, which explains why a lot of people make the changes themselves once their perception is changed.) Even after spending just 20 minutes with the reduced hole, when you go back to putting using a regular-size hole—and I've actually had some students start laughing—it looks ridiculously big. The difference in your optical perception of the hole is amazing: What once looked small and intimidating suddenly becomes large and much more possible. Whether the hole seems small and intimidating or big and possible to you—well, you're right either way, because *perception is reality*. When you change your perception of what's real, you become more responsible in aiming the club. Making the hole look larger builds your confidence instantly.

8. **15-, 20-, 25-, and 30-Foot Drill**

This drill helps you develop a feel for distance. It's strictly a distance (lag) drill between two points on a practice green. For example, putting in one direction might be a slightly uphill 25-foot left-to-right putt. When you go the other way, it would be a downhill 25-foot right-to-left putt. This trains you to instantly adapt to the break and speed changes you will encounter on the course. Do this in three ball sets, always trying to improve on the previous ball.

9. **Lag Putts**

This drill improves your lag putting by helping you develop a feel for distance. Place five or six balls in the center of the practice green. Hit the balls, one at a time, trying each time to get the ball as close as possible to the edge of the fringe without touching it. As you get better, move farther away from the fringe you're aiming at to practice longer putts.

Just like when we were kids and pitched pennies toward a wall (or tossed horseshoes, or especially for those of Italian descent, rolled Bocci balls) to see who could get it closest. Lag putting requires feel for distance. The best way to obtain feel is to practice (imagine that . . . repetition). I often will putt toward a point on the fringe of a practice green (always thirty feet or more) and try to get it as close as possible to the fringe without touching it. This has helped my feel (i.e., speed control) greatly, and I guarantee this will help yours, too.

CONCLUSION

You must develop a putting stroke that will hold up under pressure, or you'll never fulfill your scoring potential. Putting alone makes up a minimum of 43 percent of the game, which logically means in most cases (subject to your Spoke 3, Individual Analysis) you should also devote 43 percent of your practice time to putting—and in many cases more. (Logical—imagine that!)

Putting mastery isn't the impossible task many players make it out to be. Again, all it takes is some good basic information, which you now have in your hands; some periodic coaching; and tons and tons of repetitions. So go work hard, focus on the right yet simple things, do your drills, and you'll become a great putter!

PUTTING AT A GLANCE

The Fundamental Keys to Putting
- Green-reading skills
- A preshot routine
- A balanced setup
- A fluid, symmetrical motion
- A quiet body and head
- Solid ball contact
- Control over distance and speed
- Structured finish condition

9 HANDS, DON'T FAIL ME NOW
CHIPPING

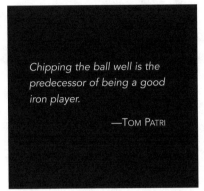

Chipping the ball well is the predecessor of being a good iron player.

—TOM PATRI

Some of the most memorable moments of professional golf are owed to the seemingly humble chip shot. This unsung hero of golf can make the difference between winning and losing major tournaments. Recall the 1987 Masters, during the play-off for the green jacket, when Larry Mize stunned Greg Norman with a single but brilliantly played chip shot (converting a score of 4 or even 5 into a birdie 3). Remember, too, Tom Watson holing an unbelievably difficult chip on the 71st hole of the 1982 U.S. Open at Pebble Beach, enabling him to go on to win the tournament over the "Golden Bear," Jack Nicklaus.

Statistically, chipping is estimated to account for 13 percent of the average round. Stated as a positive, it's an excellent opportunity to improve your bottom-line scoring significantly, especially in light of the fact that it doesn't require a great deal of time or effort to become a good chipper, nor even a large degree of athletic prowess. Considered this way, suppose you successfully reach a third of the greens in regulation and are left with 12 chips on the other holes. If you successfully convert on half of those holes (that is, you chip the ball onto the green and then sink the putt, meaning you get *up and down*), you've just saved six shots. *Six shots.* This could be the difference between being an 18 handicap and a 12. Pretty powerful stuff.

Although your chips may not give you the chance to win the Masters or the U.S. Open, this shot is critical to good scoring and, ultimately, to the development of good iron play: The technical skills involved in chipping are employed within the broad spectrum of the full golf motion. I strongly believe that *if chipping isn't a strong part of your game, good iron play won't be, either.* Chipping the ball is the predecessor to being a good iron player, because both require the ball to be compressed and spun by means of a slightly down-and-through blow. My mentor, the late Bill Strausbaugh, often applied to golf the old adage *From tiny acorns giant oak trees grow.* I often felt he was describing the relationship between chipping and iron play, because rehearsing the skills required for a broader stroke (iron play) are best learned and mastered first on a smaller scale (chipping).

OVERVIEW OF CHIPPING

CHIPPING 101: WHAT IS CHIPPING?

The chip shot is a low "running" shot, as opposed to a "lofted" shot. Generally, a chip is your best shot when you are very near the green (say, within several yards of the putting surface), no hazard or obstacle exists between your ball and the hole, and you have some degree of green to work with. The goal is to fly the ball just far enough to carry it onto the green (the most predictable surface in terms of how the ball will react when it lands) and then allow the ball to roll the balance of the distance to the hole.

A chip consists *generally* of one-third air time and two-thirds ground time. Keep in mind that this is a very generic ratio, because sometimes the conditions you encounter—the surface you are playing to (undulations, texture, grass type, and so forth, the lie of the ball, and even weather conditions such as wind and rain)—can change it. For example, if you have a downhill chip, you may land the ball just on the green and allow it to roll a great distance. If the shot is straight uphill, you may want to chip 50 percent to the hole and allow the ball to release 50 percent to the hole. In such instances, the technique doesn't change—the management of the shot does. Based on club selection, which we'll discuss below, and the conditions of the shot, all factors must be taken into account, including air-to-ground ratios.

In the pages that follow, we'll cover everything you need to know to develop a world-class chipping game. Let's get started.

FIRST THINGS FIRST: IDENTIFYING THE SHOT

The first step is, of course, to identify your shot. Is it a chip, a pitch, a lob, or a bump-and-run? Can you picture the type of shot that will give you the best chance of ending very near the hole? Once you have the picture, make sure it's *clear*. This skill comes only after some thoughtful analysis and a fair amount of trial and error, so be patient.

Once you identify the correct shot, you need to evaluate the situation further using four more steps before actually taking the shot. First, identify which of four possible forces will stop your ball; second, evaluate the conditions you're presented with; third, choose a primary landing spot; and finally, select a club. Once you have gone through these steps, you're ready to set up for the shot. Let's discuss them one at a time.

STEP ONE: IDENTIFY THE FORCE THAT WILL STOP YOUR BALL

There are only four types of force that can stop your ball:

1. **Momentum**

   The momentum (or roll) runs out, meaning the ball simply stops. This is the most likely and reliable choice.

2. **Spin of the Ball**

   To spin the ball and stop it requires a certain amount of speed and quality of contact. Unless you can create enough clubhead speed to spin the ball (which is often tough with a chip shot) and you can hit the ball perfectly, I wouldn't rely on this force.

3. **Trajectory**

This occurs when the ball is made to fly very high so that it lands softly and rolls little or no distance at all. It typically comes up with lob shots, and in my view it's not the most dependable force to rely upon.

4. **Running into an Object**

The cup, a bank, the flagstick, what have you. I would not depend on this, either, as it's the least reliable ball stopper to depend on.

STEP TWO: EVALUATING THE CONDITIONS: WHAT'S BETWEEN YOU AND THE HOLE?

1. **Undulations, Mounding, Contour, Slope**

Examine the area from which you're playing your shot and the area you're playing to. Visually inspect to see if there are any undulations or mounding in front of you. Is the shot up- or downhill? How will gravity affect the ball? Are there any other things that may affect how the ball behaves once it lands on the ground?

2. **Distance to the Target**

Get in the habit of pacing off distances to see how far you are from the hole. This helps you start to develop a database of visual pictures in your brain's computer. The more you pace off yardages, the better your control of distances will be.

3. **Speed of the Green**

Two things affect the speed of the green: the length of the grass and the firmness of the green. When evaluating the speed of the green, you can often look and see how much green there is versus brown, and how moist it is. Has it rained recently? Has it been watered recently? How about previous holes—how quick were they? Some courses let the greens grow early in the week to give them a bit of a rest and then mow them closer to speed them up quite a bit by the weekend. Some public and resort courses that are heavily played are kept slower (the grass is longer) to help absorb the traffic. Before the round, during warm-up, it's important to chip and putt to get a sense of green speed and texture.

4. **Room to Land and Roll**

Assuming we are still in the domain of a chip shot—in other words, neither a lob nor a bump-and-run is called for—the distance you stand from the green and the distance the hole is cut from your edge of the green are both highly relevant to the type and shape of shot you may wish to play. Setting aside club selection, which we'll discuss below, the alternatives available and precision required vary enormously depending on these two distances.

5. **Percent of Carry Versus Roll**

You want to predict where the ball will land and how it will react after it lands, based on the club you choose as well as the green's undulations, mounding, contours, and so on. Also, you know that this shot generally spends one-third of its time in the air, two-thirds on the ground, and since you paced off the shot in step two you can now determine mathematically where the one-third point is and then factor in conditions to see if that point makes visual sense.

WHAT'S THE LIE OF YOUR BALL LIKE?

What kind of lie are you playing from? This will greatly affect the contact quality and controlability. It will also have a direct impact on your club selection.

1. **Fringe/Fairway**

   If you are on the fringe or in the fairway, contact with the ball is not an issue. As such, on a properly executed shot you'll be able to control the ball and calculate very closely how high and far it flies and how softly it lands.

2. **Rough Conditions**

   When your ball is in the rough, contact and control may not be as certain. So there are a few things you'll want to consider:

   - **Lie Conditions.** Is the ball sitting down or up in the rough? How will it react when contacted? Might it "jump" (fly farther than you expect), or will you have to really hack at the ball to get it out?
   - **First or Second Cut of Rough.** Is it the first cut (a few inches of grass) or second cut (a few more inches)? How is the ball sitting? The object is to increase quality of contact. How will you get the ball out of the lie? Can you contact the ball itself, or will there be a little or a lot of grass between the clubface and the ball at impact?
   - **Heavy Rough.** Quality contact is a serious issue if you're in heavy rough. How do you want to approach that shot? How can you increase your chances of good contact? Have you considered altering your setup relative to the ball? Consider the ball position, the degree of loft, and the length at which you hold the club.

3. **Uphill/Downhill/Sidehill Lies**

   These lies require not only adjustments in shot execution (discussed a little later on), but also consideration of how such lies might affect the shot. For example, a shot off an uphill lie will fly higher and land softer than that off a flat lie, while the reverse is true of a downhill lie. Similarly, a shot off a lie in which the ball is above your feet will often fly left (and conversely, a ball below your feet will fly off to the right). Always place the ball closer to the uphill foot.

STEP THREE: PRIMARY VERSUS SECONDARY TARGET

When aiming at the target, you need to focus on two places: your primary landing spot, where the ball will land, and the secondary spot, where the ball will ultimately end up (the hole). The primary is actually your target, because once the ball lands it is out of your hands (no pun intended). Hitting the primary should be your sole focus. It is crucial that you identify the precise point where the ball must land in order for it to end up finishing in or near the hole once its momentum runs out. This is relevant to every short-game shot as well as to the rest of your game. The trick here is to pick a primary to achieve a secondary. *This might be the most important, and least thought about, part of chipping.* I implore you to start thinking this way all the time.

To begin thinking and seeing in precise terms, I recommend that during practice, you mark with a tee or coin the spot where you believe the ball must land—the primary target—which will then lead it to the hole, the secondary target. After each shot, evaluate carefully: Did you hit your primary target? No horseshoes here, you must hit the target. The second question is: Was the location of your primary target correct as it relates to the secondary target? In other words, did you think about and visualize the shot properly? Did you anticipate how the undulations, mounds, slopes, et cetera, would affect your ball? The shot you have in front of you will very rarely be a straight one. *It is very important that you read the shot.* Once you wear out one side of the practice green, move around the green so that you challenge the accuracy of your chip and the development of your thinking and visualization.

STEP FOUR: CLUB SELECTION

The club that will work for a particular shot is determined by lie, what you intend to carry the ball over, how far you wish the ball to fly, the desired trajectory, how you want to stop your ball, and the pace of the green. The location of your ball and slope and green speed will also influence club selection.

Here's a good place to take a hint from the pros: Make your club selection *after* you've thoroughly evaluated each of the conditions discussed above. Tour professionals evaluate conditions first, decide on the primary target, and *then* select the club that will allow them to land on their primary target and have the ball roll out with success. Adopting this tried-and-true method will improve your game immediately. Too many amateurs grab a club and head over to evaluate the shot. They use that club regardless of the conditions and their target. I call this the *square-peg-in-a-round-hole theory.* Players who do this rarely like the results of their shot. I always recommend taking three or four clubs with you instead of just one, which greatly increases the odds of having one that will work. (See the sidebar titled Rule of Thumb, on the next page.)

"BOWLING" BALLS TO GET A FEEL FOR DISTANCE

Sometimes I'll have students stand on the fringe of the green, take a ball, toss it underhand to their chosen primary landing spot, and watch it roll. I'll ask them how big a motion they had to make for that to happen. They'll tell me they didn't have to move their arm much, back or through. I'll say, "That's about the same size your pitching stroke needs to be." I'll then ask them how fast they had to move their arm, and they'll tell me, "Not very fast." To this I'll respond, "That's about how fast your arm has to move." I call this exercise bowling balls, and its purpose is simple: to get a feel for how long and fast (the answer is: not very) your arm swing needs to be to go the distance you require to land at your primary target and roll the ball to the hole.

ADD IMAGINATION TO YOUR SHORT-GAME PRACTICE

Strive for a more realistic grasp of what "feel" is. Take three clubs with you (a 5- or 6-iron, an 8-iron, and your most lofted wedge) to where you practice your short game. Take three balls and drop them in one particular starting point. Hit one ball to the same target with each club. Work your way around the perimeter of the practice green, trying your best to hit the most successful shot with each club. This will expand your feel and your imagination as well as your arsenal of short-game shots.

Don't wind up using the wrong club just because it's the only one you brought with you. Whenever you can, have your full bag handy—when you are carrying it, for instance, or you have a caddy walking with you, or you can get your cart near the ball. That's the ideal situation. When that isn't possible, the next best bet is to bring along two to four clubs for your shot instead of picking one before you've had a chance to evaluate conditions. Try to select two running and two lofting clubs. That way, when you get there, there's a pretty good chance you'll have a club along that you can use confidently for the shot at hand.

Another thing to remember is this: Chipping is not a shot that's played with a 7-iron or pitching wedge only. There are chipping situations where either a sand wedge or a 5-iron may be required. A chip shot can be played with almost every iron in your bag. It's important that you start thinking this way. Not only will your results improve, but so will your enjoyment of the game. You'll be visualizing and imagining and you won't be subject to *senseless limitations and boring repetition.*

CONSISTENT PRESHOT ROUTINE

With chip shots, as with all shots in golf, the Six-Spoke Approach requires you to use a preshot routine. During my own routine, I like to stand behind the ball, visualize the shot, step up to the ball, take two rehearsal swings, focus on my primary target one last time, look back at the ball, come to rest for just a moment, and then go. The process doesn't take much time, but from the time that I stand behind the ball until the moment the ball stops rolling, I am focused on one thing: the shot.

TECHNIQUE

The best place to learn proper setup conditions for chipping is in front of a mirror with a 7- or 8-iron and an impact bag (see Appendix C, "Tom's Top 25"). If you can't get a hold of an impact bag, you can substitute rolled-up quilts or a group of pillows against a piece of furniture that won't move. Do your drills up against the cushion. Start in slow motion to rehearse your setup. By practicing your drills in front of a mirror, you have the advantage of learning with two senses: sight and feel.

Once you've set up properly, go ahead and make a chipping motion into the impact bag. The impact bag helps you feel what it's like to deliver the club in an online condition with a forward-leaning club shaft, a flat left wrist, and a bent right wrist. Delivering the golf club to impact like this is a good way to improve your chipping, because it helps you gain a feel for compressing the ball.

THE LAUNCHING PAD: SETUP CONDITIONS

A large part of every successful shot—of any kind—is a proper launching pad. If you don't build a proper launching pad, the execution of the motion will be difficult, if not impossible. Let's go over it carefully:

- **Grip.** Neutral, or weak. Unlike the full swing, in which I endorse a slightly strong grip, in the short game I believe it is very important to use a neutral, and often a weak, grip. By this I mean the back of your left hand and the palm of your right hand should face the target—when you weaken your grip, both hands get turned more to the left of the club. When you make your chipping motion, you should have an equal amount of pressure on the two hands, so that neither hand has more control. Give them both equal responsibility for the motion.

As for firmness of grip, you'll need to experiment. A death grip will limit wrist flexibility, which will not permit natural cocking and hinging of the wrists. In contrast, a grip with a *little* less pressure will create more of a natural cocking/hinging motion (discussed in the sidebar, "Cock Versus Hinge" below).

Applying a stronger or weaker grip affects the release of the club through the impact area; a weaker grip, for example, tends to deaden the ball off the face. A light grip, plus the weight of the club, will create the natural cocking motion of the wrists that you want to achieve in your chip shots.

Although grips (in this area) are a *preference*, not a *principle*, choosing the right one for you based on your hand size and strength is essential to your success. For a detailed discussion of the three types of grip (the Vardon or overlapping grip, the interlocking grip, and the 10-finger or baseball grip) and when each is best used, please see Chapter 13.

The chipping launching pad is all too often overlooked. The ball should be *slightly* right of center, meaning just to the right of your sternum. The handle of your club should be slightly left of center (just left of your pants zipper), and your weight distribution should slightly favor your left side (i.e., weight distribution should be approximately 55 percent to the left side and 45 percent to the right).

COCK VERSUS HINGE: DO YOU KNOW THE DIFFERENCE?

Let's make sure you're clear on the difference between the hinging motion, which is crucial to the hinge and hold (discussed shortly), and the cocking motion, because they're both important. The hinging motion is what we want to happen in your chipping and pitching motions. If you hold your arm and hand out straight in front of you parallel to the ground, then make your hand move to the right, without moving your arm and while keeping your hand parallel to the ground, that's called *hinging your wrist*. If you bring your hand up so that your fingers and thumb point skyward, that's *cocking your wrist*.

In chip and pitch shots, the left wrist cocks the club up while the right hinges it. If the cocking and hinging are blended properly, this allows you to make solid contact. Avoid using too much left wrist, or you'll lift the club too steeply, or hinge the club too far to the right, or pull it too far inside. When working properly together, the wrists swing the club on the proper plane, which will result in your hitting great chips and pitches.

- **Posture and Spacing.** See "The Launching Pad" (page 163 in Chapter 13).
- **Weight Distribution.** Slightly more weight on the left foot than the right, meaning your weight is slightly left of center. We're talking 55 percent left, 45 percent right here, folks—nothing more radical than that.
- **Alignment.** Your stance should be slightly open (again, there's that word *slightly*). Most people overdo how open they are and go too far to the left of the intended line, which makes it very difficult to keep the club online through the impact area. If you can, picture yourself hitting chip shots from a relatively square position. (You should try this; I think you'll find you can hit them just fine.) *Being open is simply a matter of choosing what you're more comfortable with, not a principle of technique.*
- **Ball Position.** *Slightly* back from the center position.
- **Handle Position.** Choke down on the club slightly and move the club handle slightly forward—applying a forward-leaning club shaft. You're creating what is desired at impact—the shaft is leaning forward, your left wrist is flat, your right wrist is slightly bent, and you're delivering a slightly descending blow due to the fact that the ball is back of center and your weight is already slightly forward of center.

Once you get the conditions, you can do some rehearsals using an impact bag and a mirror. During these rehearsals, try to deliver a blow that doesn't alter your setup. At impact, you should have returned to a position where your weight is still slightly forward of center and the handle is leaning forward with a flat left wrist and bent right wrist. You want to feel this *multiple times*, and I mean maybe 20, 30, 40 times. *You can't overdo practicing this.*

MAKING THE MOTION

Chipping is basically an arm-and-shoulder stroke. Is the body rigid? No, it's not. Are arms and hands rigid? No. Wrists? No. They're not spaghetti, either. You want to feel as though the golf club is always *flowing from your arm swing through your hands*, and that there's *a rhythm to your stroke.*

IT AIN'T ROCKET SCIENCE

I tell people all the time, "This is not a complex motion." You can easily learn chipping setup conditions, the right weight distribution, grip, where the ball and the handle should be . . . and if you made an 8- or 10-inch motion to the right or left side with a descending blow and your left wrist never broke down, how much more complex does it have to be than that? I take my five-, six-, and seven-year-old students out to the edge of the green to develop some very basic setup conditions and perform quality of contact drills with an impact bag, keeping a flat left wrist and focusing simply on quality of contact (with no target involved at first). All of a sudden, I'll insert a target, and in 15 to 20 minutes these youngsters can chip a golf ball from 40 feet away to within 4 or 5 feet of the hole on a very regular basis. The moral of this story is: Let's not turn this rather simple motion into something complicated. It won't take you long to make some radical improvements, which will translate into some relatively dramatic scoring differences. Again, another benefit is that what you learn in terms of quality of contact and understanding the feeling of proper conditions at impact will transfer over to your iron play, rewarding you with improved technique in both areas.

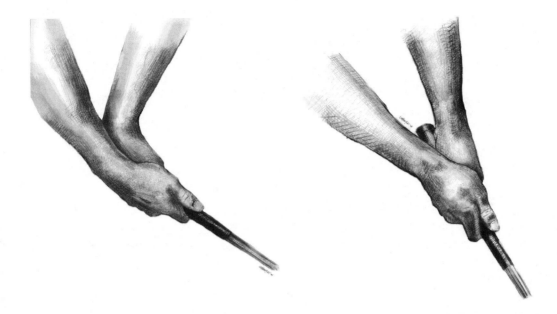

I call the illustration on the left "giant flip-o-saurus" or the "flipping pancakes" stroke, caused by flipping, scooping, or allowing your left wrist to break down—one of the most glaring fundamental faults I see in golf. Most amateurs try to "scoop" (add loft) to an already lofted club, yet each club in your bag is designed to produce a certain trajectory. You *must* reach impact with a flat left wrist. Delivering a flat left wrist to the point of impact will compress the ball and produce both the desired trajectory and proper distance for the club at hand. See illustration on the right of flat left wrist at impact.

MAIN CHIPPING MOTION: THE HINGE AND HOLD

To give you a clear mental picture of the chipping motion, imagine it as a "hinge and hold" to help keep that left wrist from breaking down. The "hinge" is the natural hinging of the right wrists in the backswing, created by the weight of the clubhead swinging. It's not something you consciously promote; rather, you allow it to happen based on the low tension levels of your hands, wrist joints, and arms when you put the club into motion. At the club level, I often see what I call a "tension convention"—golfers who look like they have two pieces of steel coming out of their shoulder joints, and two vise grips at the end of those steel beams gripping the club for dear life. You can't create a feel shot in that state. You need to be tension-free to allow a hinge and hold.

FLAT LEFT WRIST AT IMPACT

The "hold" is in fact a flat left wrist at impact. Maintain the wrist angles created in the backswing through impact and feel as if you're holding on to that position with your left wrist joint. Therefore, through impact, the back of the left wrist and clubface are in matching conditions and so attain solid, online, compressed contact.

Finally, the motion should be symmetrical, meaning equal in pace and distance in the backswing and forward swing. Incidentally, this is the best way to create a tempo and rhythm in any swinging motion. Resist the urge to use your hands to "hit" the golf ball—it's a swing, not a hit. Think *ballet*, not the *NFL*.

You should always be able to reference a flat left wrist at impact when you chip or pitch the ball, as it matches up with the clubface and compresses the golf ball. I can't overemphasize the importance of a *flat left wrist at impact*: It is a cornerstone of good iron play; in fact, it is a cornerstone of great golf.

THE ONE-LEVER

The putting and chipping strokes are called *one-levers* because your arms and shoulders create a working lever. They are where the focus of this shot should be, since they make most of the motion. The hands and wrists, although relatively quiet, should not be rigid. There is a degree of hinging in the back motion, and holding in the forward motion. Again, the hinge and hold isn't something you *promote*; rather, it's something you *allow* based on the tension levels of your hands, arms, and wrist joints when you put the club in motion.

A PIVOT IS BORN

In chipping, the pivot is born. You're on the fringe or around the green, with a swinging set of arms. Your shoulders start to create the motion, and, for the first time, a pivot is born. The body pivot should support and be proportional to the arm motion. The size of the motion with your lower body is proportional to the distance the ball needs to travel, and therefore to the length of the arm swing that's required.

I often see one of two things in dramatic fashion—either legs that are poured in concrete with hands that are content to flip at the golf ball with all kinds of breakdowns, or overactive legs (I call this the "Elvis syndrome") that violently outrace the arm swing, causing shanks and skulls. What I like is a nice, unified rhythm between how much you use your arms and legs. They should be in rhythm with one another. You don't need your

---

SWING, THEN TURN VERSUS TURN, THEN SWING

People come to me in one of two modes. They either swing and then turn, or turn and then swing. For those who turn and then swing, the body moves and the arms follow. The body activates downswing motion in their forward-swing motion, and then the arms follow, or lag behind. My job is to determine which camp each person is in, and whether they're applying the right force in the correct sequence. I tend to prefer the swing-then-turn method. I like the arms to swing and dictate the rhythm and motion of the golf swing while the body stays relatively quiet. Think of a baseball player throwing a baseball from second to first: The arm moves forward and then the body responds, rather than the body moving forward with the arm getting dragged along.

People whose bodies tend to outrace their arm swing tend to hit the golf ball to the right; those whose arms are overactive and swing past their body tend to hit it left. Since the majority of golfers hit shots to the right, generally their bodies outrace their arm swings. They don't realize that their legs are something that should support the upper body. In the 1960s and '70s we read a lot about driving our legs. Many misinterpreted this information, leading a lot of golfers to get out of sequence and hit shots to the right.

---

legs to create power during a chip, just to support your arm swing. The lower body on an average chip is relatively quiet (not very active) and responding only to the activity of your arm swing. The motion of the arm swing activates and causes a lot of things that the body has to do. You swing, then turn, not the other way around. *Allow the legs respond to a swinging set of arms.*

DOWN IS A DIRECTION, NOT A SPEED

You want to be careful to avoid the all-too-common tendency players have of nicely setting their club in the backswing, then making a violent downswing, trying to hit the ball like some crazed caveman clubbing wounded prey. Down is a direction, not a speed, and you want to make a nice rhythmic, downward motion, to allow the club to fall. Gravity, after all, is your friend.

DISTANCE IS DETERMINED BY LENGTH OF MOTION

You will find when you start to work on these concepts that to maintain your flat left wrist at impact, you have to get out of the habit of hitting the ball with your hands. What you want is a swinging set of arms. Adjust the length of the shot by simply adjusting the length of the motion. Keeping the importance of symmetry in mind, your backswing and downswing should be equal in length. You'll find far more consistency in your shots putting all this together. You'll also find that the unreliable small muscles in your hands and wrists will be replaced by the more reliable and consistent large muscles in your arms and torso. In actuality, it would be nice if, in the long term, both the body and torso and the arms and hands worked in concert with one another, with neither component trying to outrace or overpower the other.

PUTTING IT ALL TOGETHER: WHAT A CLASSIC, CORRECT CHIPPING MOTION LOOKS LIKE

CHIPPING DRILLS

Begin by practicing without a target in order to focus solely on contact quality. It's crucial that you develop sound quality of contact *first*, without the distraction of a target. Practice to a general area some 30 or 40 feet away across the green (again, focusing on quality of contact), with a forward-leaning club shaft and a slightly descending blow, having the ball come off the center of the face and feeling the compression of the golf ball against the face of the golf club. When you can hit maybe 20 or 30 balls in a row in a very solid crisp shot, *then* insert a target.

When you practice to a target, use only two or three balls with a few different clubs. When I practice, I play each shot as if I'm on the course, thinking through the details of the lie; distance to the green; where I want my ball to land (my primary target); potential obstacles, if any; proper trajectory, given the amount of green to work with; and any effect the slopes of the green will have on the ball. Obviously, this takes some serious thought, and a bit of vision to formulate the proper shot. However, the time spent developing this skill is well worth it.

1. **Main Drill: The Hinge and Hold**

   Practice the hinge and hold in front of a mirror using an impact bag. Face the mirror with proper setup conditions and then make a motion. What you should feel is a little bit of hinging motion of the right wrist in the backstroke, a rhythmic downstroke, and then, at impact, a return to the setup condition. Aligning the club back up with your left wrist, deliver a solid blow while the back of your left hand and left wrist are flat and facing the target. *Hold that position slightly through the impact area.* Doing this over and over will give you a sense of what the hinge and hold feels like.

2. **2 × 4**

   Set up with the golf ball and the clubhead alongside a 2 × 4 that you have laid on its side (see Chapter 8, "Putting," for instructions on making a practice 2 × 4). Hit several chip shots along the inside of the 2 × 4. This will help you learn to direct the face and path of the golf club. Having a reference will allow you to visually keep track of the condition of your clubface, so you can tell whether it's closed, square, or open. As you rehearse this drill, you'll become more efficient at keeping the face square. Practicing with the 2 × 4 also allows you to keep the leading edge of the club perpendicular to the board, which improves the path your club travels on. This improves your ability to aim the club and get your shots started on the line. You are in fact training your optics to relate face and path to the target.

3. **Descent Drill**

   Place a 2 × 4 parallel to your right foot in the setup condition—from your right toe area extending outward from your right foot—and place a golf ball one club-grip-length forward of the board. This makes you hinge the club upward, because if you take it back low or you'll nick the board. Then, on the downswing, you need to hold the hinge condition, because if you release you'll hit the board. By holding the condition and swinging your arms down and forward, you hit down and forward on the golf ball in a descending blow. This drill is great for learning not to make too level a chipping stroke and not trying to scoop the ball, therefore killing your contact quality, as amateurs all too often do.

4. **5-Foot-Radius Drill Using Three Clubs**

   Using four tees, place the first 5 feet short of the hole, the next 5 feet left of the hole, the third 5 feet right of the hole, and the last one 5 feet long from the hole. Now you've got a 5-foot radius around the center of the hole, and a 10-foot diameter around the hole. If you have a problem chipping to within that 10-foot circle, you probably want to work on your short game a lot more (remember—repetition is the mother of learning). This drill should be done by moving around the green to different positions and using three clubs—maybe a 7-iron, 9-iron, and pitching wedge; an 8-iron, pitching wedge, and sand wedge; or perhaps a 6-iron, 8-iron, and pitching wedge. Don't change your technique—only the clubs you use.

   The purpose is to hit different clubs at different lofts from different positions and conditions around the green and see how the ball responds and which clubs work best to put you within that 10-foot circle. You'll see, for example, that from one spot a 6-iron works best, while a pitching wedge works best from another spot. This will keep you from being a square-peg-in-a-round-hole player (see "Step Four: Club Selection," page 111), since you'll learn to use a variety of different clubs in the appropriate situations. You will have an arsenal of shots and you'll never be "handcuffed" in any situation you encounter.

5. **Primary Target Tee Drill**

   This is a visual drill that allows you to relate, see, and feel, because you will see the result, and fill your personal database with experiences.

   To do this trial-and-error drill, choose a target you want to chip the ball to. Hit a shot toward the target and try to observe, based on the club you've chosen (6-iron, 8-iron,

A Small Investment with Big Returns

At TP Golf Schools I'll typically use string to set up a 10 × 10 chipping area. I have the students go to a distance 30 or 40 feet away on the fringe to chip golf balls. I tell them all they have to do is chip the ball to the 10 × 10 area. If they get the ball anywhere in that area, they'll actually have, at most, a 5-foot putt left. They tell me they'd be thrilled with that result, and after all, it looks easy enough to hit that area from only 30 or 40 feet away. During the first 15 minutes, they chip about 5 to 10 balls apiece, and the pattern is—well, let's just say pretty scattered. There are balls everywhere. Most likely none are in the 10 × 10 area. I then introduce the concept of the primary versus secondary target, and we work on their setup conditions, using impact bag rehearsals. Then we do a second round of balls for about another 15 minutes. Boy, does the pattern change radically. There are some in the 10 × 10 area, and even the misses are relatively close. We go back with some more instruction to tighten up the fundamentals a bit, and by the third round of balls the pattern is actually quite good.

At this point I'll turn to a student with about a 30 handicap and say, "This is what you could actually do on the golf course, and after only about 45 minutes. After 45 hours or 45 days of practice, if you really worked on this skill, how many shots a round do you suppose you could save?" My student will guess (correctly) at least 10 shots. I'll say, "That's right. So now your 30 handicap minus 10 is a 20. You're instantly a 20 handicap." My students will tell me that's impossible. *No, it's not.* That's what's happening. It's what they—and you—can actually see happening. If you can just learn to chip the ball with some competence, you can save a tremendous number of shots on the golf course.

9-iron, pitching wedge . . .), where the ball lands and how far it rolls. Based on the amount of loft, when the ball lands at a certain spot, it will then roll a certain number of feet, which you can learn to predict fairly accurately with practice.

After you become more adept at selecting a primary target, test yourself by placing a tee or coin at that spot and then chipping to that precise point. During this drill, you are thinking and visualizing at a high level, pinpointing the exact primary and executing the chip to that exact spot.

ADVANCED CHIPPING TECHNIQUE

Advanced players can do several things to modify the chipping stroke. First, experiment with different launching pad conditions:

- **Grip.**
    1. Try altering the length of the handle by choking down on the club, almost to the exposed shaft, and then try "long in the grip" and "midpoint in the grip." You can use these three hold conditions or grip positions to alter the amount of leverage you create.
    2. Experiment from a strong to medium to neutral to weak grip. As you move from strong to weak, you will see the effect on the release of the golf club at the

point of impact and how the face either releases or doesn't. Some more advanced players will hit chip shots with a weak grip when they want the ball to come off the clubface very dead. They'll choose a stronger grip (as they would use on a full-swing iron shot) when they want the ball to hit the ground running (for example, when they're presented with a deeper pin position). As you get your quality of contact to improve, you'll be able to control the ball by getting it to release and run out as it finds the second or third hop on the green.

- **Weight Distribution.** How much more weight you place on your left side than your right (60–40, 70–30, 80–20 . . .) will affect the impact and the downward descent of the golf club, and will also affect how the ball will leave the face.

- **Ball Position.** Try altering in varying degrees from standard to slightly back of center to a deeper position back of center to slightly forward. These will all affect the loft of the golf club and how the ball leaves the face.

- **Handle Condition.** How far forward you put the handle (middle of your left thigh, inside your left thigh, or between your two legs) will affect the downward blow of the golf club (the *angle of attack*).

  Altering the handle position and length of the handle of any club you use (whether an L-wedge, S-wedge, pitching wedge, or what have you) will affect the trajectory and spin of the ball and, therefore, how far the ball rolls out.

- **Club Selection.** Once you have become an advanced chipper, experiment by using different clubs and other launching pad conditions. Mix and match the above conditions in a sort of trial-and-error session to see and feel how the ball will behave. In the short game, trial and error can be a wonderful teacher.

One last important tip for advanced players: It's simply not possible to revisit the feeling of the proper setup condition too often. Even advanced chippers should rehearse this regularly. You can use the impact bag and mirror routine at home to rehearse, and then take your impact bag with you to the short-game area just in case you want to revisit the feeling.

CONCLUSION

Chipping is a major component of the game of golf. On the course, many shots are saved or lost depending on chipping ability. As such, chipping is a place where you can, with relative ease, improve your scores dramatically. These shots help create momentum, hold a round together, and are thrilling to execute—limited only by your imagination. In addition, they help you build and develop the full swing.

With so much at stake, please make your visits to the short-game area a regular occurrence. Stick to the fundamentals outlined in this chapter. Experiment with as many clubs and conditions as possible. Take your time. But most of all, enjoy yourself. Your golf game will never be the same.

CHIPPING AT A GLANCE

The Fundamental Keys to Chipping

- Identify the shot as a chip shot
- One-third air time, two-thirds ground time
- Identify which of four forces will stop your ball
- Evaluate the conditions between you and the hole
- Choose primary (where the ball lands) and secondary (where the ball finishes) targets
- Select the proper club
- Develop a consistent preshot routine
- Create proper setup conditions
- The club handle should be slightly left of center
- Your weight should be slightly left of center
- The ball should be slightly left of center
- Use a one-lever (not two-lever) motion
- Hinge and hold
- A pivot is born
- Keep a flat left wrist and a bent right wrist at impact
- Down is a direction, not a speed
- Distance is determined by length and pace of motion combined with loft of club

10 ONE SHOT DOESN'T FIT ALL **MASTERING THE BUMP-AND-RUN, PITCH, AND LOB**

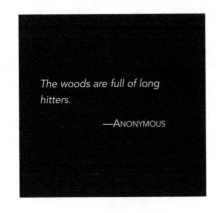

The woods are full of long hitters.

—ANONYMOUS

Lee Janzen is a genius of the short game. These skills have served him well during his career, in which he has won two U.S. Open Championships. At the 1995 Tournament Players Championships in Jacksonville, Florida, Janzen was in the lead going into the last nine holes on Sunday when his long game suddenly abandoned him. He missed *every green* on the back nine, and yet managed to shoot under par because of his short-game skills. It was an awesome display of short-game wizardry.

Short-game shots are tools to recover from an error or correct a mistake in order to save a score (converting three shots to two, for instance). You may know that the leaders on the PGA Tour—the greatest golfers in the world—hit the green only about 70 percent of the time in regulation play, which means they spend about 30 percent of their time recovering from mistakes. If these players rely on their short game a third of the time, where does that leave you?!

Short-game shots come in many sizes and shapes. I once heard Jack Nicklaus estimate that there are some 300 variations on the short-game shots to learn around the green complex—meaning within 30 yards of the hole. This chapter deals with the three most common of these variations: the bump-and-run, the pitch, and the lob. *They should be a part of every golfer's core skills*.

The key to a great short game is the ability to visualize and understand the type of shot required in the situation—to have a clear picture of how the ball will react before hitting it. This skill is vital. Players with an outstanding ability to do this include Lee Trevino, Seve Ballesteros, Raymond Floyd, and Corey Pavin. Next time you're watching golf on television, pay special attention to the short-game shots these men play in certain situations, and notice how they take time to really survey these shots long before attempting them.

You, too, must develop the ability to visualize the type of shot you are going to hit, where it's going to land, and how it's going to react when it does. If you don't know what a bump-and-run, a pitch, or a lob looks like in your mind's eye, you'll have a tough time creating them. Developing this skill comes with a clear understanding of technique and lots of trial and error (also known as practice). Because visualizing the shots is such an important component, let's go through each one to be sure you understand what they are, what they look like, and how they differ.

One final piece of advice before we move on: *These shots are best learned off the course*, because on the course you're trying to create a score and you have only one opportunity to tackle the shot. With practice, you will develop a sense of when to use them, how they feel, and what they look like, but this trial-and-error phase needs to occur before you take it to the golf course. Go to the short-game area and hit many, many shots from a variety of positions and lies. This will also help you with club selection, feel, and visualization. To develop your skills faster, as you practice, always watch the ball react and observe how it is affected by the ground.

OVERVIEW OF THE BUMP-AND-RUN, PITCH, AND LOB

One of the most striking differences among chipping and these three types of shots is their ratios of air time to ground time. The basic formulas for all four are as follows:

- Chipping: one-third air, two-thirds ground.
- Bump-and-Run: An elongated chip, which can vary from one-fifth air to five-sixths ground time, based on length of shot and terrain.
- Pitching: half air, half ground.
- Lobbing: two-thirds air, one-third ground.

Keep in mind these are all very "vanilla" formulas—starting points. Factors that will ultimately affect these ratios include your lie, the firmness of the putting surface, the topography, the location of the hole, and the existence of obstacles.

As we cover these shots, I'd like you to keep in mind my general theory of the short game: Whenever you can get the ball on the ground sooner rather than later, please do so. In other words, the more air time, the larger the swing required. The sooner you can get the ball to the ground, the more it will reduce the size of your swing, thus shrinking the potential for mechanical error.

Okay, let's go over them one at a time.

THE BUMP-AND-RUN

Under the right conditions, this shot can be a tremendous asset to your game. The motion of a bump-and-run is in fact a chipping motion, except the bump-and-run is a longer motion, usually because of the greater amount of ground you have to cover. It is often played from somewhere back in the fairway when you have an opportunity to run the ball up onto the green. But that's not the only time the shot is available. It can be played anytime the ball can roll to the secondary target with some degree of reliability.

This shot should be chosen for one or more of the following reasons: first, in windy conditions, in which a lower shot is warranted; second, where the greens are so firm that a high-flying lofted shot will result in too much bounce; and third, where the quality of the lie does not allow a pitch or high-lofted shot because the lie is tight, and making quality contact will be difficult. It should only be considered when there is nothing between you and the putting surface but short grass—no rough or long grass to grab the ball. It's also a good shot choice when you don't feel comfortable hitting a lofted golf club or one with some degree of bounce to a pin that is either close or hard to get to because of a sloping condition. In the bump-and-run, you want to make the ground your friend.

One important note: You never want to land the ball in any "violent" area. For example, you *do not* want it to land into or against a hill or steep slope; rather, you want to land the ball in a relatively flat area. It can run up or through a hill, but if it lands directly into a hill or slope, it can ricochet or be deflected and go sideways or stop very quickly. Your goal is to allow the ball to take its momentum forward and up the hill or slope by starting the run in the receptive area.

Even if you understand the bump-and-run conceptually, it will take a great deal of experience for you to gain a feel for this shot, so be patient with it. It requires a lot of experimentation to see and understand how the ball is going to come off the clubface and how it is going to react to the area in front of you. It also requires a feel for distance, which you'll acquire with experience, and an understanding of the landscape you are playing to, since this will have a tremendous impact on how the ball behaves.

CLUB SELECTION

Your bump-and-run club choices range from a 3-iron to an 8-iron. Don't forget that the club you select will have a certain amount of loft to it. So if, for example, you choose a low-lofted club such as a 3- or 4-iron, and you play the ball very far back in your stance, with the shaft leading and your weight forward, you could be playing with a zero-loft club by the time you get to impact. Therefore, be mindful that the setup positions will de-loft a club— a 7-iron may play like a 5-iron.

Before choosing your club, you need to evaluate the following:
- The quality of your lie.
- The condition and qualities of the area you're playing through.
- The condition of the putting surface—fast or slow, firm or soft, and whether it's undulated or not.
- Where you want the ball to land (your primary landing spot), and how much you want it to run after it lands.

To get a feel for different clubs and how they function in this shot, you must experiment from just off the practice green and then work your way up to 20 or 30 yards away using several different clubs to see and understand the different responses you will get based on loft, how far back you place the ball in, your stance, and different lie conditions. For example, you may wish to go as far down as a 3- or 4-iron to get that ball scurrying through the grass fronting the green.

BUMP-AND-RUN TECHNIQUE
The Launching Pad: Bump-and-Run Setup Conditions
Your setup will vary somewhat based on the conditions you encounter. The things that may vary include how far back in your stance you want to play the shot, how long or short you want to hold the lever, the length and pace of the arm swing, the loft of the club you

choose, where you want it to land, and how far you want it to run. These decisions come easier with experience (meaning practice), during which you will develop a sense for what setup conditions are called for in which situations.

You will recall that the bump-and-run is actually an elongated chip shot, and, as such, it has a launching pad similar to that of chipping:

- **Grip.** Although in the full swing I recommend using a slightly strong grip, in the short game I feel it is important to use a neutral, and often a weak, grip. This means that the back of your left hand and palm of your right hand face the target, since, as you weaken your grip, your hands get turned more to the left of the club.
- **Posture and Spacing.** See "The Launching Pad" (page 163) in Chapter 13.
- **Weight Distribution.** Your weight should be slightly forward, as when you're chipping. Again, the more forward you put your weight, the more of a descending blow you create and the more you de-loft the club.
- **Alignment.** Your stance should be slightly open (again, the key word here is *slightly*).
- **Ball Position.** As with chipping, the ball should be *slightly* back in your stance. If your lie is tighter, you'll want to play the ball farther back in your stance so you can hit down on it a bit more. The farther back the ball is, coupled with a more forward weight distribution, the more you will deliver a descending blow and de-loft the club.
- **Handle Position.** Shorten the lever for control and choke down on the club slightly. You want the shaft leaning slightly forward.

MAKING THE BUMP-AND-RUN MOTION

Refer back to our discussion in Chapter 9, Chipping, regarding the concept of having a primary and secondary target. This same concept applies to the bump-and-run. Always choose a primary target (where you want the ball to land) in order to achieve your secondary target (the place you ultimately want the ball to wind up after it lands, which is in the hole).

Hinge and Hold

Because the bump-and-run is much like a chipping motion, the techniques for these two shots are similar. Thus, the hinge and hold technique applies to the bump-and-run as well.

However, recall that the bump-and-run is a more elongated motion than the chipping motion, and may be slightly more aggressive depending on the length of the shot, the amount of ground you have to cover, and the conditions you're presented with. Both shots involve a hinge and hold, but the bump-and-run may require a more elongated motion.

PUTTING IT ALL TOGETHER: BUMP-AND-RUN DRILL

Good old-fashioned trial and error. As we discussed previously, you'll need an inordinate amount of experience to develop a feel for this specialty shot. You need to get out there and find a location where you can practice bump-and-run shots up a steep bank or over a long expanse of grass, so you can get a feel for air time–ground time ratios and how the ground affects the ball.

The Fundamental Keys to the Bump-and-Run

- It's an elongated chip shot, with less loft
- Visualize the shot playing out in your mind's eye
- Select the proper club (choices: 3- to 8-iron)
- Follow a consistent preshot routine
- Create proper setup conditions
- Hinge and hold

THE PITCH

Pitching is another short game tool that *must* be mastered. You will *never* play a round of golf in which you do not need a pitch shot. With the many obstacles on a golf course, such as mounds, ridges, and bunkers, you'll often find times when you need to pitch the ball over an obstacle to "attack a flag."

Pitch shots are usually called for when you are just off the putting surface and up to 50 yards away—in other words, anything that's not a full shot. As such, pitching the ball, whether you use a pitching wedge, sand wedge, or lob wedge, involves a partial (less than full) golf swing.

A classic high pitch shot. Notice that the length of follow-through is proportional to the amount of activity on the lower body, neither being complete and full. Both are abbreviated to control distance.

CONDITIONS TO TAKE INTO ACCOUNT

Pitch shots remind me of one of my favorite movies, *Top Gun*. In one scene, Tom Cruise's character Maverick and his flying partner Goose are pursuing another fighter plane. Maverick calls out, "He's going vertical, so am I!" Goose replies, "We're going ballistic, man. Go get him!" Pitch shots are just that: shots you use when what lies between you and your target forces you to "go vertical." They're shots that need to be lofted over an obstacle (hence the need to go vertical)—whether that be long rough, a bunker, or a mound—and will land on the ground and roll a similar distance to the hole.

CLUB SELECTION

In pitching you can choose from the pitching wedge, sand wedge, and lob wedge. Your selection depends mostly on the lie and how much room you have between the primary target and the secondary target. To anticipate accurately how a ball will react when it lands, it's best to land the ball on the green. In fact, you should land the ball on the best-conditioned surface—the putting surface, as opposed to the fringe—whenever you can. Take this into account when establishing your primary target and the distance the ball will roll to the secondary target. If the lie is not an issue, you are left with only the question of which club will permit you to fly the ball to the primary target with the proper trajectory. If the lie is poor, not only will you need to modify the setup conditions slightly, but you'll probably need to go with a little more loft as well, to improve the likelihood of better contact quality and to allow for extra roll once the ball lands. Remember, a lot of grass between the clubface and ball results in very little spin.

Most amateurs pitch with too much loft—they'll have green to work with, and they'll reach for the L-wedge (or the 60-degree wedge), *the* most lofted club. Don't make this mistake. You will *not* always need to maximize your loft when pitching, so always take loft and the amount of room you have to work with into consideration *before* choosing your club.

Incidentally, with the development in the last 10 years of the L-wedge or 60-degree wedge, pitching successfully has become a little less reliant on skill and technique. It's a wonderful instrument, which, when coupled with sound skills, can save you an ungodly number of shots around the green complex from very difficult situations.

PITCHING TECHNIQUE

I call pitching the 50–50 shot, since the launching pad is more neutral than in chipping or the bump-and-run. (See the photos on page 141 for an illustration of the proper pitch setup.

The Launching Pad: Pitch Setup Conditions
- **Grip.** A little bit weaker in both your left and right hand. Making your hands more passive or neutral will result in the ball landing softly.
- **Ball Position.** Your ball position should be centered.
- **Weight Distribution.** Your weight should be evenly distributed and neutral (again, 50–50), or slightly forward, depending on the quality of the lie.

- **Stance.** Get *slightly* closer to the ball, which will allow you to swing in a somewhat more upright plane (the farther away you are from the ball, the more horizontal the swing). A more up-and-down motion will allow you to elevate the ball.
- **Handle Position.** Your hands should be slightly ahead of the golf ball.

MAKING THE PITCH MOTION
Choose How You Want the Ball to Stop
Remember from our discussion in Chapter 9, "Chipping," that there are only four forces that can stop your ball: losing momentum, spin, trajectory, and running into an object such as the flagstick (but again, *don't* count on hitting the flagstick every time—it's not gonna happen), the cup, or a bank. Again, momentum (or lack thereof) is your best choice, as it's the most reliable method.

Choose a Primary and Secondary Target
Also recall our discussion in Chapter 9, "Chipping," on the concept of having a primary and secondary target. The trick is to *pick a primary to achieve a secondary*. It is crucial that you identify *the precise point* where the ball must land to finish *in* the hole. This will require thought and visualization.

The Two-Lever Stroke
Pitching is a two-lever stroke—there's only a slight cock/hinge, not a pure hinge and hold as in the bump-and-run and chipping. However, like the chip shots we discussed earlier, in a pitch you hold off on the clubface during the follow-through to get the ball to land as softly as you can.

Again, *a hinge of the right wrist is a horizontal motion*, while *cocking is a more vertical motion*. (For a quick review of cocking versus hinging, please go back to our discussion in Chapter 9.)

The pitch motion isn't actually that different from a normal golf swing—except that your setup condition is slightly closer to the ball, and you use a weaker grip with both hands to make the clubface behave in a slightly more neutral manner. This, in fact, presets a lot of the motion. The "one-piece takeaway" is great for producing long, boring, driving shots, but not for high, soft pitches (or lobs). To produce a pitch shot, you need the opposite of a one-piece takeaway. You need an earlier setting of the wrists (cock/hinge) to get the club shaft more vertical earlier on in the backswing. This shaft angle will help produce the high arcing shots needed for a pitchlike trajectory.

In pitching, you're making a backswing motion in which you allow the club to cock/hinge while swinging and "setting" it, very much like in a full swing. It's more of a swing-and-set motion. It gets the club shaft in what I call an inclined vertical condition, which is a source of

You can see me holding off the release of the face of the club to hit a higher, softer pitch shot. Notice how flat my left wrist is, and how the clubface is facing skyward.

If you look closely at these two photos you can detect differences in the degree of release of each clubface. The face in the first photo is more rotated than the second photo, producing a lower ball flight that will run more once it lands. The second face will produce a higher pitch that lands softly. How educated are your hands? You must master both trajectories to score. The late Paul Runyan and Harry "Lighthorse" Cooper helped me to understand how crucial the education of the hands truly is.

leverage. *Setting the shaft while swinging the arms* and the loft of the club itself are two of the factors that allow the ball to fly higher and land more softly.

A Controlled, Symmetrical Motion

The motion should be symmetrical—that is, the club swings back the same distance that it swings forward. It is critical to note that, if you want to hit a pitch shot farther, you need to focus on the length of your swing first, not its speed, to control distance.

Picture someone throwing a softball with a long, slow-moving motion, then that same pitch being made with a short, abrupt motion. The long motion will produce a high soft pitch, whereas the shorter, more abrupt one makes the ball travel in a lower, more darting manner. Same with a pitch shot—you need to create a longer, slower motion with your arm swing, not a faster, shorter one, to make your shot fly higher and land more softly. When you increase length, you are creating not more speed, but greater distance and trajectory.

PUTTING IT ALL TOGETHER: PITCHING DRILLS

1. **Swing-and-Set Hesitation Drill**

   In this drill you want to swing the club back, set the club in that vertical position, pause for two seconds, then allow the club to fall naturally and hit the shot. Do not make any concerted effort to make the club fall—the whole idea of this drill is to get a feel for gravity pulling the club down. Because you are not changing the club's direction abruptly, you can feel that gravitational pull and learn to allow gravity to be your ally.

Classic Pitching Motion, setup, backswing, and follow-through: The pitching motion is a miniature of the full swing, with a few "quiet" differences. Looking for a high, soft landing requires me to have "Gumby arms" at address (i.e., really soft and tension-free) as I swing and set the club on plane in the backswing. As I transition into downswing, I feel "freefall." My arms fall gracefully while I keep my body pivot patiently alive and there goes another "high softy."

2. **Mirror Drill**

Get in front of a full-length mirror facing the mirror. Watch as you make a backswing and then follow through; as you do so, really see and feel a symmetrical motion. Most golfers' perception of what is symmetrical in terms of length is pretty far off. In a pitch shot, you want to develop a feel for pitching the ball from a point halfway back—that is, when your left arm is parallel to the ground and the club points skyward when set—making a symmetrical through-motion in which your right arm is then parallel to the ground and the club is pointing skyward again. Please refer back to the three-photo series (above) as you practice this drill to see exactly what your motion should look like at the setup, backswing, and follow-through.

ADVANCED PITCH TECHNIQUE

Play with the length of the club and other factors to vary the trajectory and carry distance. First, hit shots holding the club in a normal full-swing grip, then hit them choking down slightly on the grip to about the midpoint, and finally hit some after choking down all the way to the bottom of the grip. Three other factors to experiment with are the way you hold the club (a grip style that is strong, neutral, or weak), the loft of the particular club in your hand (a pitching, sand, or lob wedge), and where you position the ball. With regard to ball position, play with it center, a little back from center, or forward from center, depending on the kind of trajectory and release you want to create.

Mirror Drill: I like to use the mirror to practice my swing-n-set motion to produce the shaft plane of choice (notice the slightly steeper plane for pitching).

- **Grip.** For a higher and softer shot, take a more neutral (weaker) position. The left hand, which is normally set on the club with two knuckles showing, should be set with one or no knuckles showing. Then put your right hand on the club in a somewhat weaker position (more turned to the left) as well.
- **Speed Variation.** In advanced pitching you will want to vary the speed of your arm swing, using just as much motion but with a slower arm swing pace. This creates *a lot of motion and less speed*. This, coupled with a weaker grip, will make the ball fly higher and land more softly. As we did earlier, picture a long, slow underhand toss, like that of a softball, which makes the ball go higher but land more softly. Then try shorter, crisper motions to observe a trajectory that bores more sharply through the air.

PITCH SHOTS AT A GLANCE

The Fundamental Keys to Pitch Shots
- Choose the right shot
- Visualize the shot
- Select the proper club (pitch, sand, or lob wedge)
- Use a consistent preshot routine
- Create proper setup conditions
- Choose how you want to stop the ball
- Choose a primary target, or landing spot
- Use a two-lever, symmetrical stroke

THE LOB

Picture yourself 30 yards from the pin with a deep gaping bunker in front of you and the pin tucked closely behind. I wouldn't exactly call that a green light. You'll need a lob shot to give yourself a fighting chance for par.

Lob shots come into play in just such instances: when you have to go over an obstacle, the pin is tucked very tightly behind the obstacle, and you need the ball to come to rest quickly. If you want to get to the hidden pins and save shots, you need to be able to lob the ball several times in a round.

Though a form of pitching, lob shots have a higher air time–ground time ratio than pitches. In fact, the lob is a very high shot with a soft landing.

CONDITIONS TO TAKE INTO CONSIDERATION

The nature of your lie is the key to whether you'll be able to lob the ball. Some lies just are not conducive to a lob, even though you must get over some type of mounding to get to a closely cut pin. In that case you will be forced to play away from the pin (your target). Remember, don't make a bad situation worse by turning a bogey into something uglier. If it's one of these red-light lies, meaning you cannot get the clubface on the ball with any degree of consistency, you'll need to lob or chip or pitch the ball to a different sector of the green—away from the pin.

With experience in evaluating certain conditions (as well as practice in hitting shots from various lies), you'll develop a sense of when to use these shots, and will be able to handle more difficult lies, including lies you never dreamed of playing—but start out slowly. Your focus on detail and vision will help you decide the appropriate shot for each situation.

Your practice habits will enable you to execute the shot you decide is appropriate. As with chipping, less is more. Rather than hitting several lobs in succession, place your ball in various positions and conditions during practice, because on the course, don't expect to see it land in an easy location or in the same spot twice in a row.

CLUB SELECTION: THE L-WEDGE—GET ONE, *USE* ONE

We have a rather recent invention called a 60-degree wedge; there are even 61- and 62-degree wedges. These clubs make lob shots a heck of a lot easier than they used to be. Once you have this trusty 60-degree club in your hand, you're halfway home. You can open the face slightly or a great deal (these clubs also come with varying degrees of bounce). You potentially increase the loft of the club to upward of 70 degrees by opening the face.

> ### THE LOB WEDGE CONTROVERSY
>
> *Lob wedges, though still somewhat controversial, are a relatively recent development that most juniors take for granted. As for the controversy, some folks argue that the new club has taken skill away from the short game. I think we can put these folks at ease rather quickly, though, since even with the 60-degree L-wedge available, I don't see legions of amateurs hitting them beautifully with a high, soft trajectory, no spin, and a gentle landing, stopping the ball immediately. The face of amateur golf appears to be in no danger of changing through this new technology anytime soon.*

LOBBING TECHNIQUE
The Launching Pad: Lob Setup Conditions

- **Grip.** Have your hands on the club in a very weak position. Both hands are turned slightly to the left of the center of the shaft line, so there's very little chance of releasing the clubface at all, no matter how aggressively you go at the shot. In addition, a weak grip will cause the ball to fly higher, land softly, and *not* roll. The grip varies depending on how much loft and softness you want and how much of a dead-ball syndrome you're trying to create. You don't want to create enough speed to put a spin on the ball; you want it to fly out of the air and die. Just land and stop. Period. Like a butterfly with sore feet.
- **Weight Distribution.** Dead neutral (50–50).
- **Ball Position.** In general, position the ball either a *fraction* left (forward) of center, or dead center. While this is a general rule, the ideal ranges from middle to slightly forward, depending on the lie you are playing from. If it's an uglier lie, play it more toward the center, but if it's more of an offensive (as opposed to defensive) lie, play it *slightly* left of center.
- **Handle Position.** Either straight vertical or leaning slightly forward.
- **Clubface Position.** You can open the face slightly or a great deal. However, if you're starting with a 60-degree loft and your hands are in a weak position (as they should

be), you don't need to open the clubface much—the ball will already be going high and landing soft. Anytime you start to manipulate the face of an L-wedge or even a sand wedge, you are bringing the bounce of the golf club into play. If the ball is in anything less than a pristine lie (as they tend to be from time to time, especially if the ground is firm), the club will bounce off the ground (unless you have a lot of experience with bounce) and possibly cause you to skull or drop-kick the shot, causing radically poor contact and a less-than-ideal result. If you can learn to modify your grip using the 60-degree club, you won't need to alter the clubface very much at all, avoiding the problem altogether.

MAKING THE LOB MOTION
A Relaxed, Slightly Vertical Swing

Lobbing is very much a feel shot that will take time to develop. In lobbing, you make an arm swing that is relatively relaxed and *slightly* on the vertical side. You do turn your shoulders to support the arm swing, and you do set the shaft on plane a bit earlier. Allow your body to turn your shoulders on the backswing and pivot your hips in a forward swing in sequence with the swinging of the club. You need to apply a downward, somewhat vertical force to the golf ball.

Don't consciously try to break your wrists. Allow the club to set at an angle on the backswing merely for maintaining relaxed wrist joints and the weight of the clubhead. Don't manipulate the swing—let it happen naturally and correctly out of the proper launching pad conditions. By the way, this is a consistent theme in the short game, folks: Don't try to do anything dramatic with your arms or wrists. Control your shot with your setup condition, your grip style, and the pace of your arm swing. Remember—keep it *simple*.

FRED COUPLES'S LOB SHOT

I remember staying with Freddy at the Tournament Players Championships at Sawgrass back in 1984. He won that competition despite being chased by the great Tom Watson and Seve Ballesteros, who were formidable opponents. During the third round of play on the 15th hole, a tough par 4, Freddy hit his second shot over the green, directly behind the pin, which was really close to the back of the green. It landed on some pine straw. I had scurried around in the gallery to get closer to the ball, and I remember thinking what a tough shot he had, playing it off pine straw, with the pin cut close to him and a rock-hard green running away from him to boot. At first it appeared as though he would play a bump-and-run shot up the bank behind the green, which would require perfect precision to get the ball to the speed required to stop on the top shelf of the green. When Freddy came around back there and got a good look at his lie, however, he instantly pulled out a high-lofted wedge and started making long, slow golf swings, using an arm length and pace that could put a baby to sleep. I thought, *My God, this could go anywhere*, but Freddy hit the highest, softest, most beautiful lob shot you've ever seen in your life. It landed right on the green's topshelf and stopped dead in its tracks. That day just over 20 years ago, I learned for the first time what a lob shot was all about.

You really should check out Fred Couples's lob shot. It is today, as it was then, a thing of beauty: a long, flowing motion, the ball sailing through the air in a high, flowing arc . . . then landing and stopping fast, like dead game in duck season.

You should never feel any tension in your hands, wrists, or forearms during this shot. It's a long, loose arm swing motion with a body turn/proportional pivot supporting that swinging action. The active muscles here are the inner core muscles, meaning the back and shoulder muscles in the backswing (turn) and the hip and leg muscles in the forward swing (pivot). You control the length of the shot via the speed and length of your arm swing. It will require patience to make such a long arm swing, especially when you are so close to the target. Once you get the hang of it, however, it's a fun shot to execute. Fred Couples is a great visual example of a long arm swing with a slow flowing swing pace.

PUTTING IT ALL TOGETHER: LOB DRILLS

Like the bump-and-run shot, your best drill for the lob shot is trial and error. The lob is a feel shot that requires a lot of confidence, which can only be developed with experience. Carefully adopting the technique described in this chapter, you want to make hundreds of repetitions, playing with the clubface (in terms of how square to slightly open it is) and ball position, as well as manipulating your grip. You also want to practice abruptly cocking the shaft in your backswing and getting that club up in a more vertical position in the shaft plane. There's no shortcut for this shot, folks; just good old-fashioned repetitions using solid fundamentals.

LOB SHOTS AT A GLANCE

The Fundamental Keys to Lob Shots
- Visualize the shot
- If you don't have an L-wedge (60-degree wedge), get one ASAP!
- Use a consistent preshot routine
- Create proper setup conditions
- Choose your primary target
- Understand club condition and loft

CONCLUSION: HANDICAP, SHMANDICAP (KEEPING IT REAL)

What I am interested in seeing you do is to develop into a player who can produce excellent, consistent scores. I want you to develop and reach your *real scoring potential*. You won't find any garbage in here about handicaps (they're BS), or equitable stroke control (also BS), or handicap indexes (you guessed it—BS). Country club handicaps, as far as I am concerned, are about as real as Casper the Friendly Ghost. Only real scores count.

I know you like to hit those long high ones with your driver, making those blazing iron shots onto the turf and watching the ball soar through the sky. Here's the reality check: Without a solid, repeatable short game, you'll never reach your full scoring potential— *never*. (Do you hear me? Never!) On the other hand, show me a player who can putt and chip a ball and have a couple of other short-game shots squarely in his or her back pocket, and I will show you a player with true scoring potential. The bottom line is: *If* you take the time to understand the technique, and *if* you practice over weeks and months, *you will see dramatic improvement in your scores.* So get out there and make these shots a solid part of your short-game arsenal—you'll be glad you did.

Short Game Shot Matrix

	Grip/Hand Position	Ball Position	Length of Swing	Hinge and Hold?	Weight	Club Selection
Options	(High, Middle, or Low)	(Slightly Forward of Middle, Middle, or Slightly Behind Center)	(1/4, 1/2, 3/4, or Full)	(Yes or No)	(Left Foot, Centered, Right Foot)	(Mid-Iron [6-7], Short Iron [8-9], or Wedge [PW-LW])
Chipping	Low	Slightly Behind Center	1/4	Yes	Left Foot	Short Iron
Bump & Run	Middle	Slightly Behind Center	1/4	Yes	Centered	Mid-Iron
Pitching	Middle	Middle	1/2	Yes	Centered	Wedge
Lobbing	Middle	Middle	3/4	Yes	Centered	Wedge
Sand	Middle	Slightly Forward of Center	3/4	Yes	Centered	Wedge
Putting	Middle	Slightly Forward of Center	Symetrical	Yes	Centered	Putter
Notes:	Please understand this chart is only a starting point. The lie of the ball, the condition and undulations of the green, the overall distance of the shot, and obstacles between you and the hole will all affect the above shots and the way they're played. Combinations of the above categories will allow you to be a more creative short game player.					

11 THE DARTH VADER OF GOLF
BUNKER PLAY

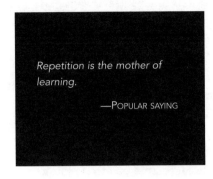

On the 72nd hole of the 1986 PGA Championship, the score was tied when Greg Norman's shot landed 12 feet from the hole and Bob Tway's landed in the bunker fronting the green. Although Norman appeared to be the more likely winner, Tway holed out his sand shot for birdie, while Norman missed his putt—obviously a stunning turn of events.

Bunker play is probably the most overtaught, overcoached, and overwritten aspect of golf. Thousands of articles have been penned on the subject, all with a somewhat different approach, and all unnecessarily difficult—piled up together, they'd look like Tolstoy's *War and Peace*. This overabundance of advice serves to create a lot of unnecessary mystique and trepidation—which is why I often call bunker play the Darth Vader of golf. As with Darth Vader, the fear bunker play evokes is not real; it is a mere figment of your imagination, brought on by a lack of *simple, clear, concise information.*

I submit that the bunker shot is probably the *easiest* shot in golf. If you understand a *few simple key principles and some key things about the sand wedge itself*—and you practice a lot (imagine that—*practice*)—you will learn to handle this shot easily. Then you will be much more relaxed *and* a better scorer around the greens.

IF THE SHOE FITS

During my early years back at the Westchester Country Club, one day in early spring one of my members, Mr. Smith, came into the pro shop singin' the blues about how bad his bunker play was; he couldn't get out of a bunker, he said, and when he did he'd skull it. I found it peculiar, because all in all Smith was a decent player who played a lot of golf. He was in his mid-to-late 50s, a single-digit handicap, and in pretty good physical condition. I grabbed a cart and we headed down to the short-game area, which featured a steep-faced practice bunker. I hopped in, threw some balls out, and asked him to hit some bunker shots. He hit one and skulled it; the next, he caught heavy and left in the bunker. He skulled another one, then hit it heavy again. Around the fifth try he hit a really nice bunker shot, then he hit another one, then hit another good one, and then another. By the time he turned around I was already gone. I had hopped out of the bunker, gotten back into the cart, and driven back up the hill.

About half an hour later he walked into the pro shop with a big grin on his face and said, "I understand." I asked him, "When was the last time you were down in that practice bunker?" He admitted it had been at least 10 or 15 years. I said, "Why don't you make it a point over the next few weeks to go down there three or four times and hit 20 or 30 bunker shots?" A month later he came to me and told me he'd played the west course and shot a 75, hitting it in four bunkers but getting up and down three times.

The moral of the story? Bunker play is a feel shot. Just as a 30-foot putt has to be lagged on a regular basis to get a feel for it, bunker shots require practice. A lot of players, even very good ones, will recognize themselves in this anecdote. If this is you—if you haven't been in a practice bunker recently—you know where you need to go.

OVERVIEW OF BUNKER PLAY

As I mentioned previously, bunker shots are basically feel shots—that is, you need to know what they feel like in terms of quality of contact with the surface and length and pace of the swing as it relates to the distance the ball is going to travel. Developing a solid bunker shot means learning a few simple concepts and making *tons* of rehearsal swings and practice shots. Once you get this technique down you'll be able to stand out on the fairway some 150 yards away and pull the trigger with confidence, because you'll know that if you land in the bunker, you will have a good chance of saving par.

The first principle to remember, which can ease some of the unnecessary tension, is that this shot is the only one in which you can miss your contact point—you can actually *miss* the shot from a technical standpoint—and still achieve an acceptable result. This is because you contact the sand first, then the ball. The sand creates the compression that causes the ball to be lofted into the air onto the putting surface.

Let's say you try to enter the sand 1 inch behind the ball, but instead you actually hit 1½ inches behind your desired contact point. Because of the porous nature of sand, if you keep that swing alive, you will still be able to get the ball out of the bunker and onto the putting surface. It may not be as close to the hole as you had hoped, but it's still a playable result. If you had been out of the bunker somewhere hitting a pitch shot, and hit ½ inch behind the ball (a "fat shot"), it wouldn't advance the ball far at all—or be very pretty.

Another key principle is that when you begin to contact exactly the right amount of sand (smaller margins of sand), you will be able to develop a tremendous amount of control, sending the ball to the target with a spin so that it stops rather quickly. This is something that likely will never be available to you out of the long grass around the green, and will create some wonderful scoring opportunities.

CONDITIONS TO TAKE INTO CONSIDERATION

To properly evaluate a bunker shot, you'll need to carefully consider the conditions in front of you: your proximity to the lip of the bunker, distance from the hole, and how much room on the green you have to work with. These factors will translate into such decisions as: How much do you want the clubface to be open? (In other words, how much trajectory do you want to create?) What's the length and pace of your swing, or, phrased slightly differently, how far do you want the ball to travel?

Most players overthink bunker play instead of working to develop a *feel* for the shot. You need to get into the bunker, take a tremendous number of rehearsal swings, and, after each one, using common sense as your guide, decide whether the shot would have worked or not. For example, if you take a rehearsal swing and make a deep gouge in the sand, you'll realize the ball might have gone 2 feet in front of you—not even close to getting out of the bunker. Or maybe you take almost no sand at all and realize that your shot would have been a skull and a home run (what I call a Babe Ruth shot).

Although it's against the rules in a real round of golf to get in the bunker and make practice swings, during bunker practice it's not, so get in there and take some swings without any golf balls to see if you can take out a quantity of sand that makes sense to you based on the distance you're trying to travel. I don't think many people take enough time to get into a bunker and understand the feeling they're trying to create in terms of the quality of contact with the surface itself, and then mentally registering what it feels like to hit a quality bunker shot.

CLUB SELECTION: MEET YOUR FRIEND, THE SAND WEDGE

Next, let's talk a little bit about the special equipment available for this shot: the sand wedge. A little understanding of how the sand wedge operates is helpful. It really is a clever little club. Go on, go get it. I'll wait here.

Take a look at it. You'll notice that a sand wedge has a very sharp (usually) leading edge. Let's rename that edge the "digger" to make it easier for explanation purposes. There is also a very heavy flange. Some people call this the bounce of the golf club. For our purposes, we'll call it the "skidder." These parts do just what their names imply: The leading edge, or digger, is used to dig into the sand when you have a less-than-pristine lie, while the skidder is used to glide through the sand when you have a pristine lie in relatively soft or medium-textured sand.

Okay, now let's use the terms *digger* and *skidder* in practice. Let's say you have a ball buried in a bunker—a fried-egg lie, as we sometimes call it. Do you apply the digger or the skidder more? Obviously, the digger, so the club will be in a more square position and can "dig" into the sand to excavate the ball. If, on the other hand, you have a nice, smooth lie sitting on fluffy sand, you want the skidder more involved so the club will slide through the sand and *not* dig in (otherwise, it will ultimately get stuck, and you will not be able to advance the ball very far).

Different types of sand call for using different parts of the sand wedge. In hard-packed sand you want to use the digger, because it's made to dig into harder, denser material in order to excavate the ball. In fluffy or soft sand you want the skidder, because the digger would slow the club so much that you'd likely leave the ball in the bunker.

The recent addition of the 60-degree club has allowed golfers to play bunker shots higher and stop them more quickly than they ever dreamed. It's a wonderful tool to have in your bag. However, depending on the conditions of the green, the length of the shot you are trying to make, and the quality of your lie, you may want to hit bunker shots with a pitching wedge, a sand wedge, a gap wedge, or the aforementioned 60-degree wedge. The shot will dictate the selection.

THE ORIGIN OF THE SAND WEDGE

The story of how this wonderful club originated is a colorful one. For those of you who are not familiar with it, I'd like to share it with you. Eugenio Sarecini, later known as Gene Sarazen, was one of only four people to win all four golf majors—the U.S. Open, the British Open, the PGA Championship, and the Masters. He is also considered by many to be the inventor of the sand wedge.

Back in the early 1930s, when our story takes place, bunkers were raked with thick-pronged rakes. This created deep furrows where the ball would nestle itself in deeply and be very difficult to excavate, especially since the most lofted golf club in existence at the time was the mashie niblick, which, in terms of loft, is equivalent to today's 8-iron. Even the finest players often were forced to play out of a bunker sideways, and in many cases away from the target. Sarazen, or—as I like to refer to him—my boy Geno, didn't dig that a whole lot (no pun intended). Geno's mind went to work on the situation, and, through a variety of influences (including Howard Hughes, who had explained to him the way air flows over a plane wing), he came up with the idea for a golf club that would be able to move through sand and excavate a ball. So off to work he went.

I am told that a family member of Geno's owned a small machine shop, and that in late 1931 he took a mashie niblick to this shop and began to heat it and bend the face, adding loft to it. He applied iron ore to the back of the mashie niblick, molding it until it became (by today's standards) a very crude flange. Then he got into some bunkers and began to excavate the ball beautifully, even in some of the worst conditions possible, elevating it over the lip of the bunker and allowing him to play in the direction of the hole. Being the clever but sneaky individual he was, he placed the club in his bag head-down to keep it a secret.

At the 1932 British Open, which took place at Prince's Golf Club in Sandwich, England, Geno was playing practice rounds with fellow competitors and hitting wonderful, high bunker shots in the direction of the hole. Each time someone raced over to see how he did it, he'd stick the clubhead down in his bag. Finally someone protested to the committee that he was carrying an illegal club. After calling him onto the carpet and examining the club, they discovered there were no rules against having a club of this type because they had never encountered one before. That being the case, Sarazen was allowed to use the club, and (wouldn't you know it?) went on to win the Open that year. How many shots do you suppose that one club was worth to him? I'm sure I speak for all of us when I say, "Thank you, Geno."

HOW HIGH? (HOW MUCH BOUNCE DO YOU NEED?)

There are so many wedges being produced with different types and degrees of bounce, it's a good idea to consult your local PGA professional as to the best choice for the amount of bounce you want to play with. Also consider the nature and texture of the sand you normally play from, because that will make a difference in your decision.

Having the right configuration of clubs in your bag (pitching, sand wedge, and 60-degree wedge) provides you with a variety of different bounces, enabling you to hit bunker shots of varied lengths and trajectories. You'll be well prepared for any situation that arises—provided, of course, that you have gone to your local practice area, thrown down a few hundred balls, and practiced over and over again under a wide variety of conditions.

BUNKER TECHNIQUE

THE LAUNCHING PAD: PROPER SETUP CONDITIONS

The launching pad in the bunker requires some slight adjustments from the launching pad of, say, pitch shots. Say it with me now: *slight, slight, slight*! So many club players I have coached in the bunkers have had problems because they have *really overdone* these adjustments.

- **Grip.** Based on the length of the shot, your grip will vary from weak to neutral to slightly strong; weak is required for a short shot, neutral for a medium one, and strong for a long one. Weaken your grip *slightly* for higher, softer, shorter bunker shots and strengthen it for longer, lower bunker shots that you want to release. The grip condition will correspond to whether you want the ball to come out high and soft or lower and more running, which will depend on where the pin is located and the type of shot you want to play. Slightly open the face of the club. Since *slightly* is a subjective word, study the photos below to see what I mean.
- **Weight Distribution.** I want your weight distribution to be 50–50 neutral. In other words, your weight should be distributed evenly over both feet.

"Before" pitching setup and "after" bunker setup: The point of these photos is to illustrate that a pitch shot setup and a sand shot setup have very few slight differences. The only real difference is I'd like you to feel *slightly* more open to the target in the bunker shot setup.

- **Ball Position.** Here's a trick question: Where do you position the ball in a bunker shot? Time's up . . . wrong answer (and the rest of you, put your hands down). In a bunker shot, *you are not trying to hit the ball, because you are not trying to make club-to-ball contact.* Therefore you don't position the ball, but in fact, address the point in the sand at which you wish the club to enter the sand. What you want is to set the club at a point in the sand somewhere *behind the ball* to allow that cushion of sand to excavate it from the bunker. Instead of focusing on the ball, focus on a point in the sand where you want the club to enter. Make sense? Good . . . let's keep going.

  Now I want that point (generically speaking) where you want to enter the sand to be somewhere at center or just slightly left of center, which would make the ball *appear* well forward of center. In the bunker you want to get the point in the sand (the impact area) centered, which will in fact keep the ball slightly forward of center, because if the impact area is always centered for how much sand you are going to take (1 inch, 2 inches, 3 inches . . .), the ball will be a corresponding distance (1, 2, 3 inches . . .) forward of center.

- **Stance.** Your stance should be *slightly* open. Please note that this is a preference on my part, and not a required principle of technique.

- **Handle Position.** Handle position should be neutral.

- **Clubface Position.** I get the question all the time: How open or closed should the face be when hitting the shot? The answer is in the distance you need that little white dimpled monster to travel. How much you want the face open depends on the conditions in front of you. This means considering how high the bunker lip is, how far the ball needs to travel, and how much trajectory you will need to accomplish your goal in stopping the ball, all of which determine how much loft you'll need. This will affect how you set the clubface for the shot. The lie may also affect your decision. If it's a short shot, you want a more open condition. A longer shot would call for a squarer face condition.

  In any case you never want the face to be totally square, unless you have a severely buried lie. (Recall our previous digger discussion.)

BUNKER PLAY STANCE: PREFERENCE VERSUS PRINCIPLE

When I demonstrate bunker play at TP Golf Schools for the first time, I'll often "lead the witness" by asking my students, "You should definitely have an open stance when you hit a bunker shot, right?" They'll nod and tell me, yes, they've read that a million times. I'll then proceed to severely close my stance and hit a perfectly fine, high and soft bunker shot out of the sand up on the green. I'll say to them, "Okay, why did that work?" They'll look at me, dumbfounded, and say they have no idea. The answer, my friends, is that an open stance while hitting a bunker shot is a *preference*, not a *principle*. However, most amateurs go so far open off the intended line that they can't get the ball started in the direction of the hole. In your setup, how far open or closed your stance needs to be will depend on the type of shot you have to hit. Opening your stance slightly is a preference. You need to be very careful in bunker play, and in most short-game shots, in understanding the difference between preferences and principles in technique.

THE BUNKER SHOT MOTION

You have probably heard all of the following about bunker shots: You should set the club a little more quickly in your backswing and/or cock your wrists sooner, take the club back a little outside, swing the club down a little more abruptly, maybe try to swing across your body lines and hold off your finish with the face open . . . Holy smokes! How much can you think about in an action that takes two seconds to perform? Erase all this, take a deep breath, and remember the following: There are only three key principles of bunker play that dictate the type of bunker shot you hit:

1. **Amount of Face**
   Square to slightly open.
2. **Amount of Swing, or the Length and Pace of the Motion**
   This relates to how far you want the ball to travel. The greater the distance you need the ball to travel, the longer your swing and slower the pace—this will create a higher, softer shot. The shorter the distance, the shorter the swing motion and the faster the pace, which creates a lower, more "boring" bunker shot.
3. **Amount of Sand, or How Much Sand You Will Displace**
   This is the amount of sand you want to excavate from behind the golf ball (which determines how far back from the ball you want the club to enter the sand). Once again, it's based on the distance you want the ball to travel. If you displace a lot of sand, the ball will not go as far as it would if you took less sand during the shot. There is a distance correlation here. Therefore, you need to pick a spot where you want the club to enter the sand. To understand sand displacement as it relates to distance, there is a huge experience factor. (I'm referring, of course, to that practice thing again!)

If you control these three things—how you position the face of the club, the length and pace of your swing, and where the club enters the sand—and then make a very normal, short-game pitch-shot-type swing, you can hit a more than adequate bunker shot. That's all there really is to it, folks. Really. While there are some advanced techniques out there, and a few specialty shots you can learn (and should at some point), if you can just remember these three things, you can execute quality bunker shots.

As you develop and improve your bunker play skills, here's another simple concept that will help you. There are only three possible priorities when hitting a bunker shot: (1) getting the ball out of the sand, (2) getting the ball close to the hole, and (3) holing the bunker shot. When you attempt a bunker shot, pick one of these priorities and focus on it. Nothing more, nothing less. If you're a new player, getting out of the bunker would be a noble accomplishment. An intermediate priority might be to decrease the dispersion of balls you hit in a practice session, getting the ball a little tighter and closer to the pin as your skill level improves. As for advanced players, if you can get out of a bunker under normal circumstances, in a halfway-decent lie, you should be thinking about the possibility of holing that shot out. You need to have a clear vision—a plan—before you hit each and every shot in your golf life, bunker shots included. Like a 30-foot putt, it's a shot you should be capable of holing occasionally. After all, if you can hole those long putts occasionally, then *why not a bunker shot?*

PUTTING IT ALL TOGETHER: WHAT A CLASSIC
BUNKER SHOT LOOKS LIKE

BUNKER SHOT PRACTICE DRILLS

Okay, kids, here's where we get to play in the sandbox! Roll up your sleeves and get into that practice bunker. Instead of the pail and shovel you used as a kid, bring your sand wedge, some balls, and maybe a canteen, since you will be there a while.

Don't be like the hordes who overthink bunker play. Instead of just working to develop a feel for the shot, try practicing sand contact. Get in the bunker and practice a bunch of different shots, watching the depth of your divots. Virtually every good golf complex (not only private ones, but public as well) will have a short-game practice area with sand. Find the good one(s) in your area.

Make a bunch of practice swings to try to develop a level divot pattern. Most people get too vertical on their bunker shots. I want to see longer, thinner patterns of sand divots. Longer, shallower patterns can spin the ball more than when you have a gouging effect that pushes it out and puts an overspin on it, making it land and roll a great distance. Simply getting into the bunker, practicing, and watching the divot patterns will make you a better bunker player.

Also, during bunker shot practice, it is crucial that you rehearse your swings as if they're the real deal—as if you're playing under real course conditions—but with one key difference. As we all know, during real-time play you cannot contact the sand before a shot

Here I'm abbreviating my follow-through intentionally. I hit these shots with a shorter and crisper stroke, sort of a punch shot in a bunker, if you will. This promotes a lower trajectory and a shot that will roll out or release toward the pin.

without incurring a penalty. But you *do* have the unique opportunity while practicing your bunker game to make these rehearsal swings, so take advantage. Again, you need to feel the contact with the sand, decide where the club is going to enter the sand, and determine the amount of exertion it will take to move that small bit of earth out of the bunker with the ball going along for the ride. That said, do make rehearsal swings during practice time, and make them as realistic as possible.

Practice Step One: Develop Your Divot

In this step you will learn to develop a shallow divot using the bounce of the club. Once that's perfected, you will then head to practice step two.

Before you hit *any* shots, I want you to perfect your bunker divot. For an average-length sand shot, you should create a divot that is about the length of a hot dog and as deep as a wallet on payday. Play with the amount of face, and with how the skidder moves through the sand in terms of depth and length. Work on this step *a lot*. It is key to developing your sand technique.

As you do, simply try to splash out some sand, leaving long, level displacements. If the divots are deep, the skidder is not being used properly and your angle of attack is too steep. You do not want to leave deep gouges of sand; on the other hand, you do not want to avoid contacting any sand.

Feel the bounce, slide through the sand. You should feel less resistance than you would from the turf of the fairway.

Practice Step Two: Hitting Behind the Ball

This second step is where you will learn to enter the sand at a specific, desired point; once this is perfected, you will then head to step three.

Okay, now that you have perfected your divot in step one, drop some balls. I want you to work on where the club enters the sand. Mark a line about 1 to 2 inches behind the ball. Practice entering the sand at this spot. You may be surprised by how much you are missing the mark. This is understandable, since every shot in golf requires contact with the ball except this one.

Once you are consistently hitting your mark and forming a hot-dog-long, wallet-deep divot, you should be pleased with the results you're beginning to see. Go ahead, drop some balls, and give it a go.

Practice Step Three: Exploring Different Types of Shots

Now that your divots and entry point in the sand have been refined, you're ready to explore and perfect different types of bunker shots.

As you become more adept and confident with the average-length shot, you can begin to work on different lengths, different lies, and even different types of sand. You'll find with the variety of shots you may need to tweak your technique a

DOCTOR BUNKER: A GROUP DRILL FOR BETTER BUNKER PLAY

Here's a group drill you can add if you and your playing buddies want to work on these shots together. It's called Doctor Bunker, and it's more like a game than a drill. It's a fun way to improve your bunker play, and I can personally vouch for its benefits. Buddy Alexander, my dear friend and head golf coach at the University of Florida, taught me this drill years ago.

It's a similar game to horse in basketball. The first player to pick the shot would, for example, bury a ball in the bunker or put it in the side of the slope or some other difficult position. Then the golfer hits the shot, and everyone has to match or beat it to earn a point or position in the game. Competing under this pressure helps develop the mental and physical skills needed to make these shots second nature on the golf course.

bit. (What's the key concept here again, folks? *Slightly*.) For example, short shots generally require up to four possible slight adjustments, although you may not need all four, since two alone may provide a result. These adjustments are: a shorter swing, a slower tempo, more face, and displacement of a little more sand.

ADVANCED BUNKER PLAY

The following are techniques and tips to be applied *only* after you're confident in your ability to get out of the bunker in what might be termed "normal situations," to keep the ball on the putting surface, and to start to close the dispersion pattern of how far from the hole you're finishing. At that point, and not before, you're ready to move to a more advanced level of bunker play.

Advanced Club Selection

One advanced bunker play technique is to experiment with the type of equipment you choose. You can play some very long bunker shots across a long deep green with a pitching wedge. You can play medium shots with a sand wedge and short bunker shots with a lob wedge.

The Advanced Launching Pad: Setup Conditions

The most helpful drill is to experiment with how you position your hands on the club, meaning how strong or weak your grip is. As discussed previously, there are strong, medium, and weak grips. These all affect how the ball comes out of the bunker. If it's a short bunker shot you want to hit, you'll need a weak grip; this will prevent you from releasing the face at all, which would deaden the shot even more. A very strong grip will tend to release the face slightly, so you'll hit the ball lower and it will land running a bit more.

Face condition changes are also a good way to elevate skill level. If a pin is tucked close to a bunker, there isn't much room to work with, so you want to hit a higher and softer shot. This requires playing a club in a much more open face condition and manipulating the shaft (that is, getting the shaft to swing back in a more vertical plane) to create the desired shot.

Also start varying the length and pace of your swing. The single most important factor in getting shorter shots that are higher and softer is the ability to put your hands on the club in a weaker position and turn both left and right hands more to the left on the club in a very weak position.

If, for example, I had a pin cut close to me, with little green to work with, or with the green sloping away from me, I'd have the club in a very open position, with my hands on the club in a weak position, and I would make a long, slow golf swing to produce that higher, softer bunker shot.

Conversely, on a longer bunker shot with the pin farther away from me—here I need the ball to fly farther and then release more—I would have the club in a slightly open position with a stronger grip, and make a shorter, crisper motion so the ball comes out lower and lands and releases more. It's a swing that almost looks like a punch shot motion, with a shorter backswing, a more abrupt downward motion, and an abbreviated follow-through with a stronger grip and a square clubface to get the ball out lower then land and release more.

A lot of this is trial and error—playing around with different types of shots and varying launching pad conditions to see how you can use them to manipulate and control the club and ball under the different circumstances that arise.

CONCLUSION

If you can integrate this information, these few key principles, then you can learn to hit some nifty little bunker shots in a variety of situations. The principles we've covered may sound simplistic, but that's as it should be. You will not be one of those people who over-think bunker play, because now you know better. By keeping it simple, and keeping the three keys in mind as you practice this shot, you'll be well on your way to adding solid bunker play to your bag.

BUNKER PLAY AT A GLANCE

The Fundamental Keys to Bunker Play
- Know how different types of sand affect your shot
- Get familiar with the sand and lob wedge, the digger, and the skidder
- Create proper launching pad conditions
- Avoid the tendency to overthink the shot, feel the shot, practice the shot
- Consider how open or closed the clubface should be, the length and pace of the swing, and the amount of sand you want to displace
- Choose one of three priorities when hitting a shot: out, on, or in

12 INTRODUCTION TO THE FULL SWING
GOLF MECHANICS 101

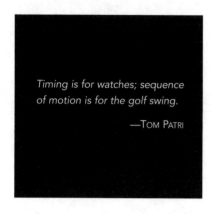

Timing is for watches; sequence of motion is for the golf swing.

—Tom Patri

We all like to see the ball fly high and straight, with crisp contact that achieves distances most of us can only dream of, but in truth the ideal full golf swing is much like the ever-elusive Holy Grail. The complexity of the motion and the skills required make it a difficult task. This is not meant to discourage you, but to inspire you to seek it, with the understanding that you will continue this search throughout your golf life. That's what the process of learning to play golf should be about—not a destination, but a journey, in which you are always growing and evolving. It's important to keep your pursuit one of excellence, and not some ill-fated attempt to find a quick fix. Achieving your full swing's full potential is the most complicated and difficult task you will face in golf—an ever-improving work in progress.

Equally important is a consistent effort based on *sound fundamentals*. Switching from one approach to another and chasing after each new piece of advice haphazardly will ultimately prove frustrating and futile. It never really makes sense to take or seek advice from anyone other than your coach; on the flip side, you should probably never offer advice to others, either. If you follow the sound and simple advice that follows in the next two chapters, you will come to understand these principles and your hard work will pay off with much more consistent ball striking.

As I've mentioned previously, golf is not taught, it is learned. One important ingredient of this process is to construct a proper learning arena. If you are provided with solid instruc-

SHORT-GAME SHOTS: YOUR SECRET ARSENAL

I mentioned in the short game section that even the world's golf leaders hit about 70 percent of fairways and 70 percent of greens in regulation, which means they miss around 30 percent of each. Some of them get on hot streaks where they hit higher percentages on the fairways and greens, but over the course of a year the average always comes out to around 70 percent. That's how difficult it is to repeat the golf swing. Your full swing is a work in progress and will go through peaks and valleys. Yes, improving your full swing will shave shots off your score, but given its complex nature you will not be able to achieve as radical an improvement as you will by improving your short game. I hope this will encourage you to put a secret weapon in your arsenal: developing your short-game shots while you continue to work on your full swing.

tion (such as that contained in this book) and a visual model of your swing (using a practice mirror and/or a videotape), you have been given the best opportunity to begin to create your own individual golf motion. You will start to *see* and then *feel* it over time. This doesn't necessarily mean you'll create a pretty swing, or even a classical swing. It means you'll create a swing that works, consistently, day in and day out—for *you*.

THERE'S NO SUCH THING AS "THE" PERFECT SWING

There's no one correct swing. Otherwise, there would be no difference between Fred Couples and Jim Furyk. Lee Trevino's swing would look just like Tom Watson's or Raymond Floyd's, and the tournaments would come down to a putting contest each week. The gentlemen mentioned here have each found a swing that, although somewhat unconventional, and in some cases definitely not pretty, works for them day in and day out. Compare these players with Tiger Woods and Stuart Appleby, whose swings are more classic and conventional. Yet what all of these players' swings have in common is that they're effective and repeatable, and *that* is what's important. While the fundamentals must be learned, strive to develop your own *individual golf motion*—one that accommodates your dominant natural tendencies.

DISCOVERING YOUR DOMINANT NATURAL TENDENCIES

Back in the early 1990s two very fine LPGA Tour players, Cathy Johnston-Forbes and Missie Berteotti, were students of mine. Like all of us, they both had Achilles' heels in their swings. I worked with both of them for a long period of time, which allowed me to learn and document what I call *dominant natural tendencies*. I utilized this important knowledge to keep them on track. Like all players, they have swings as individual as their fingerprints.

Rarely does a longtime student come to me with a new issue, something wildly different from everything I've seen before. We all exhibit dominant natural tendencies, whether negative or positive. One of the benefits of working with the same coach over time is that a competent one will document your tendencies. When things go wrong in your golf game, you can usually look back at two or three key points in your swing to get things back on track fairly quickly.

REAL LEARNING TAKES TIME

The thought and effort you give to the concepts covered in these chapters while on the practice range, rather than the course, are important. You need to learn to feel the correct positions, then incorporate them into a motion, which will require discovery and assimilation. You can't do this during an actual swing because, given its speed, it leaves little time for reflection or for learning. You need to take time to understand and implement and review these sections again and again, and revisit the other five Spokes often to be sure they continue to work together. The other five Spokes—Body, Mind, Analysis, Time Management, and Equipment—should always be part of the journey.

OVERVIEW OF THE GOLF SWING

It's important that you understand the three physical principles that govern the golf swing: symmetrics, physics, and geometry. Understanding these basic principles will give you a "big picture" to work from.

The fact that a sound golf swing follows certain physical and scientific principles is a good thing. If you master the mechanics, taking into account your individual body type and the interaction of the swing's parts, that swing will not only be repeatable, but will allow you to compress the ball as well as control it.

- **Symmetrics.** The backward and forward motions of a good golf swing are basically mirror images of one another—they are *symmetrical*. These mirror images include folding joints, turning shoulders, and rotating hips, blended with a proper distribution of weight, an on-plane shaft and arms, and a square clubface. *While slight differences exist because of a static start*, working conceptually toward a symmetrical swing will lead to better results. I call this concept as it relates to the golf swing *symmetrics*.

- **Physics.** By this I mean the various sources that contribute to speed development in the golf motion. As mentioned in Spoke 1, The Body, the golf swing is a sequence of events in which the body transfers energy in a kinetic link. In the backswing, rotational forces build up in the shoulders while the hips and lower body create resistance. This, as well as the leverage created in the elbows and wrists, is the source of the power and speed that build up and are stored for, then released during, the downswing. To maximize your power and speed, proper sequencing must be understood and then tapped into.

WHAT IS COMPRESSION?

You've heard the word compression *several times now in the short-game area, and it'll come up again in the full swing. When you make really sound, quality contact with the ball, you should feel as if you're compressing the golf ball against the face of the club. The ball, when struck properly by the clubface, actually becomes almost egg shaped for a moment. If you've never seen a high-speed film of the ball being compressed, try to get a hold of a high-speed camera and see it for yourself. It's important that you understand compression conceptually, and seeing it will vividly solidify the concept in your mind.*

Halfway Back: Notice the amount of armswing is proportional to the amount of shoulder turn. This means the swing is well timed. I refer to this as being "in sequence."

Another source of power during the swing is proper weight distribution, which is actually a physical as well as a symmetrical occurrence, in both the backswing and the through-motion. For most players, except those with a high degree of flexibility, the backswing is a posted-up condition to the right side— the right side of the body stays firm, and grounds your body. As you commence your downswing and begin to release the club, there is a posted-up condition to the left side—again, the body stays grounded by standing firm on that side, as opposed to swaying. Your two legs are your two points of stability throughout the swing. The right leg stabilizes the top of the backswing, and the left side stabilizes the finish condition.

I like to feel and see two things in a chest-on view of a "loaded backswing": (1) a 90 degree rotation of the torso and (2) a distribution of weight over the right leg. Notice both in this photo.

I'm a big fan of what I refer to as "posting up" into your left side (I also sometimes call this "vertical left"). By this I mean that you should see a vertical line from your left leg, your torso, and continuing to the front of your face.

One of the real difficulties of golf is that its motion is unlike that of other sports. In tennis, for example, your body is rotating horizontally while the tennis racket is swinging horizontally. In baseball, your body is turning or pivoting horizontally and your bat is swinging horizontally, so you are working with like planes.

Golf is very different. You have to coordinate opposing planes or motions. You have inclined verticals running into rotated horizontals. (Hockey, by the way, has similar vertical and horizontal motions.) If you imagine a Ferris wheel inside a rotating merry-go-round in a perfectly timed sequence, you have a golf swing. It's a circle on an incline (the Ferris wheel), which has an inclined vertical aspect running into the horizontal motion (the merry-go-round). You're trying to visualize those two motions and sequence them. This is a basic explanation of the golf swing that my mentor, Bill Strausbaugh, taught me many years ago. I've found it's a great way for people to understand and conceptualize the geometric shapes of the golf swing.

My mentor, Bill Strausbaugh, was in my estimation one of the greatest teaching and coaching minds this game has ever known. He often would describe the golf motion as a Ferris wheel running into a merry-go-round, with the Ferris wheel as the vertical component (the arms and club falling), and the merry-go-round as the horizontal component (the body unwinding). One of the great (but solvable) mysteries of golf is the proper sequencing of these two components of the golf motion.

- **Geometry.** This refers to the shape of the swing. It is based predominantly on the player's body type—tall, short, heavy (large boned), thin (long limbed), and the degree of flexibility. While these are basic categories, each of us has our own unique geometric shape. You must understand and learn to work with your individual shape to develop a geometric swing that makes sense for you. Because your swing style is unique and personal to your particular physical makeup, do not try to emulate others. In fact, in most cases trying to imitate other players' swings is a mistake.

Okay, now that we've covered the basic concepts of symmetrics, physics, and geometry, here's the advanced formula: The golf swing is (1) the coordination and sequencing of the rotational (centrifugal force) motions, (2) weight distribution, and (3) the inclined up-and-down (leverage) motions, which, when tied together (assuming a square clubface and an on-plane shaft), produce your own personal best ball flight. This is the essence of what you are trying to achieve.

CONCLUSION

As we move on to the fundamentals of the swing, I want you to stop listening to about 99 percent of the golf instruction you see or hear elsewhere, and stick to learning and understanding the basic fundamentals needed for a sound swing motion. In fact, as teaching and coaching the game evolves, I find more and more that my job entails not allowing students to get derailed by all the information they accumulate from other sources. In other words, *golf is severely overtaught and largely undercoached.* Stick to the basic fundamentals, which we will cover in the chapters that follow, practice the drills provided faithfully, and you will achieve real, lasting changes that will lead you to great success in your golf.

TOM'S LONG GAME LESSON NOTES

I. Set-up
  A. Grip
    1. Left Hand: _____
    2. Right Hand: _____
  B. Posture
    1. Upper Body: _____
    2. Lower Body: _____
  C. Alignment/Ball Position: _____
  D. Pre-Shot Routine: _____
  Drills: _____

II. Body Motion
  A. Backswing
    1. Upper Body/Arm Swing: _____
    2. Lower Body: _____
  B. Downswing
    1. Upper Body/Arm Swing: _____
    2. Lower Body: _____

III. Swing Plane/Cubface
  A. Backswing: _____
  B. Downswing: _____
  Drills: _____

IV. Mental Conditioning/Physical Conditioning: _____

This is the format for the notes I provide to students after a full-swing lesson. You should prepare and keep similar notes after every lesson.

13 THE BOOKENDS **THE LAUNCHING PAD AND FINISH CONDITION**

If you've ever watched golf professionals play, you've probably noticed they go through a unique routine before every shot. What you may or may not have observed closely is how consistent each player's routine actually is. If you go back and review tapes from the 1960s of Jack Nicklaus, making a note of how many steps behind the golf ball he started from, what hand the golf club was in, how he walked up to the golf ball, what he set down in what order (clubhead first, then his right foot, then the left foot), the obligatory waggle of the club, how many times he looked at the target . . . and then you compared this with one from the 1980s—or from any segment of his professional career, for that matter—you would find them to be remarkably similar, if not precisely identical. That's a very definite reason why Jack is Jack.

A preshot routine is a consistent, repeatable set of actions leading up to the motion itself. *What's the big deal?* you ask. It's this: *The most important and fundamental instruments you play golf with—your body and your mind—recognize these signals and translate them into the desired performance.* It's a psychological and tactical tool, without which creating a consistent, repeatable swing is impossible.

Equally vital to the success of your full swing are your setup conditions, which I call the launching pad. If the launching pad for your shot is not fundamentally sound, a compensating adjustment will almost always occur during the swing. Because the swing happens in less than two seconds and at around 90 miles an hour, taking off without a proper launching pad is risky. Most students of golf fail to realize the significance. They are eager for me to *fix* their golf swing, and when I start correcting their launching pad, they look at me like they're thinking, *No, not my setup, my swing!*—as if the two are somehow unrelated. Yet because a correct launching pad is so vital to a sound swing motion, *the only sure way to cure your full-swing ills is to start with the launching pad.* Once there (for the first time), most students are amazed with their ball flight results. Only then do they start to understand and feel that the launching pad enables them to achieve swing positions that were previously unattainable.

Building both a solid consistent preshot routine and launching pad isn't as much work as it sounds, since although they are indeed two separate steps, they go hand in hand. Once you've proceeded through your preshot routine, you've already begun to build a wonderful launching pad for putting your golf swing in motion.

Aside from these two important factors, we need to concern ourselves here with one other related aspect: the finish condition. Now, I know what you may be thinking: *Whoa, TP, wait a minute! We just got to the full swing and already you're skipping all the way to the*

CHECK YOUR LAUNCHING PAD REGULARLY

The launching pad is to be checked frequently for the rest of your golf journey. Check it in the mirror or a window, using your shadow, on video . . . You can never spend too much time on a daily basis checking and rechecking the fundamentals of a correct launching pad. Every single Tour player I've ever worked with, whether on the LPGA, PGA, or the Senior Tour, has said to me at every lesson, "Hey, TP, when we start our session today, would you mind looking at my setup to see if it's in good shape?" In 25 years, not one amateur player has ever said that to me. Professionals understand the importance of the proper launching pad conditions. They know that if the launching pad isn't taken care of first, their swing has very little chance of being successful.

finish *condition?* That's right. And there's an excellent reason why we cover both the setup and finish conditions here, and it has to do with a handy little thing known as the mind–body connection.

In other words, in addition to building and utilizing a sound preshot routine and parlaying that into a sound launching pad, we take the same concept of using a consistent, correct routine to pre-program the mind to make a successful golf swing one step farther. We apply the concept to the entire full swing to help train the body to make the correct motion. I call this approach *Bookends* because together, they form the framework of your swing. It has been used with great success by hundreds of my students over the years.

Let me briefly explain. Two keys that help create a mental shortcut to a sound golf swing are the proper launching pad conditions and a fully released, balanced finish condition. The reason for this is simple: To get from a perfect start to a perfect finish, a correct swing has to have occurred, and *the body will respond accordingly in between.* By training the mind and body to "feel" the correct beginning position and finish position, the rest of the swing mechanics start to fall into place. This eliminates some of the work in trying to perfect each swing segment separately, which often yields mixed results. *The mind fills in the blanks.*

Think of an actor who must shift his facial expression from joy to misery on cue during each performance. The number of muscles and movements in this transition is enormous, but he does not focus on working each individual muscle. Instead, he practices smiling, then frowning, and he often begins the rehearsal process using a mirror to monitor his results. Once he has developed the appropriate expressions, shifting from one to the other becomes automatic through the mind–body connection.

Too often golfers concentrate on every little movement in their swing, as if it's a process of connect the dots; in so doing they make learning the golf swing unnecessarily difficult, slow, and extremely awkward, if not impossible. By concentrating on the Bookends—the correct start and finish conditions—your mind and body can and will work together, freeing the rest of the swing to fall *naturally* into place.

Let's go through these one at a time. First, we'll delve a little more deeply into the preshot routine, which we discussed briefly in Spoke 2, The Mind, by developing an effective preshot routine that works for you.

A good routine only takes moments. Slow play, on the other hand, is due to a lack of routine. Disorganized players scramble to pick their club, get their yardage, figure out what the wind is doing . . . If you time touring professionals, you'll find that they take between 8 and 20 seconds for their preshot routine through the actual shot (with the exception of Jack Nicklaus, who was and is notoriously slow). They each have a set routine that covers everything, whether they're compiling information necessary to pick a club, setting their yardage, evaluating the wind condition or the position of the pin, or moving through their preshot routine. Most Tour players are fairly brisk because they don't want to get static, which can lead to becoming too mechanical and analytical. Aaron Baddeley, for example, is a young Australian player who takes almost no time to putt. The idea of having a routine, aside from consistency, is to keep a flow and develop a rhythm for a round of golf.

Most players' routines on the LPGA and PGA Tours mirror who they are in terms of personality. For example, Lanny Wadkins, who is a PGA champion and a fine Senior Tour player, has an extremely brisk routine. He goes about 120 miles an hour at all times. He has one speed: *go*. Contrast this with Jack Nicklaus, a slow-moving turtle who strolls through life. That's his style. He's extremely methodical; to him, everything is a step-by-step process. That's who Jack is. A routine should mirror who you are. I think many amateur players are in danger of trying to change who they are. Don't make this mistake. Your routine should match the pace you bring to other aspects of your life; the difference is that your routine has to be organized in order to keep you organized in the process.

OVERVIEW OF THE PRESHOT ROUTINE

The first crucial step, from which everything else we do in the full swing (as well as the short game) follows, is the preshot routine. It is your full-swing foundation, because it sets the tone for your swing. A proper preshot routine aims and aligns you, postures your body, positions your golf ball, and allows you to be relaxed, so you can put the club in motion with a level of consistency not otherwise attainable. It also serves to reduce the potential for tension in your swing. A solid routine followed on *every shot* serves to quiet your mind, even when the pressure is on, and forces you to focus on the process leading up to, as opposed to the result of, the shot.

Because of its importance, I want you to take time to carefully develop or refine your preshot routine. Though I encourage you to watch touring professionals and analyze their preshot routines, I do *not* want you simply to copy their routines. They are only examples of successful routines. Your job is to develop one you're comfortable with and that works for *you*.

CREATING YOUR OWN PRESHOT ROUTINE

The following are what I have observed to be the seven characteristics common to comfortable and reasonable preshot routines. Again, these are *merely guidelines*, and are not meant to define precisely what works for you:

1. Players often start behind the golf ball and begin with a realistic rehearsal swing while looking down the line of the shot. They then turn and face the golf ball, clearly sighting the target line.

2. With their right hand on the club, they then walk to the golf ball in a wide semicircle, slightly behind and leading up to the ball, careful not to get past the ultimate ball position, placing the clubhead down behind the golf ball (possibly using an intermediate target in front of them, maybe 2 to 3 feet away, that they've picked out previously from behind the ball), and making sure that the club *faces* where they want to go.

3. Stepping in, they place their right foot parallel with the clubface, then place their left hand very gently on the club. Some players may want to build the grip and feed both hands in together. Note that steps 2 and 3 may occur simultaneously.

4. They position their left foot.

5. They drop their right foot back slightly to the right. The placement of the left and right foot will define ball position and will require training.

6. They take a couple of looks at the target while making some casual waggles with the golf club, coming to rest very quietly, with no tension in the arms (or anywhere else, for that matter), and finally . . .

7. They put the club in motion with a trigger (say, with the slight cock of the head à la Jack Nicklaus, or a slight kick of the right knee à la Gary Player, or slight swivel of the hips à la Arnold Palmer—whatever their personal trigger is that puts the club in motion). I recommend that you never remain at rest very long and that you have a definite trigger to jump-start the motion consistently.

The most important thing you are trying to accomplish is to create a preshot routine that allows you to put your golf machine in motion the same way every time—and then stick to it! Spend a lot of time developing your preshot routine, and then utilize that routine regularly. Remember the story about Nick Faldo and David Leadbetter in Spoke 2, The Mind. Even the greatest players in the world devote a great deal of time and attention to getting their routine down perfectly. They understand that it's crucial to their success.

MOVING FROM THE PRESHOT ROUTINE INTO THE LAUNCHING PAD

There are three critical junctures where the preshot routine and the launching pad strengthen each other. These key junctures should be thought through and practiced as you develop both your preshot routine and your launching pad. They are:

1. **When Making the Rehearsal Swing**

   Make it the real deal. When you're standing behind the golf ball making that rehearsal swing, it should be a real adaptation in terms of length and pace, ability to contact a little grass at the apex point (the bottom of your motion), holding your finish, and observing your balance.

2. **When Visualizing the Shot**

   Go to the movies. When you take that last look down the target line before you take that long walk in a wide circle as you approach the ball itself, it's a crucial moment in which you need to visualize (and I mean really *see*) what you're about to do. I'm talking about a real picture—what Jack Nicklaus called "going to the movies," because he actually saw himself making the swing. I sincerely believe that part of why Jack is the greatest player of all time is that he had the clearest mental pictures of all time.

3. **When Checking the Distance and Spacing from the Ball**

   Step out, step in. This is the moment when you first place your right hand (or in some cases both hands), reach for the ball with the golf club, and step in with your right foot simultaneously (as discussed previously). It's your first opportunity to determine your spacing from the golf ball. At this point say to yourself, *Am I too close or too far?* If you're too close or too far, step out and step in again. You'll often see Tour players doing just that: stepping in, stepping out, and again trying to get a feel for their distance from the ball, making sure it's just right. Spacing to the golf ball accurately is critical because it's going to set up and affect a lot of things—most important, the shape of your swing. If you're too far away, you'll swing too flat. Too close, you'll likely swing too upright and outside the proper path in a disconnected manner. Setting it just right sets up the golf club for a better, if not perfect, plane in your backswing. One way to learn to get it just right is to practice standing way too close. Bring the club behind the ball and step in with your right foot, to get a feel for that. Then do the same thing standing much too far away. Start with these overdoses and then tweak and refine them until you get a feel for the correct distance.

THE LAUNCHING PAD: THE FIRST BOOKEND

Sound fundamentals must be solidly in place throughout the golf swing. In my view, the most critical fundamentals to grasp are those that make up the launching pad.

While the launching pad, or setup, is static, the swing is dynamic—it's the motion. But the truth is, if the launching pad is not fundamentally sound, a compensating adjustment in the swing will be required, and a countless number of swing flaws can result. That's why we spend tons of time on the launching pad—it has a tremendous impact on the swing, and when properly set it yields dramatic results.

SYMMETRY IN THE SETUP

As in many areas of the game, symmetry is crucial in the launching pad. When you set up the launching pad correctly, you should be able to draw an imaginary line from the middle of the top of your head, directly through your body, that bisects your legs (stance) at an equal distance from each heel, *with one exception*: Your spine angle may feel slightly tilted to the right, and you feel a little more weight on the right side of your body than the left. Here's why: God

Having a balanced and neutral launching pad is crucial. The factors to strive for here are: (1) feeling the weight in the middle of your feet—heel to toe—as well as from the insteps to the outsides of the feet, (2) having your head slightly behind the ball, and (3) having your arms relaxed and hanging from the shoulder joints. From this position, you're ready to load up your backswing. If you don't feel balanced in your launching pad, *do not* put the club in motion!

gave you two arms of the same length, and when you put your hands on the golf club in a traditional grip, you place your right hand slightly below the left. Because your arms are the same length and the right hand is lower than the left, this causes your right shoulder to be lower than the left. That's the only thing that will interrupt the otherwise total symmetry.

THE FULL-SWING LAUNCHING PAD:
PROPER SETUP CONDITIONS

The seven basic tenets of the launching pad consist of grip, alignment, posture and spacing, weight distribution, ball position, stance and foot position, and tension levels.

1. **Grip**

   I'm a big believer in using a relatively strong grip. This means placing the club a little more in your left fingers with the heel pad on the top of the club (the pad below the pinkie, as opposed to the muscle pad, which is located under the left thumb), so that you should see at least two, *possibly* three, knuckles of your left hand. There should also be a V formed by your thumb and forefinger pointing toward your right shoulder. We call that putting the left hand in a relatively strong position. Your right hand will be based somewhat more in the fingertips due to being in a more neutral condition than the left. Your palm should be more facing the right side or back side of the grip. The thumb of your left hand should fit beautifully into the lifeline of your right hand—between the heel pad and the muscle pad. God made your right-hand lifeline so you could put the left-hand grip right in there perfectly and play beautiful golf. This right-hand position is known as a relatively neutral condition.

   Do not skimp on the process of learning your grip! If you do, you'll find yourself forever making compensations in your golf swing that sabotage any possibility of consistent trajectory, ball flight, or contact quality. Your grip is like the steering wheel of your car. Without a good one, you'll have real problems.

I strongly recommend having the left hand in a slightly strong position on the club and the right hand very neutral. I personally do not buy into the light grip pressure adage, but instead prefer medium grip pressure for most of my students (although some of my more advanced players have done quite well with a borderline firm pressure).

THE THREE TYPES OF GRIP

There are three types of grip. Keep in mind that none of these is wrong—they are all *preferences*, not *principles*. However, it's vital that your preference leads to good performance. On that note, a discussion of the three types of grip is in order, which will help you decide which works best for you.

- **The Vardon Grip (aka the Overlapping Grip).** The vast majority of people in my profession teach (and their students play) using the Vardon grip, in which the pinkie of the right hand overlaps the crease between the pointer finger and the middle finger of the left hand.

  Let's talk for a moment about the origin of this grip. Harry Vardon was a hooker—of his golf ball, that is. He had unusually large hands. He came up with the Vardon grip because he wanted to take a portion of his right hand off the golf club, since he felt it led him to release the golf club too early and hook his ball. He wanted to prevent that. And you know what? Not many of you out there who are playing average rounds of golf are hookers of the golf ball. So *why* would you want to use a grip that's designed to prevent the club from releasing? You *want* the club to release. Unless you hook the ball and have huge hands (which eliminates all but a very tiny percentage of you), I'd strongly advise against this grip, because it's probably sabotaging your technique.

- **The Interlocking Grip** involves the joining of your two hands in another way, placing the pinkie between the pointer finger and the middle finger of the left hand and kind of hooking it in between there and joining them together. Jack Nicklaus made this grip his own throughout his entire career. As an instructor, my *preference* is to teach this grip to men with medium to large-sized hands or individuals who have strong, relatively athletic hands.

- **The 10-Finger Grip (aka the Baseball Grip).** Place your hands side by side on the club. You're not changing the positions of the hands, but changing their condition in that they are not linked together; rather, they are placed side by side. As an instructor my *preference* is to teach this grip to juniors, women, and men with smaller or medium-sized hands, or any individuals with physically weak hands.

Whichever grip you decide to use, the ability to put your hands on the golf club in a position that's fundamentally sound is essential. By the way, there is an excellent teaching aid called the form grip that can help you get to know the feel of a proper grip (see Appendix C, Tom's Top 25).

In the Vardon, or Overlapping Grip, the pinky of the right hand rests in between the pointer and middle fingers of the left.

The Interlocking Grip is similar to the Vardon, except the pinky of the right hand bisects the same two fingers of the left hand.

The 10-finger or Baseball Grip is the one I strongly encourage for the vast majority of women as well as men with medium or small hands. In this grip, the hands are placed in close proximity to each other but they do not join or overlap in any manner.

2. Alignment

So that they can build a sound launching pad, a large percentage of the PGA and LPGA Tour players place something on the ground when they practice, be it a golf club, an umbrella, or even a 2 × 4. Vijay Singh, for example, always has something on the ground when practicing. Good players, knowing that their body line––target line relationship is a vital component to putting the club on plane in each and every swing, realize that it is very easy to fall out of alignment one way or another. These tools help them get back on track. If you're not practicing with an alignment aid, you should be. You should also be using a second item, which allows you to train yourself in both proper alignment and ball position: the T-Tech. The T-Tech is a brilliant yet simple teaching aid that allows you to visually define both your alignment and ball position as they relate to the target line.

You will rarely see tour players *not* using an aid while practicing to help them define and maintain their alignment and ball position. Great players know the critical importance of proper setup fundamentals and that proper alignment and ball position are crucial to success. Do yourself a huge favor—use setup aids.

When I recommend these devices, people often say to me, "But Tom, I'm not going to have the boards or other aids available to me on the golf course, so why should I use them when I practice?" If you use them during practice—and it's imperative, really, that you do—you are developing an *optical* sense, a little chip in your brain that gets programmed to sense a *relationship* to the target line and ball position. Every ball you hit during practice without them is a waste of time.

3. Posture and Spacing

It's been my experience that the better golfers posture themselves to the golf ball within 3 inches of their natural height—someone who is 5 foot 10, for instance, wouldn't stoop to a posture below 5 foot 7. This is simply an observation I have made. How can you get too short in your posture? If you move too far away from the golf ball, bend too much from the waist, overflex your knees, make your stance too wide, or carry your hands too low in address position. Any one of these would affect your posture. I always advise students to stand in a relatively tall, athletic-ready position. I've observed during more than 20 years of teaching that most people get too far from the ball. I estimate that fewer than 5 percent stand too close. My recommendation is that you should feel borderline too close versus too far from the ball. A corollary of posture is the position of the knees. Knees should be slightly flexed, but no more so than when you're standing and talking to someone in a normal conversation. I often see knees flexed too deeply; this means the weight is no longer centered in the feet, causing the player to get out of balance. In addition, overflexing the

DOES YOUR DISTANCE NEED A REALITY CHECK?

Some years ago at the Buick Classic, I ran into a buddy of mine, Ken Venturi, who's a great guy and a U.S. Open champion. John Cook, who is also a wonderful PGA Tour player, and who throughout his career relied on Ken to help him with his game, was there as well. They were headed over to the range so Ken could take a look at John's swing, as he was having trouble with his ball striking, and they allowed me to tag along. The first thing Kenny observed was that John was too far from the ball and asked him to move a little closer. John shuffled in a bit to get into a closer and taller position. Before he could even take the club away on the first attempt, Ken asked him to move in a little closer. John looked at him as if to say, *I just did*, but Ken insisted he move in a little more, so he did. Let me note right here that often players' *perceptions* of how close they are to the ball and how close they *actually* are can be totally different. Anyway, John edged closer and then hit one; it was a little better than what he'd been hitting before. Ken asked him to move even closer. Immediately John replied, "Kenny, if I get any closer to the ball it's going to be behind me." Ignoring his objection, Ken encouraged him to move in closer again. John did, although at that point, he felt like he was standing on top of the ball. To Kenny and I, who were objective observers, it didn't appear that way. The total change John made that afternoon was maybe an inch, but to John it felt dramatic. Bottom line, however, was that after 20 or 30 minutes had transpired and John was the distance from the ball Ken wanted him to be, John's quality of contact had changed dramatically and he was much happier with his results.

Anyone can have this problem. Our perception and reality often don't match. That's why we all need periodic coaching. However, the real moral of the story is this: There's often a fine line between playing wonderful golf and playing really sloppy golf. Small adjustments can sometimes work wonders.

knees kills the pivoting action of the hips. Again, slightly flexed is best, in a neutral position (not pinched in or out). Bend slightly forward from the waist. In fact, I'd rather see you reach the golf ball because you created a spine tilt toward the ball in your pelvic region than by overflexing your knees again. Overflexing kills the pivoting action of the hips.

Regarding the proper shoulder and arm position, once you assume your posture—that is, with a slight knee flex, and tilting your spine forward through your pelvic region—wherever your arms would normally hang vertically downward at that moment is where they should be placed. They should hang very naturally and form a V in front of your body. I don't like the arms to be manipulated, meaning I don't want you to hold them out away from your body or pinched in toward it.

I also don't want any tension in your arms, shoulders, neck, or upper chest region. I do want your head aligned with your spine, which will keep your spine from rounding and will keep it relatively straight. It will also promote a wonderfully tall athletic posture that allows your arms to swing in front of your body with plenty of freedom.

4. **Weight Distribution**
Weight distribution should be almost 50–50, with maybe slightly more weight on the right than the left. You should also feel as if your weight is equally distributed from heel to toe.

5. **Ball Position**
Correct ball position is based on the length and loft of the club you are about to use. If you point with your index finger to your sternum, that's the center of your body. That's the point where wedges should be placed. Your left breast is where the 5-iron would be placed, and your left armpit is the driver position. Notice that as the club gets longer,

BALL POSITION

Imagine setting up a 5-iron under your left breast and then taking that 5-iron and moving it dramatically back in your stance, maybe even outside your right foot. The clubface will appear slightly open. So if your ball is placed even a little too far back in your stance, the clubface is not going to be consistent with a normal swinging motion. It will be open at impact, and your weight distribution on your right foot will be too late, causing your shot to go right or be fat. Conversely, if you take the same 5-iron and place it outside your left foot, you'll immediately notice that the club appears to be closed and your weight is dramatically forward in your stance. Your angle of attack will be too steep and the club will shut down too soon, causing you to pull the ball or hit it thin. That's a dramatic illustration. Please understand that a golf ball struck at 200 yards in distance with 1 degree of open clubface will go approximately 33 yards offline. Therefore, ball position is vital to direction as well as quality of contact. Correct ball position is unquestionably a fundamental *principle*, not a *preference*.

wedge through driver, the ball position moves gradually forward. If you put the pointer finger of your right hand on your sternum and the pointer finger of your left hand on your armpit, you'll note that it's not a great distance—maybe 6 inches, depending on your body size. You've got to fit 13 clubs (excluding, of course, the putter) incrementally within that space. The changes are very slight, and yet good ball position is absolutely essential—it's a *principle*, not a *preference*, of contact quality and direction control.

6. **Stance and Foot Position**
   - **Stance.** This has a lot to do with people's athleticism, flexibility, and range of motion, but as a general rule I'd like the insteps of your feet to be set *shoulder-width* apart.

     Here's a simple stance drill (remember, I like simple): When you finish your golf swing, your right knee should be able to post up and physically touch your left knee. If you can do this, it's a good indicator that you can pivot your hips and create some centrifugal force with your pelvic region, allowing you to transfer weight from your right side to your left side during the downswing and deliver force to the golf ball (meaning *compress* it). Once you get into the longer clubs, if you want to alter this a *touch*, that's fine with me, but I advise against getting too far away from this parameter.

   - **Foot Position.** Your feet should be slightly fanned out, because this allows your hips to turn with more freedom. I'd like you, right now, to pigeon-toe your feet in—really, really pigeon-toe them in—and then try to turn your hips and fan your feet out 2 to 3 degrees in each direction. You'll see there's obviously a difference in your ability to rotate your hips. Having freedom in your hips is a good thing.

     If you tend to over-rotate your right hip in your backswing, you might want to square that foot a little more. If you're having trouble getting through the ball on your left side, you might want to flare the left foot out a little more, because that's going to have a lot to do with your ability to pivot. Use some trial and error and fool around with this a little bit.

7. **Tension Levels**

   Ahh, tension . . . my favorite topic in the launching pad. I'll address it very simply: There should be *none*. Remember, there's a reason we call it a golf "swing." I feel the arms and

THE IMPORTANCE OF BALANCE IN THE FULL SWING

Balance is extremely overlooked in golf—in fact, it's almost ignored. However, with the hitting surface—the clubface—being as small as it is (compare it with, say, tennis), and with the amount of speed created in a golf swing, balance becomes a crucial factor in your ability to make center-face contact. To evaluate your balance, make some complete swings at normal speeds with your eyes closed. If you are in perfect balance at the completion of each motion, that's terrific; stick with it. If not, you may want to work on the tempo, meaning the pace, of your golf swing. Pace and balance are related.

Good balance often begins with proper footwork. Try to imagine a dancer with bad footwork—not a pretty picture, is it? When you reach both the top of your swing and then impact, you want to be standing solidly on both feet. This enables you to load and store energy with maximum efficiency, as well as deliver a solid blow to the ball. Only after impact do you begin to leave your right foot as a result of your hips pivoting through impact and into the follow-through.

body should be in the most relaxed condition possible at address to assure freedom and repeatability of motion. Be aware that physical tension begins in your *mind*. In your launching pad, you should feel relaxed, tension-free, and ready to put your golf machine in motion. If there's *any* hint of tension in your launching pad, step away and start again.

Once you feel that you have developed a sound and repeatable preshot routine that leads to a pure launching pad, the next thing you want to do is begin your golf motion. So, naturally, I will fast-forward from here to the finish condition.

THE SECOND BOOKEND: A BALANCED FINISH CONDITION

The finish condition is an invaluable tool in helping you develop a sound golf motion. If that position is proper, you can hang there for quite a while. You're relaxed, balanced, observant. If your finish condition has flaws, it tells the story of your motion, which provides wonderful clues as to what's going on in your swing.

So let's talk about the conditions of the finish. They should consist of the following:

1. **Proper Footwork.**

   Left foot flat, right foot vertical on toe. This shows me a complete transfer of weight. If I see *creases* in your right shoe's toe area, then your right foot is probably supporting too much weight.

2. **A Straight Left Leg.**

   This means straight but not locked, and with your belt buckle directly over your left foot, knees together, right knee behind and touching your left knee. Your knees and thighs should be close enough together that it is difficult to slide a piece of paper between them. This is all a result of freely pivoting hips.

3. **Levelness.**

   The following should be level (relative to the tilt of your spine at address):
   • The shoulders.
   • The hip/pelvic region.
   • The head, with your eyes level and looking at the horizon.

4. **A Vertical Spinal Column.**

   This should be self-explanatory, but let's just say your spine should be vertically in line with your left leg. You will then be fully "posted up" (released).

5. **A Feeling of Balance.**

   This balance is dictated by your own personal "speed limit"—your ability to swing at a controlled pace. Proper balance reflects a pace that, given your physical attributes, allows you to maintain control in a properly sequenced motion.

Great athletic motions always appear to have wonderful balance. A proper golf motion is no different. I could have stayed in this position comfortably for a long time admiring the flight of the ball. There is a direct relationship between great balance and proper tempo—that is, a controlled pace.

Using a mirror, compare your finish condition to the illustration at the right. When working in front of a mirror, line yourself up as if to hit a shot into the mirror. First, carefully set up your launching pad. Once you are in the launching pad position, simulate impact. From this impact position, go immediately to the finish condition, without making a backswing. This drill (one of my favorites) is called a post-up drill, and it's designed to get you from impact to the fully released finish condition. It is an isolation drill. When you reach the finish, hold it, then check it thoroughly and make any needed tweaks. Using the previous discussion as a checklist, go over your finish condition one item at a time until you have checked and perfected each. By monitoring your finish condition visually and making the proper changes until it is correct, you will develop a sense for what a correct finish position feels like (and believe me, your brain is taking notes as you do this).

You want to get in front of that mirror and do this post-up drill hundreds, if not thousands, of times, on a regular basis, to train your body to get into a static impact condition and move through your pivoting action, your arms' reactions, your body rotation, your shoulders turning through the impact area into completion, and posting up into your left side until you reach a balanced vertical level condition. You want to take mental notes on what happened and how your body got from point A to point B. When you practice this, your body becomes more instinctual about reaching a balanced finish condition from a proper launching pad. As you do this drill, using the mirror and illustrations, *pay careful attention to detail*, meticulously checking and perfecting your launching pad and your finish condition. And guess what? You can't get to a good finish condition from a bad swing motion . . . it doesn't work that way. Soon that in-between part will start to fall naturally into place.

Another way to learn the proper finish condition is to have someone videotape your swing. When you replay the film, stop on your finish condition to study and compare it with the illustration in this book. Then work on tweaking your finish condition until it is perfect.

Another thing you can do, in addition to using a mirror and/or video, is to clip out photos from your favorite golf magazine of two or three players whom you think have beautiful finish conditions. If I were going to pick out two, I'd choose Stuart Appleby and Annika Sorenstam, both wonderful golfers. I would tape up a picture of each on my full-length mirror at home and then, with a club (or without one, simply putting my hands in front of me), do some post-up drills. I'd go to the finish condition, as described above, and compare myself in the mirror with what Stuart and Annika look like. Then I'd make tweaks and refinements to get my finish into a similar condition. Of course, as you do this, your finish won't be identical to that of the players you choose because your body type won't be identical to theirs. The important thing is that as you emulate these players, you train your body where you want it to go, and in the process learn what muscle groups you need to utilize, and in what sequence, to accomplish this. It's a very proactive way to train your body and mind.

COMMON FINISH FAULTS, AND HOW TO CURE THEM

Below, you'll find what I consider the most common finish faults. Understand that the best way to correct a motor skill flaw is to replace it with something else. If A is incorrect, you want to give it B. You must give the body something to replace the flaw with.

Symptom: Right-foot flop. This is when your right foot is not vertical; instead, your right heel is flopped over closer to the target line than your toes.

Cure: A right-foot flop means your body is out of balance, or not in sequence, and your pivot isn't very level. It also may be a sign of what I call *spin-out*, meaning a sequence or pace of the lower body that is not proportional to the unwinding of your upper body in the overall swing motion.

Improper footwork tells many tales. For example, it frequently indicates poor balance and/or bad sequence of motion. Bad footwork = Big problems.

I want you to slow things down a bit and make some slow-motion rehearsals by placing your hands on your hips and simply pivoting your lower body (hips, legs, and feet) so you can end up in the proper condition described above—left foot flat, right foot pointing vertically, knees touching. What sequence occurred and at what speed? You need to learn to pivot and use your feet correctly beginning in slow motion and working up to a faster pace, so you can learn to coordinate it properly first and then *gradually* add speed to the sequence. After you've done that for a while, grab a golf club and make some practice motions, again coordinating the swinging of your arm with the pivoting of your legs and feet, and then later on introduce live action using a golf ball. Doing it full speed before you have the coordination down is like turning the CD player up to high volume, then switching it on. You'd blow the speakers, not to mention your eardrums. Practicing this way is akin to turning on the CD player and adjusting the volume gradually until it's just right.

Symptom: Finishing with your right shoulder higher than your left.

Cure: Usually this means the club shaft has come from an outside path that is steep and not balanced. Again, here is a way that the finish is going to train and help the in-between. By learning what it feels like to have a level post-up spine condition—one in which you're supported by a level spine—your body learns how to get into a more level, vertical finish that's very balanced and posted up (supported) over your left leg. You're also training yourself to route the golf club differently—in more of an on-plane condition—in the downswing. In other words, you're correcting, from the finish backward, the over-the-top imbalance of your swing. Your golf club won't be able to come from over the top if the desired result is a vertical, level, balanced finish. You have to come from a different direction to achieve that finish condition, so you're forcing your golf swing to perform properly.

If the right shoulder finishes higher than the left, the swing was likely an "over the top chop." Quieting the upper body and jumpstarting the lower body should help solve this problem.

Symptom: Finishing with your upper torso behind your lower body; reverse C—inverted spine.

This is the ol' "hang on snoopy." It creates a need to overwork the hands and arms. It really stresses the timing, not to mention the back. I always strongly encourage my students to finish in a more level condition.

Many difficulties in golf can be traced to a reverse pivot. It is just not possible to deliver a solid, powerful blow to a golf ball (or to throw a baseball—just picture stepping back to toss a ball). Good footwork will permit the transfer of weight to the right side.

As your footwork goes, so goes your legwork, a key piece of the weight transportation vehicle. Finishing with the right leg touching (or almost touching) the left leg is critical.

Cure: First of all, this causes severe back problems. It also contributes to right shots, fat shots, and hand flips. In addition, it is *not* a balanced condition. How many more reasons do you need *not* to do this?

By working to a vertical level posted-up condition, you're eliminating this potential for injury and achieving a better distribution of weight in your through-motion. Imagine throwing a baseball from a short to first with your spine moving in the opposite direction your arm is traveling. That makes no sense at all. First, there would be no velocity on the throw, and it would be very difficult to throw the ball in the intended direction. So why would you do that in golf? Anytime you want to direct something on a line with any velocity, your spine has to follow and move in conjunction (directionally) with the swinging or throwing motion of your arms.

Symptom: Staying on your back foot.

Cure: This is a result of improper weight displacement during the downswing. It causes an exaggerated in-to-out swing path, making your chances of having a square clubface at impact rather slim. To cure this, have your coach grip your right hand, as if to shake your hand, and then pull you through to a balanced, complete finish to give you a feel for proper weight displacement and a proper finish condition.

Symptom: Finishing with a large gap between your knees; your right knee points right.

Cure: My nickname for this is the *sideways shuffle*. This is a warning sign that your hips did not rotate correctly or completely, which effectively deprives the swing of a major power source.

Symptom: Finishing with your head still down.

Cure: The edict that you should keep your head down throughout the swing is, I believe, one of the two greatest myths in golf instruction (the other one is the "rule" of keeping your left arm straight). If you take a moment to think about it, you'll realize this advice doesn't make sense. Beginning from a static position, you are attempting to generate a force great enough to move the club at 90 miles an hour or more. There's no chance you can do that while keeping your head still or down. The average adult head weighs 10 to 15 pounds and, being attached to the body, as it generally is, the laws of physics simply won't permit it to remain stationary.

The head should stay only *relatively* still, not *totally* still, until the moment of impact; then it should rotate in sequence with the body and arms through completion of the swing. This means remaining level with the horizon and posting up over your left side. If instead your head hangs back and to the right, this will interfere with the pivoting of your body and inhibit the full distribution of your weight onto your left side.

As I previously mentioned, one of my favorite golf swings is Annika Sorenstam's. She is one of the world's straightest, most consistent and solid ball strikers. Her tournament record serves as adequate proof of this. Watch her on television, paying attention as her club approaches the ball. Her head is actually turning left, toward the target. Most people think the head should be looking down at the ball, even after contact. Sorenstam is proof to the contrary. When she reaches her finish condition, every part of her—eyes, head, shoulders, waist, and knees—is level, and her spine is posted up over her left leg. These perfect finish positions would be physically impossible if she kept her head down.

I think people like Annika are ahead of their time. By changing the way we understand the role of the eyes and head as a factor in golf club release, they will change the way golf is taught in the future.

You'll notice players vary as to when they release their head and how long they keep it stationary. Let's use Tiger Woods as an example here. How long does it take for Tiger to go from impact to finish? A fraction of a second. At impact, his head appears to be looking at the golf ball or, as an amateur might say, looking down. But at the finish he's looking out at the target, trying to find his ball in flight and see what the result of his shot was. There was very little opposition of his swinging motion from his head. It was not an anchor; he did not stay there forever. Obviously, then, he had to release it just after impact.

CONCLUSION

By developing a sound and consistent preshot routine that leads to a proper launching pad, you are setting the stage for a sound golf motion. When one of the professional tours stops in your area, I strongly encourage you to attend the event. While there, spend a good deal of time at the range, focusing on each player's launching pad. From player to player you'll notice a remarkable consistency in posture, ball position, and so on. Skip over the ball striking (for now) and observe these pros' finish condition. It is quite beautiful—free, balanced, and level.

It is my strong belief, borne out by years of experience with hundreds of students, that if you meticulously develop a sound launching pad and finish condition, you will create more lasting and positive changes to your dynamic swing much faster and much more easily than you could if you dissected each segment of the swing and tried to develop it separately. Using the Bookends trains your body and mind and reduces the learning curve greatly.

We'll turn next to the in-between: backswing, crossroads, downswing, and follow-through. You should move on to this *only* after your Bookends are both fundamentally sound and decidedly consistent. When you're ready, I'll be waiting to guide you through these final technique areas of the full swing.

14

HOUSTON, WE HAVE IGNITION
PERFECTING THE BACKSWING, CROSSROADS, DOWNSWING, AND FOLLOW-THROUGH

If the ball feels light, you're doing something right.

—CHARLES SORRELL

Now that we've covered the Bookends and you've developed a wonderfully solid framework, it's time to take a look at the in-between—the backswing, crossroads, downswing, and follow-through. This chapter completes the fundamentals of a mechanically sound golf swing.

THE BACKSWING

In the following pages we will discuss the backswing in great detail. I want to make it clear up front, however, that people spend way too much time worrying about their backswing. Whenever I walk along the practice tee, I see so many golfers tied up in knots trying to analyze the different parts of their backswing. They're muttering, "Are my shoulders turned back enough?" "Is my club on plane?" "Is my clubface square?" and the like. Contrary to popular belief, you don't need a technically perfect backswing to play good golf. Just look at the success of some of the world's greatest all-time professionals, such as Fred Couples, Raymond Floyd, Nancy Lopez, and Jim Furyk. From a technical standpoint, these professionals have very imperfect backswings, but what they do have is an uncanny ability to deliver the club precisely to impact. They know what perfect impact looks like, feels like, and sounds like, and even with swings some would describe as downright ugly they manage to strike the ball well on a consistent basis. You should learn from this, too.

When students come to me fretting over a problem with their backswing, I tell them, "Relax. We're okay." As long as you can address the ball in a decent athletic position and develop a sound launching pad, *you have some leeway in your backswing motion*. I like to teach people how to use the swing they've got to deliver the club to the ball online and powerfully. Understand that yes, we will always be striving to simplify your backswing, but we will not get stuck there. Of course, sometimes students have major backswing problems and really need help. But in many cases the backswings people have are not as far off as they believe. After working with an impact drill (see page 178), they often forget they came to me with a backswing problem.

BACKSWING TECHNIQUE

The backswing is a great source of power. It's what allows you to load your club, much like cocking the hammer back on a .45-caliber gun, causing the ball to explode with great force. Top professionals and world-class amateurs hit shots with admirable length, trajectory, and accuracy because they make a backswing that is athletic, repeatable, and powerful.

There should be a balance in any backswing between the distribution of weight and the rotational aspect of the upper body. When I observe what are, in my opinion, great backswings on the PGA and LPGA Tours, I notice a balance between how much those players displace their weight from the launching pad condition into the right side as well as how much they rotate their various body parts. The distribution of weight to the right and the coiling of the upper body against a resistant lower body (a grounded base) is what creates the power. While sometimes the radius of the arm swing, the hinging and cocking of the wrists, and the on-plane condition of the club shaft are factors, for now we're just talking about inner mass movement. When the body is properly loaded and released, it creates a powerful force.

THE KEYS TO A SOLID BACKSWING
Proper Initiation

Properly initiating the backswing is key. The most effective way to consistently derive power is to initiate the swing with your back muscles. While some will argue for targeting the shoulders, I strongly encourage you to initiate and control your backswing with the biggest and strongest muscle group in your body—your back muscles. (It is called a *back*swing, after all.) As will become obvious to you as you work on this, the back-muscle-based approach makes it easy for you to coil your body behind the ball, and thus helps you swing the club on the proper plane consistently.

While the back muscles play a very strong role, I'd be remiss—or rather, dead wrong—if I didn't also say that the turning mechanism of the upper body and the momentum of the arms swinging to the right in the backswing aid this shifting of weight. The arm swing, ultimately blended with the back muscles turning the torso, loads the gun, if you will. In the long term I would like the marriage of these two components to be a perfect and equal blend of responsibility.

While *in general* I favor the big-muscle theory, because *most* people who come to me need to focus on their inner mass (upper torso and shoulders), there are others (yours truly included) who have more success focusing on their arm swing and allowing their inner mass movement to tag along (see Forefront Drill in the "Downswing and Follow-through Drills" section of this chapter). Whichever one you focus on is fine—as long as you get there. Different folks need different buttons pushed at times. Do a little trial and error to find out which one allows you to achieve a powerfully loaded backswing position.

Blending of the Three Directions—Back, In, and Up

The club's initial directional movement is backward, followed by an inward, then an upward, direction—in fact, a perfect blending of the three. As with other mechanics of the backswing, however, getting hung up on these directions will do you in. Suffice it to say that these motions will follow naturally from a solid launching pad and a fundamentally sound loading.

Freely Swinging Arms

You can't do a wonderful job of moving your big muscles and achieve the displacement of weight and turning of your shoulders to the right if there is too much tension in your arm swing or your arms aren't swinging freely. On the other hand, while this big-muscle-based (meaning inner-mass-based) movement is happening—if your arms are swinging with a tremendous amount of freedom—it can be a wonderful and powerful thing. (Does Davis Love III come to mind here, or what?) Crucial to the golf swing is speed. If you have tension in your shoulders, inner mass, arms, hands, or elsewhere, you will reduce the speed of your swing *dramatically*. Controlling your backswing with your back is the correct approach because it is an excellent tension reducer, thus allowing those arms to swing freely.

Turning Behind the Ball

Now that you've found the best way for you to properly initiate your backswing, the next step is to coil behind the golf ball—a powerful twist of your trunk. To coil something, you need to turn or wind up against something else that is stable. To use archery as an analogy, it is the tension created by pulling the bowstring against the stationary bow itself that ultimately propels the arrow. In the golf swing this tension is created by winding the upper body against a stable lower body. As we discussed in the setup, your knees are nicely, but not overly, flexed. This flex, especially in your right knee, is maintained throughout the backswing. Your hip movement is rotational. Your pelvic region rotates half as much as whatever your shoulders do. With a 90-degree shoulder turn, you should have about a 45-degree hip turn. (This is a generic example, of course, since some people might be in the 95–47 or even 85–35 range, depending on their flexibility.) A slide is when your hips move laterally instead of rotationally. This seriously impedes the winding action, because it prevents you from turning against a stable base, putting you in a very weak position.

Weight Distribution

Next, let's deal with the upper body. I strongly encourage my students to create as much distance or as large an angle as they can between their left shoulder and left hip. This is done by allowing the head to move freely to the right and as far as possible to the outside edge of the right foot, but not beyond (in other words, pushing it to the outer edge of your body lines, yet staying within those confines). Once you have achieved this position, you will find you have displaced your weight well behind the ball. This, in concert with a tightly coiled upper body against a stable lower body, will put you in a powerful position.

JUMP-STARTING THE TORSO WITH FREE-SWINGING ARMS

If your arms are truly relaxed and allowed to swing freely, not only might they move as a result of the torso turn, but the arm swing might be a jump start for the torso. The exception here is those players who have trouble moving their inner mass. If that's you, you might want to use the arm swing as a jump start. It all depends on your individual needs.

I love this teaching aid, called a right angle. The right arm structures the left, not vice versa.

Maintaining the Radius of Your Arm Swing

Radius is a speed source for you. The key here is to achieve and maintain good extension, rather than trying not to bend your left arm, because if you stand there and think about wanting to keep your left arm straight, you will only create tension. You should allow your arm to swing wide and with some freedom, while focusing on and feeling the bend in your right arm that allows it to support and structure your left arm at the top of your backswing. So long as you are careful not to bend your right arm by more than 90 degrees, the left arm will be in a relatively extended condition and will not flex beyond an acceptable amount; you will thus maintain excellent width/extension in your swing. In other words, *your right arm should structure your left in the backswing.* (Note: You want to mirror this on your forward swing as well, because your left elbow joint and right arm will determine and the radius of your swing, which will greatly enhance that swing's speed.)

Waist-High Shaft and Face

One key for me in the backswing is where shaft and clubface are at the swing's halfway point. When the club has been swung back to about waist level, the club shaft should be parallel to the target line and level with the ground. The clubhead should be somewhere between slightly facedown and having its toe straight up. Where exactly you are with the face depends on your body type and the type of ball shape you are trying to attain. If you're in the wrong position at the halfway point, you'll need to make unwanted compensations.

I find that many of my amateur students show me some positions and conditions here that I'm not particularly fond of. Things that I don't want to see include the clubface facing the ground at waist height, and the club past toe-up at waist height. Facedown is a shut position; if the toe is over-rotated past vertical, this suggests a fanning of the golf club and laying off of the shaft. Either issue requires resquaring the clubface at impact, which, as I've said all along, is not easy or recommended.

Staying on Plane

First of all, let's simplify the term *swing plane.* Look at yourself in the mirror, turning so that your backswing is in a down-the-line position. I'd like to see your left arm bisect your right shoulder at the top of your backswing. It's a generic checkpoint to see if it's on plane or not.

If you're a tall, thin body type, I might allow you to see your left arm a little above your right shoulder at the top of the backswing. If you have a shorter and rounder body type, I might be okay with your left forearm just a fraction below your left shoulder at the top of the backswing. If you're more or less average in height and build, I'd like to see the left forearm bisect your right shoulder, indicating to me that the arm swing is on plane.

If you could take a couple of steps back and see yourself when you're on plane, just shy of the top of the backswing, before your left arm got into position, your shaft might have passed through identical positions.

Cocking/Hinging the Wrists

I'm a proponent of the big-muscle, free-arm-swing style, so cocking/hinging of the wrists isn't something I spend much time on. The wrist cock/hinge largely follows the body and arm movements and should be allowed to do so due to the lack of tension and the weight of the clubhead. Remember: I want to see *absolutely no tension*. (If you like to set the club early, obviously you will cock/hinge your wrists earlier in the backswing. For examples of this, watch Seve Ballesteros's and Johnny Miller's swings.) For a refresher on cocking versus hinging of the wrists, please go back to our discussion of this in Chapter 9, "Chipping."

This illustrates, from the "caddie" or chest view, what you want to accomplish: a fully turned shoulder rotation with the left shoulder appearing to be turned over the right thigh. About 80 percent of your body mass also should appear to be distributed over the right thigh—meaning about 80 percent of your body weight should be on the right side. Now you're loaded and ready to explode.

THE THREE BACKSWING TYPES

Let's talk about the three backswing types and which is best for you. Each type will create different ball flights, trajectories, and shapes.

1. **The One-Piece Takeaway** seems to be the backswing students are most commonly taught. The name refers to the requirement that you move your arms and hands together (in "one piece") as you initiate the swing. I strongly disagree with this approach. For most amateurs, this type of backswing causes severe tension in the arm swing joints (located in the rotator cuffs, the elbows, and the wrists). This tension will likely seep into your shoulders and hips—the rotational forces in your swing. When this happens, you've lost before you've even started. It often leads also to disconnection between arm swing and body rotation. There are times and ways for this type of takeaway to be used correctly, but please use caution here, folks, because it is often over-taught and undercoached.

2. **The Early Set** is probably the second most popular backswing. The term *early set* refers to the early angle created between the club shaft and the left forearm. This set is

caused by purposely hinging the right wrist and cocking the left one. Any intentional physical exertion leads to tension. In most cases, then, I ask you to use caution in applying this method, too. I often see overlift and a lack of body turn when this method has not been properly coached.

3. **The Lag Load.** The backswing method I like best is the lag load. In the early initiation of movement, the arms are free of tension, and the turning of your back muscles briefly precedes your arm swing. You should use very moderate grip pressure and be very relaxed. Initiate the backswing by slowly turning your lower *back* (yes, you read that correctly) away from the ball, and keeping your arms and hands passive. Your back muscles will cause your trunk to pivot, which will cause you to briefly leave your arms and clubhead behind— at address. Your hands and arms follow your back. If it's done properly, the last thing to move in this backswing is the clubhead. That's why it's called a *lag load*. Keep those arms supple, and rest assured that you will not lose control of the club as you do so.

While I generally prefer to see lag load backswings, this is based on preference, not principle. Experiment and see which backswing type works best for you, basing your choice on your body type and physical constraints.

Though there are three types of backswings, they fall into two categories: those with high tension levels (the one-piece takeaway and early set), and that with soft, supple tension levels (the lag load). I call players who employ those with high tension levels "hitters" and those with the soft supple swings "swingers." Examples of Tour professionals who are hitters include Greg Norman and Arnold Palmer. Swingers include Fred Couples, the late Sam Snead, Mickey Wright, and Al Geiberger. As you explore these backswings, keep this question in mind: As you age (which brings with it a decrease in flexibility and range of motion), which style do you think will work best for you? Here's a hint: Hitting (at least for distance) becomes more and more of an issue as you get older. A good swinger, on the other hand, can last a long time. Sam Snead was a perfect example of this.

KEEP A SOFT, NOT STIFF, LEFT ARM

One of the most widely taught and misunderstood concepts in golf is that of keeping a straight or stiff left arm. People feel this keeps their swing structured, but the truth is, adhering to this advice creates tension, which is the opposite of what you want to achieve in your swing. You want your swing to produce momentum and speed, yet tension inhibits speed. The left arm is one half of your arm swing, and it will, when compared with the right arm, be, of course, straighter. But ramrod straight is a mistake: You're sacrificing half the combined power of your arms. When you use a lag load swing, which initiates the swing using the back muscles, you allow your left arm to remain soft and slightly bent at the elbow from the backswing and into the first part of the downswing. A soft left arm also produces a more fully extended club, which gives the backswing greater power. Your left arm will straighten at impact, but this should happen naturally and not be forced. To achieve this lag load and soft left arm you must avoid the temptation to hit the ball hard. With a little practice, you'll get the hang of it and start seeing positive results. Though it may seem counterintuitive, becoming a swinger instead of a hitter will in fact give you *more* speed and power in your swing, not less.

How to Lose a Reverse Pivot

If you hit a lot of radically bad shots, there's a good possibility you have a reverse pivot problem. A reverse pivot is when you shift your weight toward the target during the backswing. As the club moves back, your head and club are supposed to be simultaneously rotating away from the target, while the hips rotate from left to right.

A common cause of the reverse pivot is the hands "lifting" the club back or swinging the club too vertically. Taking the club back with your hands puts you on dangerous ground to begin with, since this often encourages lifting, instead of swinging, the club back. When you lift the club, your right knee straightens while your left shoulder dips downward. This position is about as helpful as wearing a straitjacket.

Reverse Pivot Drill

To get rid of a reverse pivot, you need to find a steeply inclined sidehill lie to work with. (Not to get deep or anything, but I call this the "Hill of Wisdom.") Choose a spot where the ball is above your feet at knee level. If a reverse pivot is your problem, you'll find you're hitting the ground well behind the ball from this position. To make proper contact, try swinging around your body in a more circular motion. Keep your shoulders level by starting the swing with them, as opposed to your hands or arms. Let your arms follow your shoulders, not the other way around.

Try making 20 to 30 shots with a 5- or 6-iron from a sidehill lie, starting with smaller swings and building up gradually to full ones. The stance will become more comfortable to you, and you'll start to increase quality of contact. As you do, you'll see that most of your shots are now heading left. That's a good sign. Your shoulders will begin to feel more level as you hit more of these sidehill shots, and your swing will feel more level, as though the club is going around you rather than toward the sky. Once you have felt this radically different swing pattern, go back to the level practice area with the same swing motion in mind and hit more 5- or 6-iron shots. Don't panic if your shots start out low and to the left—that's what you want to happen at first. Eventually your body will try to drift back toward its old, ingrained bad habits, and your job will be to find a midpoint between the flat feeling of your sidehill swing and the vertical feeling you were used to before. This happy medium is known as being *on plane*. Keep doing this sidehill drill, and over time you'll replace your poor habits with correct ones.

Reverse Pivot: I always tell people simply don't oppose or resist the direction in which the club is swinging. In other words, if the club swings to your right (backswing), *follow it*. If it swings left (follow-through), *follow it*. It doesn't make any sense for your club to swing to the right and your body to the left.

To get an idea of what a marvelous arm swing looks like, check out Davis Love III's backswing. Surely his body type aids in this, with his long limbs, but nevertheless it is a thing of beauty. And let's not leave out Fred Couples, Ernie Els, or Vijay Singh. These guys will play forever.

BACKSWING DRILL: THE IMPACT BAG

Here's the drill I referred to earlier. It's terrific for teaching you to use your swing to deliver the club to impact on line and in a powerful, accurate manner. This drill should be done in front of a mirror. Use the mirror to inspect your technique only after you have swung. That way you can see the impact position *after having felt it first*. This drill should be done at half your normal speed to really develop that feel.

The drill has four steps:

1. Take a few practice swings into the impact bag. Don't make full swings; only take the club back to about waist level. This is just to get a feel for impact and assurance that it doesn't hurt. No speed, no aggression—simply feel contact with the bag.
2. Check your weight distribution and clubface condition at impact. Most students have a disproportionate amount of weight on their right foot at impact. Check to see if you are doing this. If so, correct the situation, then take a few more swings into the bag. At this point your weight should become spread more equally between your feet.

   Another problem to be aware of is an open clubface. Check yourself (or have your coach do it) to make sure your clubface is square and not too open at impact. What does it *feel* like to square the clubface?
3. Next, make some full swings into the bag. In all likelihood you will be amazed, because you will feel something new and strange to you: what it's like to be well balanced and deliver a square clubface at impact. Do this at half speed.
4. Finally, take several more swings, trying to get the toe to hit the bag first. This will feel awkward initially, as if the club is way too closed, but don't let that deter you. *Powerful and balanced* is what you want to begin feeling. This will occur with practice, as you begin to release the clubface naturally.

THE CROSSROADS

Bill Strausbaugh called the transition point when the backswing ends and the downswing begins the crossroads. This moment should be a very patient, quiet moment when the club is allowed to come to rest for a brief instant—not in a manipulated or predetermined stop in the swing, but like a pendulum when it stops traveling in one direction and begins to travel in another. All too often this is the moment when most players try to add a little something to their effort by racing out of their backswing, which destroys this very fragile sequence of positions leading to impact. It's important that you allow the golf club to settle

BACKSWING TROUBLESHOOTING GUIDE

The following are problems to watch out for in the backswing:

- **Tension** is the number one culprit in troubled backswings. This scourge inhibits the inner mass movement, and thus interferes with the creation of speed, which is crucial in the full swing. One of the things I ask students to do is pretend they're swinging the club like the cartoon character Gumby, the original "rubber band man," with unbelievable flexibility and range of motion. I'll ask them to make some swings where they feel there is zero tension in their wrist, elbow, and shoulder joints. I want them to swing the club around their body in kind of a "Gumby" manner, as if the clubhead is floppy. You can really feel the weight of the clubhead when you do this. That's not too far from the way Freddy Couples, Ernie Els, and Vijay Singh play golf. People who are swingers of the club, like these two men, really sense and feel the clubhead swinging around their body with very little tension in their extremities. If you do this—act a bit like Gumby—then put the ball on a slight tee and hit some shots, you'll probably hit some really nice ones and find you're not working very hard to attain a high degree of speed in your swing.

- **Clubface Problems.** First, understand what square, open, and closed look like on top of your backswing. Just understanding this often helps people get rid of some problems in this area. Sometimes I'll ask students to take the club to the top of their backswing, then I'll reach up, grab the shaft, hold it in place, and ask them to turn around to look at the face. Regardless of what face condition they're showing me, they usually cannot tell me whether it's open, square, or closed. They're guessing, and most often they guess wrong. So let's go over it.

    By *face*, I'm referring to the leading edge of the club, and by *toe*, I mean the end point of the clubhead farthest from the shaft. If the toe at the top of your backswing is pointing straight down, that would be open. If the face of your club is facing straight up at the sky, that would be closed. If the clubface is at a 45-degree angle at the top, that's considered square. To sum up: Toe-down is open; faceup toward the sky is closed; 45-degree angle is square. In front of a mirror, put your club into a backswing. Then tweak the face until it's at a 45-degree angle so you can feel what it's like when your club is in that condition. By saving this feel in your mental database, you can replicate it.

- **Club Shaft Plane Problems.** A good way to check to see if your shaft is on plane is to make a backswing halfway back where your arm is parallel to the ground. At that point the shaft should be cocked/hinged vertically upward, forming a 90-degree angle with your left forearm. The butt of your club should be pointing toward the target line extended. The target line is an imaginary line that goes through the ball in either direction indefinitely. If the butt of your club points toward the target line, your shaft is on plane. If the butt is pointed downward or inside the line, the shaft is too vertical. If the butt points above your target line away from you in the foreground, that means your shaft is under plane. You'll want to practice your backswing halfway back to get the butt of the club pointing directly at the target line on which the ball rests.

---

at the top and fall naturally out of your backswing. Let gravity take its course—at the rate of 32 feet per second squared, it's an adequate physical force on the club, and needs no additional push from you. Isaac Newton, as I mentioned earlier, was the first golf instructor, because he understood the constancy of gravity. Remember, this road to impact is a very *gradual* increase in speed, not a sudden one.

YOU CALL IT TIMING, I CALL IT SEQUENCING

The sequencing of the golf swing has a lot to do with what goes on as you (1) put the club in motion to start your swing, and (2) start down out of transition. Some people call it timing; I call it sequencing. Either way, it's the ability to get the arms and the body to dance

SEQUENCING PROBLEMS AND HOW TO CURE THEM

As far as sequencing is concerned, people at the club level come to me in one of two ways. They are either (1) a turner, then swinger; or (2) a swinger, then turner. The turners, then swingers generally have trouble with the club not catching up to their body, leaving the golf ball to the right and/or hitting thin shots. Swingers, then turners unwind their shoulders too early, which results in hitting pulls, pull slices, or pull hooks. What you want to do is to blend the two aspects—the swinging and the turning—together. For those who have either of these problems, I do different things.

For example, if someone comes to me who's an early turner (turner then swinger), I'll have him hit some shots flat footed and let the club swing past his body feeling that he is actively releasing the face. All of a sudden, he goes from being a slicer to a hooker of the golf ball (which is a great shape to move toward if your ball flights have been historically weak). Then we work to modify this and blend the two together to find a middle ground. After all, if you put together a hooker and a slicer, you get the ideal golfer: one who hits the ball straight.

If someone comes to me who's a swinger then a turner and hitting shots to the left, pulling shots, or pulling hook shots, first I'm going to get her to release her body a little sooner and get her arms a little bit behind her body in terms of the sequencing of the motion. I'll do some early pivot drills, or I'll place her hand (palm) on top of a golf club (when the club is standing vertically) that is aligned with right foot, then I'll swing her right arm back into the top of her backswing, back down to impact, and stop at impact, where her shoulders will be square but her hips and lower body should feel radically open. So I've got to clear her lower body sooner to get her arms in behind her body turn. The point is to get her to feel her body unwinding and her arms in a more passive state.

I saw Davis Love, Jr. show someone this drill, oh, about a million years ago and have never forgotten it. Place your left hand on top of a club that is vertical and opposite your right toe. Place your right hand in a setup position and swing it back and return to impact. The premise is to keep the left hand stable/mounted opposite the right so you cannot spin your shoulder and that you have to swing your right arm under your left. Two things to keep in mind here: the shoulders are square at impact (never spinning open) and the armswing is on plane. No over the top chop! This greatly helps your plane sequence.

with one another as the motion starts, as well as move together at a transition, both of which are critical junctures in the swing. The problem for someone who hits balls out to the right (aka thin), or can't square the clubface, is usually that the body is outracing the arm swing. Folks who hit hooks or pulls are often unwinding their shoulders or swinging their arms down too early or across the target line. And, in all cases, violent movement destroys proper sequencing.

THE DOWNSWING AND FOLLOW-THROUGH

With the completion of your backswing, you are now behind the ball with your weight loaded into your right side, and a coiled trunk. Now it's time to initiate the downswing. Those swiveling Elvis hips are ready for action, but please: Don't let Elvis out too early!

I often ask people, "What happens first: down or through?" Some people feel that the club falls first; others say it slots itself first, and after it's gotten a bit of a head start and moved down plane slightly, they can begin to unwind their body. However it is stated, the people who get it right imply that down happens first. After all, the ball is below you and the target is out in front of you. (Logical, no?) Even though we often refer to the second half of the swinging motion as the downswing, this area of movement, in fact, has two distinct directions—down and through. If we logically examine the motion, down precedes through.

When initiating the downswing, the problem for many people is that they unwind their shoulders before the club has had a chance to drop. If you're at the top of your backswing with your hands at the top, and you do nothing with your hands but simply begin to unwind your shoulders, you'll notice that the club seems to go out and off plane (or "over the top," as students often say). I call this unsavory condition the *over-the-top chop*. What you want to happen at the start of the backswing is to let the club fall *slightly*—a brief head start—and *then* allow your body to unwind, causing the clubface to square up. In fact, what I'd like to see ideally is these two actions blended together. That's when you'll hit shots solidly and squarely and right down the line. I call this process the *down and through*, because what you are doing is letting your arms fall down and then turning the body through, trying to blend those two things together in a smooth sequence. A player's ability to understand this *sequence of golf motion* is vital to improvement.

You should swing down and *then* through. After all, the ball comes before the target in terms of sequence. However, the impulse to hit the ball leads all too often to the "over the top chop." The 2 × 4 drill is handy for these cases—in 20 plus years I've never seen it hurt anyone (except perhaps their pride) or break a club, but I've seen it correct a lot of paths.

AT IMPACT, YOU'RE ONLY HALFWAY HOME

Golf is a target game, and the ball is located at midpoint in the motion. In other words, when the clubhead reaches the ball, the motion is only half over. Players who direct their focus to completing their motion into a full balanced finish have the right idea. This way of thinking—in terms of completion—will produce the best results.

Another key aspect of the downswing is the pivot, which, alas, is often lacking. I am often reminded of the time in the early 1980s at the back of the range at Greenleafe in Haines City, Florida, when Dave Leadbetter and I were watching several amateur players. They were hitting shots off the right foot and coming over the top by throwing the club to the outside and winding their shoulders early—not a pretty picture. Dave turned to me and said, "If I could give everybody something for Christmas, I'd give them a pivot." He made a motion in which he "slotted" the club with his arms, then pivoted his hips. "If I could teach them to drop it and then turn it," he continued, "they could really play some golf." It made such a lasting impression on me that I'll never forget it.

So if I could blend a free-falling set of arms with a pivoted set of hips, we'd have the perfect golf machine on the *downside* and the *forward side*. As you will recall from Chapter 12, "Introduction to the Full Swing," the swing can be described as a Ferris wheel running into a merry-go-round. This image may help you conceptualize what you are trying to achieve. Also, a good way to remember this is repeating the phrase *divot, then pivot* (another way of saying *down, then through*) to ensure a proper downswing sequence.

THE SLICE: THE COMMON COLD OF GOLF

Many golfers are habitual slicers. We've been discussing the *drop, then turn* in this chapter. The two principal causes of the common slice are improper face and path conditions; this is often due to turning the body before swinging the club. Too often I see players' torsos facing the target even before the club has hit the ball. Their hands, holding the club, are well behind the torso. This is out of sync, and they are in "the dead zone." There is no way to hit anything but a high banana to the right—or occasionally a snap hook—as a violent compensation.

Unless all the greens on your course are located where a right fielder would stand, we need to fix this problem. The good news is, we can do so easily. Most likely, the cause is in your sequence—more specifically, in your ability to understand how and when the parts move.

Let me explain. The two primary moving parts in the golf swing are the arms and torso. These parts rotate and swing within their own plane, ideally in sequence with one another.

In golfers who tend to slice, the path of the swing usually is interrupted because the turn precedes the drop; the club is then swung from the outside and, as a result, over the top. To remedy this problem, work on the sequencing discussed above—that is, allow the club to fall before you begin to unwind your shoulders.

Another problem is that at impact, most golfers are out in front of their arm swing. What they need to do is delay their body turn so they can deliver the clubface to impact in the correct position and at the right time.

One way to slow down or delay is to do some drills where you create a launching pad in which you feel your stance is very closed. Once you've done this, make a few rehearsal swings that feel like the club is really falling to the inside and swinging from in to out with a *huge* amount of forearm rotation, where your right forearm passes over your left forearm at impact. Do this many times, feeling the club swinging from in to out of the closed stance with your forearm rotation, and seeing the ball start to the right then shape back to the left—exactly the opposite of what the cause of the slice is. You're now well on your way to curing your slice.

THE HOOK: THE RARE DISORDER OF AMATEUR GOLF

For you rare birds out there who over-rotate your clubface and cause shapes from right to left, let's go over hooks and how to cure them. I always believe that the best way to fix major ills is to go to the opposite end of the spectrum, then eventually get back to the ideal middle ground. Most hookers aim too far to the right, swing too much from an in-to-out path, and over-rotate the clubface. This is rather simplistic, but here's how I handle classic hookers. I take them to the far right side of the driving range and ask them to feel as though they're aiming too far left for their taste. I'll have them show me what they think is a radically outside-to-in golf swing. For players who habitually aim too far to the right—swinging from inside to out—this makes for a very unusual feeling. They usually feel they're very much over the top, but, in actuality they're swinging the golf club on a very linear plane. I'll even video it to prove to them that it was very online instead of way over the top as they perceived it to be. For the first time, they realize they have to sense what they think is an extreme exaggeration of the condition they're trying to work toward to get to that middle ground. Initially they won't hit very many good shots, because they can't time or sequence this motion—it's too foreign to them. As a coach, I guide them through the process for a while to keep them confident and committed to repeating it until the sequence and timing of their body parts can catch up to the mechanical and physical change.

DOWNSWING AND FOLLOW-THROUGH DRILLS
Forefront Drill

This drill helps you load your right side more effectively. In fact, I've never seen anybody make a forefront swing and not hit the club in a perfect plane. To perform the drill, address the ball and then place the club 36 inches in front of it. Swing the club back over the ball in an otherwise normal swing motion, and then continue your downswing and hit the shot. As you do this, try to create more momentum to allow yourself to better load your backswing. Be careful, here, though. Sometimes from the static start, a player gets just that—very static, which creates tension, and doesn't create any momentum. (That's bad.) Momentum will help you get turned and loaded into your backswing more effectively.

Progressive Drill One: The Drop, Then Turn Drill

Make a full backswing and, leaving your back turned toward the target so as not to unwind it, feel the club definitely dropping first in a vertical downward motion. Once you feel the club dropping down, unwind your body until the club squares at a static impact condition (against an imaginary golf ball). Rehearse this sequence 15 or 20 times. Again, turn to the right, leaving your back facing the target. Drop your arms, turn your torso back to square (impact), and sequence your arms falling and body turning in a different manner than you're used to.

Progressive Drill Two: The Shoulder Drill

First, cross your arms, place your hands on the opposite shoulders, and turn your shoulders horizontally, to learn what a good level shoulder turn feels like. Do this in front of a mirror if you can (always "see and feel" when you can). Next, hold your arms across your chest and pivot your hips to the left to feel the pivot of your hips going to the other side while releasing your right heel off the ground and joining your knees up together in the follow-through condition. The idea here is to take the club out of the mix for a while, in order to feel what your inner mass is doing. Once you feel a level set of shoulders turning to the right in the backswing, and horizontally against a braced lower body, and then when you change direction, feel your right shoulder working slightly under the left, you have become acquainted with the proper sequencing and positioning of the inner mass movements of either shoulder.

Criss-cross your hands to opposite shoulders holding a club at shoulder level cross-wise. Then, assuming your regular address position and posture turn so the shaft turns level into your backswing position until it is over your right leg. Then return by pivoting your left leg into a full finish position. At finish you would like the shaft to be level with the ground and you should be "posted up" vertical from head to toe over your left foot.

Progressive Drill Three: Free-Swinging Arms

Now add a free-swinging set of arms to the progressive drills described already. Allow your arms to swing tension-free to the right in your backswing in a proper shoulder plane (the right shoulder working under the left shoulder as discussed for the shoulder drill), allowing your arms to fall freely by means of gravitational force, not exertion. If you do this, you'll have a very powerful on-plane motion approaching the golf ball from a very shallow angle of attack rather than a steep one, and you'll really be in business.

CONCLUSION

This is the most dangerous chapter in the book.

And if you're thinking that's the strangest conclusion you've read in a golf publication, ever—well, folks, it is. Still, maybe it explains why I believe that the Bookends discussed in the preceding chapter are so vital to your development. This chapter—while necessary to complete coverage of the technical fundamentals of golf—actually contains so much segmented, detailed information that it takes away from the athletic endeavor you're trying to create. The same holds true, I believe, for all published golf information on this subject.

Athletic endeavors are *motions*. I don't think anyone has ever been taught to throw a baseball in a step-by-step, segmented, chopped-up manner. But that's the way we go about teaching golf. Although I believe the information in this chapter is wonderful food for thought and conversation, I really don't think it's the way you ought to be learning this motion. You didn't learn how to play baseball, football, or basketball this way. No one will try to teach you how to scoop a ball from second base and then turn and pivot and throw it to first base in separate steps. All these motions are learned instinctually—we watch the person before us do it, and then step up and try it ourselves. If we don't do it right, we do it again, watching what happens. Later, we make certain instinctual tweaks to perfect what we're doing.

When people come to the tee for lessons or coaching sessions with me, as time goes on, I try to become less and less technical and more and more instinctual in the way I present information to them. I don't want you to get too caught up in the mechanics and lose sight of this. So please be careful.

START SMALL FOR BIG GAINS

Try to learn the correct motion on a smaller scale before you bring it to the full swing. Try using a pitching wedge or 9-iron to hit some shots three-quarters back to three-quarters through in length, using right shoulder to left shoulder as a length-of-swing reference. Hitting shots with tempo and sequencing is a good way to learn to feel these things first. Let the club fall and then turn, drop, then turn . . . feeling the club falling as you begin the weight shift to your left side.

If you make some motions on both sides of your golf swing—the backswing and the follow-through—at a three-quarter pace, trying to feel the club drop and turn, and to feel the inner mass rotate as you allow your weight to shift to your right leg on the backswing, you will start to recognize the proper sequencing of these many moving parts blending themselves into a golf swing . . . imagine that!

WATCH YOUR TEMPO

Tempo is a topic frequently discussed but rarely defined when it comes to golf. Your arm swing and body pivot are two vital functions of the golf motion. Ideally, the motion has the swinging of the arms and pivoting of the body moving at relatively similar paces. If the pace between your arms and body is a tie, your swing is in tempo.

15 GOLF VERSUS THE GOLF SWING
BRINGING IT TO THE COURSE

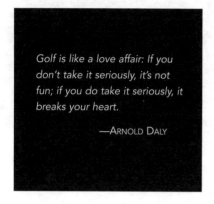

> Golf is like a love affair: If you don't take it seriously, it's not fun; if you do take it seriously, it breaks your heart.
>
> —ARNOLD DALY

> By concentrating on precision, one arrives at technique; but by concentrating on technique, one does not arrive at precision.
>
> —BRUNO WALTER

Sadly, I've seen many students who demonstrate excellent ball-striking skills on the practice tee, along with wonderful short-game skills, but can't translate those skills successfully to the course. In fact, this problem is pervasive enough that I felt it essential to include a chapter on course management to help many of you bridge this gap.

The previous chapters comprising Spoke 6, Technique, have focused largely on developing mechanical or technical skills, which, if done properly, happens off the golf course during practice. It's important to realize, however, that golf includes two arenas that are separate, but both necessary, for a successful end product: (1) the golf-swing arena, and (2) and the golf-game arena. The first arena is where players spend most of their golf day, working on mechanics and trying to perfect the golf motion. This is where golfers spend time and effort on instruction and practice; when fundamentals are learned, digested, ingrained, and eventually translated into acquired skills.

In the second arena, the golf game, our minds should not be consumed by the mechanical process but, rather, by the playing process—making sound, strategic decisions and creating a score. It should depend mostly on a feel or instinct for the course and specific situations, which only develops over time with experience. It's also the part where we're supposed to be having fun.

What I do for a living is teach the golf swing. My job is to make your golf swing more sound and repeatable; to give you some consistency of motion where you can rely on attaining your ball flight and contact quality repeatedly. When you take this to the course, though, you want to play, not practice, the game. So in addition to teaching the technical side of golf, it is my job to coach you as a player of the game. You want to go out there, enjoy yourself, and create a satisfactory score. People often confuse these two things. Those who understand this best are usually those who have played other sports.

Borrowing an example from basketball, Bobby Knight is known as an excellent teacher of the fundamentals of the game, such as sound fundamental defense. He's also known as an excellent game coach, which is a very different arena. He'll coach his players how to react to certain situations they might encounter during the course of the game as it's played against a real opponent. Likewise, my job is to teach the fundamental mechanics of the golf swing on the practice tee and in the short-game practice area as well as coach how to play the game on the course.

I have seen some people whom I like to call *all-American driving range players*. They demonstrate terrific skills on the range but can't get it done on the golf course. In my world, that's a failure. If you're interested in hitting prettier shots, then don't join a club, join a range. You'll save time, money, and aggravation, as you won't have any holes available to you. If you're interested in playing better golf, however, you need to become a gamer as opposed to merely a practicer. You need to gain on-course skills.

Of course, if your technique is generally poor, the problem certainly won't be solved by translating those poor skills onto the golf course. But if your technique off the course is in good shape, have no fear: It *is* possible to get you onto the course with these skills intact—it's just that sometimes it takes a little thought, some effort, and some sound, understandable coaching.

THE RIGHT PRACTICE PROGRESSION

Ideally, the learning process goes like this: First you take a golf lesson and spend a fair amount of time developing what you learned. Then you play a practice round by yourself—that is, putting your clubs on the back of a golf cart and hitting a couple of extra drives and approaches, chips, pitches, and putts as you work your way through nine holes. Next, pay attention to those feelings you are trying to develop—not the verbal commands your coach gave you. I don't want a little devil on your right shoulder screaming in your ear, *Coach said do this!* and *Coach said do that!* I want you to have already reached the point—through practice, repetitions, and drills—where these fundamentals are part of your natural golf motion. At this point you are rehearsing your game in a practice round setting before taking it out into live action (say, a Saturday morning game with the boys, when you're trying to win that $5 Nassau). The practice round is the link, or *bridge time* as I call it, between learning time, the lesson, and application time, when it's time to score. Bridge time should be considered part of, and essential to, the learning process.

Do not get into the habit of trying to develop your golf swing on the golf course. Trust me: *It's not going to work.* It hasn't worked up until now, has it? Once you get it to the first tee, just let it happen. If you are still trying to figure out how to initiate the golf swing, or where the club should be in the downswing, or when to turn your hips on the first tee, you're in for a long afternoon and it's not gonna be pretty. Play golf as the target game that it is, not as a mechanical, segmented, and choppy series of movements with no flow or relationship to a target. As a golfer, you are in fact an athlete reacting to a target.

A DIFFERENT GAME EVERY TIME

No two rounds of golf are exactly alike. Even a golf course, though roughly the same, will be a little different every time. Different types of weather—temperature, wind, rain—present different challenges. Players themselves change from day to day, as do other factors, such as the equipment they use or the

> To be aware of targets throughout your round of golf—as opposed to being totally preoccupied with hitting the ball—is a big step for a golfer. It's the difference between playing and spending eighteen holes trying to make golf swings.
>
> —JIM MCLEAN

companions they play with. The golfers who best understand and adapt to these changing conditions will be the most successful on the course. You need to develop the ability to adapt and play on the course, and not become overly focused or "stuck" in whatever swing segment you're currently working on.

Learning to adapt well to changing conditions means being ready for anything. The only way to do this is to simulate various course conditions during your practice. As Rick Jensen and I discussed in some detail back in Spoke 2, The Mind, all players should practice in a way that closely replicates conditions they will likely face on the golf course. This will allow them to overcome the natural tendency to be intimidated, or worse, blindsided by changes. Instead they will be able to face them head-on, because they are familiar with them— "been there, done that." This involves practicing in the wind or rain, playing from various lies, playing in and around trees and bunkers, . . . Similarly, during your bridge time, drop a few balls—not in the middle of the fairway, but in the rough and even the trees. Around the green, hit shots from all the nasty spots. See what works and what needs further work. Only then can players be truly adaptable to the broad variety of changes and conditions they will face in a given round. I remember a conversation I had with Jack Burke some years ago. For those who may not remember him, he's a former Masters and PGA champion and former Ryder Cup captain. Although he was a world-class player, he may even be a better teacher of the game of golf. He told me that a player should go to the first tee expecting to have to recover from adversity instantly. In other words, be ready for the worst so you're never taken by surprise. It's not a negative thought—just a matter of expectations. If you step up to the first tee expecting to hit it 290 yards down the middle of the fairway, hit an approach shot close to the pin, and then sink your putt—well, you're living in a dream world. Check your ego at the door, and it'll help you keep it together.

DANCE WITH THE LADY YOU BROUGHT THAT DAY

Nobody works harder on the practice range than Vijay Singh. He often spends 12 hours a day hitting literally thousands of balls to develop and perfect his swing mechanics. When he leaves the range and heads onto the course, though, he leaves behind all those drills, techniques, and mechanics and plays with whatever swing he brought to the course that day. He focuses on his target, clears his mind, and takes each shot as if it's his last.

Contrast this with Gary, a determined amateur who practices every day after his dental office closes. When he ventures onto the course after hours of working on technique and creating a beautiful, sound swing, Gary spends most of his time concentrating on the mechanics and not on the feel of his swing—with disastrous results. He doesn't understand that practice is over, and that when he reaches the first tee it's time to clear his mind and let his body take over. He is tied up in mental knots on the course.

Similarly, among the least constructive things you can do is to go straight from a lesson to the golf course—which, unfortunately, is exactly what many students do. They head for the first tee while still mentally working on their golf swing, with various *Coach said this*, *Coach said that* reminders rattling around their heads. They make what should be a free-flowing swing motion into a choppy, segmented thing that has no rhythm because their minds are busy playing a game of connect the dots. The fact is, no one can concentrate with all that noise going on in their heads, especially in an activity where the actual motion happens in such a short time period.

On any particular day you may develop a tendency or problem in your swing—say, curving the ball too much to the right when normally you don't have this problem. Go ahead and take this to the course, playing by feel, trying to recover from shots affected by the problem, and managing the situation as best you can. As I always say, "You dance with the lady you brought that day." Manage your shot pattern. Don't look for a new date once the dance has started. So if, for example, you're out there hitting slices you don't like, then stand on the right side of the tee box, aim down the left side of the fairway, and let that dog slice. If it's hooks you're hitting, stand on the left side of the tee box and to the right side of the fairway and let that baby do its thing. Work on getting rid of the problem later, off the course. And although the golf course is not the place to fix your swing or your ball flight, you don't want to leave it there, either. Get to work on it as soon as you come in. In any event, you'll have many more pleasant experiences while playing what we call damage-control golf. If you don't have your game with you that day (and trust me—it won't come to the course with you each time), deal with it as best you can and hammer it out later. Think of yourself as a world-class basketball coach whose star player suddenly twists his ankle during warm-ups and is out for an important game. Suddenly you've lost your game plan. If you're still going to win that game, you've got to be able to adapt, think on your feet, and react accordingly. You've gotta come up with a new game, instantly. World-class golfers do this all the time. If they find when they warm up that things are not going the way they'd like and it's minutes before tee time, they're able to take the shot shape they've got and manage it around the course as best they can. That's the sign of a true player, one who can adapt without their A game, and still go out there and be competitive that day.

EVERY DAY ANOTHER POSSIBILITY

Every year I give hundreds of playing lessons. Over the years I've begun to spend more time on the course with my students because I realize there is a greater need for me to spend time there, teaching and coaching. Every time I go out with a student I realize, unfortunately, how little the average player really understands the game of golf and how it's played, how decisions are made, and what factors are taken into account when evaluating a shot or picking a club. And the more time I've spent with world-class players on any of the tours, the clearer it is to me that they think their way around the golf course, and when they're not even hitting their best shots—they're minimizing their errors.

If over the next year all the average players out there spent 50 percent of their learning and coaching time in the short-game arena, and the other 50 percent on the golf course (with their coach walking and talking them through their decisions), the world of amateur golf would see a dramatic scoring change—in the right direction. I want you to realize the possibilities here. If for one year you committed yourself to spending half your golf practice time perfecting all aspects of your short game—putting, chipping, pitching, lobbing, and bunker play—and the other half with your coach on the golf course working through such decisions as how to handle trouble shots that arise or how to handle shot selections, different pin positions, wind conditions, and lie conditions, you would *radically* improve your golf game.

COURSE MANAGEMENT 101

When trying to execute trouble shots of whatever type—from the trees, out of a bunker—amateur golfers tend toward some common mistakes that all too often lead losing additional shots. Let's take a closer look at some of these.

DON'T GO FOR THE ONE-IN-A-MILLION SHOT

One of the most prevalent golf mistakes is not playing the odds. Instead, amateurs try to pull off the one-in-a-million shot. My advice to you is: *don't.* Remember why you got into that tight spot in the first place: because you were not in complete command of your golf motion. The odds of suddenly gaining complete control of your ball are slim, at best, especially in a tight situation. I often wonder what makes players think they can suddenly thread the needle between two branches, or hit a shot out of an awkward lie over water with a 200-yard carry. Golf is like chess. You must constantly evaluate and reevaluate your next move, responding to your opponent (who, in this case, is the course). Unless you hit an absolutely perfect drive exactly where you were looking, even if it's just 10 yards from where you were looking and is still in the fairway, you'll need to reevaluate, because it's nevertheless at a different angle from the pin.

When you're in a tough situation, the best stretegy is to get your ball safely back into play, and the best way to do this is by carefully rehearsing the shot you're about to execute several times (which is a sounder and safer bet than a long-odds shot), rethinking your game plan carefully, and taking note of everything surrounding you. Don't turn one swing into multiple lost strokes.

HOW TO HANDLE THE ROUGH

It's safe to say you'll encounter the rough a few times along the way. While making a bogey from the rough is no cause for embarrassment, what *is* a shame is turning a bogey into a much higher number by getting too ambitious with your shots, and all because of a lie condition you can't totally control. Here's how to handle five tough shots from the rough to help minimize the damage:

1. **The Flier Lie**

   Perhaps the most deceptive lie is the *flier lie*—when you're in the intermediate cut of rough and the ball sits up instead of getting buried. This type of lie lulls you into a false sense of security. Don't be fooled! Whenever grass is trapped at impact between the clubface and ball, the ball spins less and goes much farther. The ball will jump out of the rough hot and release more when it lands, making distance control difficult, if not impossible (kind of like a knuckle ball in baseball). So how should you handle these tricky shots?

   First, go down at least two clubs. For example, if you're 150 yards from the green and would normally use a 7-iron, go to a 9-iron and choke down on your grip a bit. Then go ahead and hit it. Better to undershoot the green a little than play the next shot from way behind it. Don't let the ball get wildly away from you. In this situation it is always best to try to keep your ball between you and the flag. That way, par is still a real possibility.

2. **The High-Lofted Shot**

   Uh-oh. You're 20 yards from a green that slopes away from you, and there's a closely tucked pin. Making matters worse is that bunker or pond between you and the green, and the rough beneath you. Overcoming these obstacles while trying to land the ball softly seems like a tall order. Remember what we have worked on (see the lobbing sections of Chapter 10). You'll need to make a longer, slower swing. Picture yourself tossing a softball underhand over the plate: long, slow, with an almost exaggerated motion. Don't fall into the common trap of letting impatience or sheer panic overcome you. Take many rehearsal swings to feel the shot. Also, be careful to use enough loft, play the ball centered in your stance, weaken your grip slightly, and then hit the prettiest high, soft lob shot you can, smiling as you walk up and tap it in. Oh yeah! Ten feet past is better than plugged in the front bunker.

3. **The Greenside Chip**

   Whenever you play a chip out of deep grass you should anticipate little or no spin. What you want to do is swing from the arms and shoulders, hinge the club a little faster, and allow the clubhead to fall at the back of the ball into the rough with a shorter-than-normal follow-through. Remember your primary and secondary target strategies from Chapter 9, "Chipping," and use them here.
   - **From an Uphill Lie/Pitch.** This lie isn't as tough as it looks. Having an uphill launch angle increases the loft of your already lofted club, so use a less lofted club. Getting

the clubhead into the grass will cause the ball to pop up and out. Be careful not to overdo the loft by opening the clubface more or sliding the club under the ball. Then swing level with the slope, keep your weight evenly distributed, make sure your shoulders are parallel to the incline of the hill, and place the ball slightly closer to your front foot. The ball is closer to the uphill foot.

- **From a Downhill Lie/Pitch.** This is a tough lie. Unlike the uphill lie, you want to increase loft here as much as possible because the downward slope will de-loft the club. Also, be sure to place the ball closer to your back foot, keep the angle of your shoulders consistent with the incline, open your clubface more, and swing along the downward slope of the hill. Allow the ball to pop up and out and plan for a greater amount of roll. Make many rehearsals and feel the club bottom out where you want it to.

4. **Going Against the Grain**

   When grass is growing against you from the rough, it serves to grab and impede your club immediately, making it feel as if you've hit a wall. The best strategy here is to hit to safety. For starters, you do not want to try to force the ball out of the rough with a long club. Instead, use a punch shot to get the ball on the fairway to an intermediate diagonal target that will give you the greatest margin of error. Also, keep your clubface more open (the grass will tend to grab the hosel and shut the face down), apply more pressure with your left hand (to control the face), choke down on the grip more (for control), maximize the loft of your club, and abbreviate your follow-through.

5. **The Basic Recovery**

   Check your lie. Can you reasonably expect to reach the green? If the answer is no, then pick a target on the fairway from which you are confident you can play the next shot to the hole. Don't make the mistake of trying to use the wrong club—a fairway wood, a 3-iron—to force the ball to the hole when the odds oppose you. Don't try to apply sheer physical strength over technique and strategy—you'll just make a bad situation worse. Swinging harder will most likely serve only to throw off your balance, making quality contact virtually impossible. Also, very heavy rough has the effect of grabbing the hosel of the club, shutting down the face at impact, and killing the distance, direction, and trajectory of your shot. You'll need to go with greater loft to counteract this effect. Furthermore, you need to open your clubface slightly, position the ball in the center of your stance, increase the weight on your left side for a more descending blow, and increase your left-hand grip pressure to control the face.

HOW TO HANDLE SLOPING LIES
Uphill and Downhill Lies

The golf ball must always be played closer to the uphill foot—how much closer depends on how drastic the uphill or downhill lie is. Try to level your body's lines—shoulders and hips—to the inclination of the hill instead of trying to oppose the hill. Many of us try to lean up into the hill, because that's the way we try to balance ourselves and counter its gravitational effects. You should instead try to match the slope of the hill, despite feeling slightly out of balance.

Sidehill Lies

Obviously, there are two types of sidehill lies: those in which the ball is below your feet, and those in which the ball is above your feet.

- **Above Your Feet.** Choke down on the club slightly to compensate for the ball being closer to you. Stay tall in your posture. The ball will try to come out and shape itself to match the nature of the hill, so when the ball is above your feet, it's going to shape to your *left*.
- **Below Your Feet.** Conversely, when the ball is below your feet, it is going to shape to your *right*. Moreover, you'll want to bend more from the waist and hold the club as long as you can to accommodate the sidehill lie.

In either of these situations you're going to feel out of balance, so it's important for you to take many more rehearsals than you would for a standard shot. Alter your preshot routine accordingly. If, for example, you normally take one practice swing, take three, four, or five practice swings to really understand the nature of what you're going to face so that your comfort level is up when executing the shot.

PUNCH SHOTS

This is a must-have shot for windy days or low-lying tree limbs. A common mistake among nonprofessionals is taking way too little loft, hoping that's all they need to do, and then actually driving the ball into the turf without ever getting it airborne. You'll *always* need some degree of loft because in your punch shot launching pad, you need to move the ball *slightly* back of center, play your hand position *slightly* forward, and *slightly* hood the face. These three factors will aid you in helping the ball fly lower. The only additional swing adjustments you may choose to make are to choke down on the grip and to make a *slightly* shorter back-swing and follow-through to better control your club in this trouble shot situation.

CONCLUSION

One of the reasons people aren't prepared for the golf course is that during their preparation time, they don't practice the way they play. For example, there may be a hole or two on your home golf course where you want to or should hit a 3-wood or a long iron off the tee. If so, do you practice hitting any of these shots on the range? Or perhaps there are a couple of holes where you typically hit an errant drive and have to play a partial wedge shot around the green. Let's say you normally hit your pitching wedge 100 yards, but now you have to hit one 85 yards with a lower trajectory because of the wind direction. Naturally, then, you need to practice hitting partial wedges in varying trajectories to be able to handle these situations. Let me ask you this: Have you worked on your bunker game this week at all? Have you hit any punch shots on the range? Have you practiced any bump-and-run shots this week? Or practiced any lag putts from what you'd call an extraordinary distance, say 40 or 50 feet? You might encounter that on your first green today. In other words, does your preparation on the range during your practice time really prepare you for anything you may encounter on the golf course? This is what you need to aim for during your practice time. If you expect the unexpected, and you're prepared to deal with it head-on because you have practiced a variety of situations that may come up during play, you will indeed have learned to manage the course well. The best way to do this? Spend time during practice altering your shots to prepare for situations that may come up, and spend time on the course with your coach talking you through the various unexpected situations that arise. As they say, forewarned is forearmed. Now get out there and play!

APPENDIX A: **FINDING A GOOD GOLF-SPECIFIC SPORTS THERAPIST**

As you can see by this short list, golf-specific sports therapy is a fairly new field, but if you live near or will be vacationing near any of these places, I highly recommend you see any of the people listed here. They're all terrific specialists in the area of golf.

New York/Connecticut Metropolitan Area
Eanna Rushe
BioSport Technologies LLC
76 Valley Road
Greenwich (Cos Cob), CT 06807
(203) 661-8330
Cell: (914) 588-6457
rushe@biosporttechnologies.com (or biosporttechnologies.com)
www.biosporttechnologies.com

Chris Welch (Biomechanics)
ZenoLINK
1827 North Cafferty Hill Road
Endicott, NY 13760
(607) 786-9262

Naples, Florida
Kathy Vacondios
Director of Fitness
Health Club of Naples/The Fairway Fitness
info@fairwayfitness.com
(239) 293-3613

West Palm Beach, Florida
Randy Myers
PGA National in Palm Beach
400 Avenue of the Champions
Palm Beach Gardens, FL 33418
(561) 627-4444
Randym@floridagolfing.com

Southern California

Pete Egoscue

Pain Relief, Performance Through Postural Therapy and Exercise

The Egoscue Method

12707 High Bluff Drive, Suite 150

San Diego, CA 92130

(800) 995-8434

admin@egoscue.com

www.egoscue.com

The Egoscue method clinics and sports programs are located throughout the United States and in Europe. Check the Web site for the location nearest you.

Nationally

Body Balance for Performance

Golf Health and Fitness Training

(888) FIT-GOLF

www.fitgolf.com

There are more than 60 locations throughout the United States.

APPENDIX B: **FINDING A MIND COACH IN YOUR AREA**

The following is a list of great golf mind coaches within the United States:

Rick Jensen, Ph.D.
Performance Center at PGA National
6347 Northwest 72 Way
Parkland, FL 33067
(954) 752-3333
Fax: (954) 752-3600
DrRJensen@aol.com
www.pgaperformancecenter.com

Bob Rotella, Ph.D.
3183 Kingsbridge Trail
Keswick, VA 22947
(434) 296-7872
Fax: (434) 296-8665

Dr. Richard H. Coop
Professor of Educational Psychology
University of North Carolina at Chapel Hill
118 Peabody Hall
Chapel Hill, NC 27599
dcoop@email.unc.edu

Robert Winters, Ph.D.
Mindpower Sports
8835 Great Cove Drive
Orlando, FL 32819
(407) 264-4222
www.mindpowersports.com

Deborah Graham, PhD
Licensed Counseling and Sport Psychologist
Co-Director of GolfPsych, Inc.
P.O. Box 1976
Boerne, TX 78006-6976
(830) 537-5044 or (888) 270-4653
Fax: (830) 537-5048
jstabler@golfpsych.com

Fred Shoemaker—Extraordinary Golf Corporation
P.O. Box 22731
Carmel CA 93922
(831) 625-1900 or (800) 541-2444
Fax: (831) 625-1976
email@extraordinarygolf.com
www.extraordinarygolf.com

APPENDIX C:
TOM'S TOP 25

Here are the 25 top training devices I recommend for helping your golf game.

All Areas

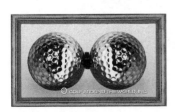

1. Golf metronome

2. T-Tech

Short Game

3. Pin balls

4. No 3-Putt cup reducer (hole reducer)

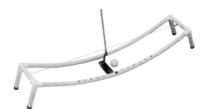

5. High Tech putting track

6. Bee Line (putt string)

7. Mentor mirror

8. Xtend align

Chipping Tools

9. Chip-N-Pitch (shaft extension)

10. Tac-Tic Wrist

Full Swing

11. PowerSwing fan

12 Right angle 2 (also for pitching)

13. Swing extender

14. Swing wave

15. Plane stick

16. Swingyd (pronounced *swing guide*)

17. PVC mirror (full-size mirror)

18. Figure 8 strap

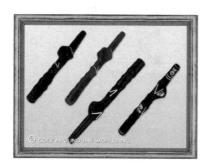

19. Form grip

20. Heavy hitter driver and iron

21. Impact bag

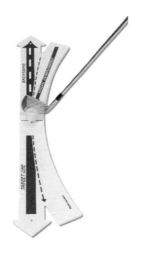

22. Inpact trac

23. Player's Image mirror

24. SwingSpeed RADAR

25. Homemade 2x4 (see Chapter 8, "Putting," for instructions)

And one more excellent,multiple-use teaching aid is the 4Xi-promotion. This new and handy aid is used to improve putting, chipping, the full swing, and core flexibility, and it's also a connection tool. To find out more about the 4Xi-promotion, or to order one, go to www.squareshot.com or call (800) 819-9063.

Photos courtesy of Golf Around the World, Inc.

Where to Find Them

An excellent company that carries all of these products (except the 2 × 4, of course, which is homemade, and the 4Xi, although it will be available from them in the near future) is Golf Around the World, Inc., owned and operated by Dr. Gary Wiren and his son, Dane Wiren. They are experts in the field of training aids, second to none. Visit their Web site at www.golfaroundtheworld.com or call (561) 848-8896 or (in the United States) (800) 824-4279.

APPENDIX D:
WHERE TO GET YOUR CLUBS FITTED

To find a qualified club fitter in your area, contact any of the following:

Titleist
Acushnet Company
P.O. Box 965
333 Bridge Street
Fairhaven, MA 02719-0965
(800) 225-8500 or (508) 979-2000
http://www.titleist.com

Henry-Griffitts, Inc.
P.O. Box 1630
Hayden Lake, ID 86835-1630
(208) 772-8505 or (800) 445-4653
Fax: (208) 772-9632
http://www.henry-griffitts.com

Callaway Golf Company
Corporate Headquarters
2180 Rutherford Road
Carlsbad, CA 92008-7328
(760) 931-1771
http://callawaygolf.com

Taylor Made
5545 Fermi Court
Carlsbad, CA 92008-7324
(760) 918-6000
http://www.taylormadegolf.com

Tom Patri
TP Golf Schools
183 Burnt Pine Drive
Naples, FL 34119
(239) 455-9179
Fax: (239) 455-2923
tpatri@mindspring.com

Or contact your local PGA section for information and a referral. To find the section nearest you, go to www.pga.com/home/sections/index.cfm.

APPENDIX E:
RECOMMENDED READING

Here are some books I highly recommend for winter or off-season reading:

Beach, Dick E., and Bob Ford. *Golf: The Body, The Mind, The Game*. New York: Villard, 1995. Note: This book is currently out of print.

Boomer, Percy. *On Learning Golf: A Valuable Guide to Better Golf*. New York: Knopf, 1946.

Coop, Richard H., and Gary Wiren. *The New Golf Mind*. New York: Fireside, 1995.

Coop, Richard H., with Bill Fields. *Mind Over Golf*. Hoboken, NJ: Hungry Minds, Inc., 1997.

Draovitch, Pete and Wayne Wescott. *Complete Conditioning for Golf*. Champaign, IL: Human Kinetics Publishers, 1999.

Egoscue, Peter, with Roger Gittines. *The Egoscue Method of Health Through Motion: Revolutionary Program That Lets You Rediscover the Body's Power to Rejuvenate It*. New York: Perennial, 1993.

Els, Ernie, and David Herman. *Ernie Els' Guide to Golf Fitness: Take Strokes Off Your Game and Add Yards to Your Drive*. Three Rivers, MI: Three Rivers Press, 2001.

Enhager, Kjell. *Quantum Golf: The Path to Golf Mastery*. New York: Warner Books, 1992. Note: This book is currently out of print.

Farnsworth, Dr. Craig L. *See It and Sink It: Mastering Putting Through Peak Visual Performance*. New York: HarperSource, 1997.

Gallwey, W. Timothy. *The Inner Game of Golf*. New York: Random House, 1998.

Hebron, Michael. *See and Feel the Inside, Move the Outside*. Smithtown, NY: Smithtown Landing Country Club, 1990. Note: This book is currently out of print.

Jobe, Dr. Frank W., and Diane R. Moynes. *30 Exercises for Better Golf*. Fredonia, WI: Champion Press, 1986. Note: This book is currently out of print.

Love, Davis III. *Every Shot I Take: Lessons Learned About Golf, Life, and a Father's Love*. New York: Simon & Schuster, 1997.

Millman, Dan. *Way of the Peaceful Warrior*. Novato, CA: New World Library, 2000.

Mumford, Carey. *Golf's Best Kept Secret*. Note: This book is currently out of print.

Murphy, Michael. *Golf in the Kingdom*. New York: Penguin USA, 1997.

Penick, Harvey. *Harvey Penick's Little Red Book: Lessons and Teachings from a Lifetime of Golf*. New York: Simon & Schuster, 1999.

Rotella, Bob, with Bob Cullen. *Golf Is a Game of Confidence*. New York: Simon & Schuster Trade, 2001.

———. *Golf Is Not a Game of Perfect*. New York: Simon & Schuster, 1995.

Shoemaker, Fred, and Pete Shoemaker. *Extraordinary Golf: The Art of the Possible*. Perigee, 1997.

APPENDIX F:
CHOOSING THE RIGHT COACH FOR YOU

Coaches can help you spot problems, offer solutions, and track your progress while providing professional, objective feedback. While coaches cannot teach you to play golf, they can teach you to *learn* to play golf. That is, they can provide you with suggestions and teach you the fundamentals of the game, but the true learning takes place while you are practicing and actually learning to incorporate this technique into your game. This cannot take place on the golf course or during lesson time.

When selecting a coach, you want someone whose philosophy and style work *for you*. This is an individual choice. As with equipment, when it comes to coaches, one size doesn't fit all. Your coach's personality, style, and approach to teaching golf should be a good fit and make sense to you.

The first step in finding a qualified golf teacher in your area is to check out *Golf Magazine*'s Top 100 Teachers in America. You can find this feature annually in the February issue of the magazine or on its Web site, www.golfonline.com. Once you've narrowed the list to a few people you're interested in working with, the next step is to call each prospective coach to ask a few questions.

Choose a coach carefully: You want to get the most out of the time and hard-earned money you spend. Finding a quality teacher is the easy part; choosing one who matches your personality and learning style takes a little more digging. Narrow your list to 10 potential coaches, for instance, and you might find a good match with only 1 of them.

First, you'll want to ask about teaching philosophy. There are many different philosophies and approaches to teaching golf. Some coaches, for example, start from the hole and work backward. Some focus on setup, others on playing conditions. See if a coach's philosophy sounds logical and sequential to you.

You also need to be comfortable with the person from a personality and communication (or style) standpoint. Two coaches might explain the same thing very differently, and one might click better and/or sooner for you. In short, some communication styles work better than others for a particular individual. There are also a variety of personalities out there, and again, you need to find the right fit. For example, some coaches (such as yours truly) are not hand holders, and could be better described as part coach, part drill sergeant. That style works well for a lot of people, but it isn't for everyone.

One final note: While good coaches are in high demand, that shouldn't mean they won't take the time to answer a few questions from a prospective client. I once had a man who came to me after some investigation. While it turned out we were a good match, the reason he chose me initially is that of 10 coaches he called to ask a couple of questions, I was the only one who returned his call.

Here are some questions to ask when selecting a golf teacher:

- How long have you been teaching?
- Do you have a specialty area—short game, full swing?
- Do you have any objection to working with a high handicapper? (If applicable.)
- Tell me a little about your teaching philosophy.
- Are you seasonal in your location? (Some teachers teach in different locations at different times of the year.)
- What days and hours do you teach?
- How far in advance are you booked?
- What's your rate? (But remember, sports fans—if you pay with peanuts, you get monkeys. Do you question what you pay your doctor?)

APPENDIX G: **GLOSSARY OF GOLF TERMS**

Address: Another term for your setup position.

Advancement Shot: A shot in which your goal is not to reach the green, either by choice or by necessity.

Approach Shot: A shot in which your goal is to reach the green.

Apron: Also called the fringe, this is the closely mown grassy area between the putting green and the fairway or rough.

Backswing: The beginning of the swing in which the club goes up and back from the ground to up above your head.

Bent Grass: A type of grass, typically found on courses in the northeastern United States.

Bermuda: A type of grass, typically found on courses in the southern and western United States.

Birdie: A score of one stroke less than par on a hole.

Blade: The bottom edge or clubhead of an iron. Also, a particular type of putter.

Bounce: The flange of a sand wedge.

Bunker: A hole or depression around a green or in or along a fairway, usually, but not always, filled with sand.

Closed Stance: A setup condition (also called a hook stance) in which you line up to the right of the target. For a right-handed player, your right foot and right shoulder are drawn back to your chest cavity and facing slightly away from the target line, or closed to the target line.

Clubface: The front of the club, which faces the target and where the lines are located on the club. It's also the area of the club used to strike the ball.

Collar (of the Rough): The section of grass where the apron meets the rough.

Compression: The act of delivering force to the golf ball.

Draw: When a ball is hit and the sidespin causes it to move gradually from right to left during flight. The opposite of a fade. (Please do not confuse this with a *hook*.)

Driver: The longest of clubs, created for distance and thus most often used off the tee (also referred to as a 1-wood).

Duck Hook: A sharp left turn of the ball.

Face: The surface of a clubhead used for hitting the ball.

Fade: When a ball is hit and the sidespin forces it to move slowly from left to right. The opposite of a draw. (Please do not confuse this with a *slice*.)

Fat Shot: See *heavy*.

Flange: The part of the bottom of the clubhead beginning at the blade.

Follow-Through: The part of the swing from impact with the ball until the end.

Fringe: See *apron*.

Gap Wedge: A lofted wedge used to fill a gap in loft, most often between the pitch and the sand wedge (often 52 or 54 degrees).

Green: The term commonly used to describe the putting surface, but it can also refer to the entire golf course.

Grip: The position of the hands on the club; also, the part at the top of the shaft used for holding the club.

Heavy: When the clubhead hits the ground before making contact with the ball. Also called a fat shot.

Heel: The clubface area closest to the shaft.

Hole: The space between the tee and green; also, the hole on the green.

Hook: When the ball is hit and the sidespin forces it to move from right to left. It is more severe than a draw.

Hosel: The part of the club where the shaft is inserted into and attaches to the clubhead.

Lag: A long putt, the aim of which is to stop near to the hole.

Lie: The angle or slope of the ground where the ball sits. Also, the angle of the clubhead in relation to its shaft.

Lob Shot: A shot that goes up high and comes straight down without much roll.

Loft: The angle of the clubface in relation to the ground.

Makeable: A putt that's likely to succeed.

Open Stance: A setup condition in which you are lined up to the left of the target. For a right-handed player, your left foot, hip, and shoulder are drawn back slightly to the left, causing your chest cavity to face slightly away from the target line. The body feels open toward the target line.

PGA: The Professional Golfers' Association.

Pin: The thin pole that marks the hole; also called a flagstick.

Pitch: A type of elongated chip shot that travels with a high arc and soft landing, sometimes with backspin.

Pitch-and-Run: A pitch shot with less loft and backspin that travels farther on the green after it lands.

Pivot: A rotating motion of the pelvis and hips during the golf swing in which a coiling and uncoiling motion is made that transfers weight from the back leg in the backswing to the front foot in the downswing, creating a source of power in the swing.

Posture: The leg and body position employed during setup.

Professional: A golfer who potentially earns payment for playing in tournaments or for teaching golf.

Pull: A ball that starts out left of the target and often continues to curve left.

Punch: A shot played against wind or from a trouble spot (such as the woods) that is low and controlled.

Push: A ball that starts out right of the target and often continues to curve right.

Putt: A shot executed on or near the putting green with the intent of landing in the hole.

Putter: A club used for putts that has a negligible degree (say, 4 degrees) of loft.

Putting Green: The closely mown grassy area surrounding the hole designed for putts.

Reverse Pivot: A hip-and-pelvis motion in which the weight is incorrectly transferred during the golf swing.

Rolling the Pill: Slang for making the ball roll on the green.

Rough: Thick grass found on the sides of the fairways and often around greens.

Setup: The address position from which you strike a ball.

Shank: A shot in which the ball ricochets to the right off the hosel of the club.

Short Game: Putting, chipping, pitching, lobbing, bump-and-running, and sand shots.

Skulling: When the ball is struck above its center and, as a result, does not achieve its intended trajectory and travels too far. See also *thin*.

Slice: When the ball curves to the right; more severe than a fade.

Square Stance: When your feet and body are placed in a position parallel to the intended target.

Stance: Where your feet are placed at setup.

Sweet Spot: The exact center of the clubface (and where its mass is often greatest).

Takeaway: When the backswing begins.

Tee: The place where the ball is hit from at the start of a hole; also, the small wooden peg that you set the ball on in order to strike it.

Tee Box: The place from which players take their first shot at each hole.

Thin: A shot where the club hits the ball at its center or above, causing it to go low or along the ground. Also known as a skulled shot.

Toe: The end of the clubhead beyond the sweet spot and farthest from the shaft.

Top: A shot in which the clubhead strikes the top part of the ball and the ball goes into the ground then pops up; it usually doesn't go far.

Touch: Also called feel, this is a learned skill for accurately judging the distance that the ball will travel.

Trajectory: The height or arc of the ball flight.

Turn: The coiling motion in the golf swing; also the point halfway between the front nine and the back nine.

Up and Down: Usually a short-game shot that lands near the hole, enabling you to 1-putt the ball into the hole.

Wedge: A high-lofted iron club used in short-game shots; it can be a pitching, sand, or lob wedge.

Weight Transfer: During the swing, body weight is transferred from one foot to the other; when properly executed, this creates power.

Wood: A club with a large head (made of metal or wood) used for distance shots.

INDEX